PROOF OF LIFE

STEVEN SUTTIE

I'd like to dedicate this book to my mum.
(But more on that later.)

I'd like to take this opportunity to thank my loyal and growing gang of readers. I really do appreciate your support, your kind comments and your endless likes and shares on social media. It is very humbling, and I hope you don't mind me borrowing your names to use for the characters in my stories.

I hope you enjoy this brand new Miller adventure 😊

Prologue

Wednesday 15th May
Greenlife Windows Factory, Stalybridge

"Right, thanks for coming." Said Susan McKenzie, the head of Human Resources. "Please take a seat."

Mike Jenkins pulled the chair back abruptly and slumped into the chair. His supervisor Terry Holdsworth looked at him disapprovingly.

"Right Mike, I think you know why we are here?" said Susan in a soft but authoritative tone. Mike shrugged and glared at the table top. He began fidgeting with his mucky hands.

"Terry, just for the avoidance of doubt, can you please inform Mike why we have called the meeting."

Terry looked embarrassed having to discuss the details in front of a lady. He took a deep breath.

"Well, it's been said by a few people that it was Mike who blocked the toilets up and flooded the lavs."

"Do you have anything to say about that Mike?" asked Susan, ever-so-nicely.

"Yes, I do as it goes. I'm sick of getting blamed for anything that goes on around here. I'm not even allowed to take a dump now!" Mike let out an exaggerated breath of frustration. It fooled neither of his superiors, who looked at one another. Susan could see that Terry felt awkward with this, so she took the lead.

"Well Mike, we're all adults, so let's put a stop to the pretence. You've been seen walking around the factory with a model poo that you made out of malt loaf. We've got it on the factory CCTV where you were moulding it in your hands and laughing to yourself. You were clearly seen pushing bits of sweetcorn into it, as well."

Mike let out another rasp of air, continuing to stare at both of his hands on the table top.

"You've been seen leaving your model poo on other members of staff's work benches all morning. And now, a very similar looking object has blocked the toilets and flooded them. Now if you can present me with your model poo, we'll know that this wasn't the object that blocked up the toilet." Susan paused dramatically.

"Can you?"

Mike puffed out again. After a long pause he defiantly said "No."

"Well, as you are aware this isn't your first warning for your general conduct in the workplace. So, under the circumstances, I'm afraid that we have no alternative, we are going to suspend you…"

"Is this a joke?" snapped Mike.

"…on full pay, while we do a thorough investigation," continued Susan, without acknowledging the outburst. "We'll write to you to invite you to a further meeting in due course. Now I must ask you to leave the premises immediately, and don't come back until you have been invited to do so." Susan retained a professional expression as Mike angrily stood and pushed the chair away with the back of his legs.

"Absolute joke! This firm is going down the pan!" He said huffily.

Without hesitation Susan looked up and replied. "Which is more than can be said for the malt-loaf turd."

Mike stormed out of the meeting room, leaving the door wide-open as he stomped down the corridor.

"Thirty-five years old that bloke," said Terry. "You'd not guess it would you? My grandkids are more mature!"

"I know. But did you say he's a good worker?" asked Susan, now displaying her usual, friendly smile.

"When he puts his back into it, he's the best grafter on the shop-floor. But once he starts mucking about, he's just a pain in the neck." Terry looked genuinely frustrated.

"Right, well don't worry. We'll sort it. Thanks Terry."

Susan touched Terry's shoulder lightly, feeling quite charmed by how embarrassed the supervisor had been by the malt-loaf incident. "You're a real gentleman."

"Oh, it's his lad I feel sorry for. My son goes to the same school as Mike's lad. He's forever turning up with a black-eye or a swollen jaw. I'm just hoping Mike doesn't take this out on the youngster."

Chapter One

DCI Andy Miller was standing in the rain outside a scruffy-looking red-bricked terraced house in Urmston. He and his colleague DI Keith Saunders were here on an unscheduled visit to interview a witness to a shooting which had occurred a few days earlier. The witness had already given an account to CID officers when the incident had happened, but the victim of the shooting had since died, and the case had become much more serious now, and had been handed up to Miller and his team at the Serious Crimes Investigation Unit. It was suspected that this shooting was linked to another one, two weeks earlier, seven miles away in Fallowfield.

But the witness wasn't answering the door.

"She's definitely in. I heard her shouting at someone when we first arrived."

"I know. I saw the curtain twitch a minute ago." Said Saunders quietly out of the side of his mouth.

"Well, she won't know us. She might think we're just debt-collectors or summat." Miller was feeling grumpy as the relentless rain bounced up from the pavement.

"Hello, Lisa Cummiskey. Are you in there? It's the police!" Shouted Saunders through the letterbox. There was an unmistakable smell released from the flap, the mouth-watering waft of bacon frying.

"Hello Lisa, it's the police. Need a quick word about the shooting you witnessed on Friday." Saunders was speaking politely. But there was still no response.

"Lisa!" He raised his voice this time. Saunders was also getting sick of this rain, he was soaked to the bone.

"Nah, she's having none of it. Probably scared, I bet some mate has warned her off helping us when she's told them that she's given a statement. It's understandable, I suppose. Come on." Miller walked towards his car, got in, and looked around to the back-seat to find something to dry his face and hands with. There was nothing, so he took his jacket off and used his shirt sleeves to try and soak up some of the water.

"Jesus. We should have phoned first."

"The number she left with CID won't connect. I think this Lisa Cummiskey wants to forget about the whole thing."

"What are you going to do?" asked Saunders, himself wriggling out of his soaking coat. The windows in the car were steaming up.

"I'll send Jo round. She'll sort it." Miller was talking about one of his DCs, Jo Rudovsky, the department's specialist "people-person."

"Yeah, that'll work."

Miller turned the car's ignition key, and began blasting the windows with the hot-air in a bid to de-steam them, when his phone started ringing.

"It's Dixon," he said as he pulled the phone from his pocket. "Hello Sir."

"Oh, Andy, hello. It's Dixon." Miller looked at Saunders and they both grinned.

"Yes, hi Sir," said Miller again, trying not to laugh at Dixon's weird telephone manner.

"Where are you?"

"I'll give you a clue Sir, I'm currently in the town which is only famous for being the birthplace of Morrisey."

"Morrisey who?" asked Dixon, sounding a little eager to get on with the conversation.

"Urmston, Sir. The town that inspired such wonderful songs as Everyday is like Sunday, and Heaven knows I'm Miserable Now."

"Right, well, I need a word actually. When will you be back here?"

"Not sure Sir, got a few interviews to do about the fatal shooting in Stretford on Friday."

"Oh, I see. Well, something's come up. I might need to take you off this one."

"Oh? What's come in?"

"Well, a schoolboy was reported missing a few days ago. He's known to run away from home, long history apparently. He'd been gone overnight when his father rang it in."

"How old?"

"Fifteen."

"And how long has he been missing?"

"Six days."

"Oh right. Shit. It's Wednesday today, so he was last seen Thursday?"

"That's right, as we understand it."

"But presumably something's come to light?" Miller knew that his elite detectives wouldn't be dragged into a missing teenager enquiry, especially one who had a history of disappearing, unless there was a very good reason.

"Yes, something rather peculiar has come up. His teacher has also disappeared, at roughly the same time from what we understand. The two have a very strained relationship. It's starting to look extremely iffy."

Miller looked across at Saunders in the passenger seat. They both raised their eyebrows.

"Okay, well if you can reallocate this murder investigation, I'll head back to HQ and we'll get cracking."

"Thank you, Andy. Come straight up to my office when you get back, I've got the file on my desk. I'll pass your shooting case back to Stretford CID. It has now slipped down our priority list somewhat."

Chapter Two

Miller and Saunders listened carefully to their boss, DCS Dixon, as he gave an overview of this rather suspicious missing-persons inquiry. Once they'd been informed of the basics and heard the essential details about each missing person, coupled with the fact that an altercation had taken place at the school between the two missing persons the previous Thursday morning, Miller and Saunders both recognised that this was going to be a significant investigation.

They finished up with Dixon and headed down to the SCIU floor. All of the team's detectives were in the office. DC Rudovsky and her partner DC Peter Kenyon were working on their investigation, while DCs Bill Chapman, Mike Worthington and Helen Grant were all working individually on their own case-loads. They all looked surprised to see their superiors, DI Saunders, and DCI Miller walking back into the office.

"Aw, we thought we'd got rid of you two for the day!" said Rudovsky, with a disappointed look on her face.

"Oh, aye?" said Miller. "Planning an early dart were you Jo?"

"No. Nothing like that Sir. I just can't stand looking at your face. So, its ace when it's not here."

"It's hard to believe that you're angling for a promotion Jo. It really is." Miller smiled at the DC and nudged Saunders to follow him into his office. Saunders closed the door.

"Right mate, sit down. You heard what Dixon said about this lot." Miller threw the file onto his desk, and sat down himself. "Got any thoughts?"

Saunders thought for a few seconds. There was no evidence of any crimes taking place. All that existed was a very dodgy looking coincidence. Eventually, he spoke.

"I think it's quite strange. But I'm not jumping the gun just yet Sir. Dixon gave me the impression that he's come to the conclusion that some harm has come to the young lad, and that the teacher is responsible. I've not quite reached that conclusion yet. So, I'll proceed cautiously with an open-mind for now."

"Well, that's best practise Keith. But it does stink, it has to be said."

"I'm not so sure. I'll know more once I've looked into the teacher's background, and sussed out what this young lad is all about." Saunders was undoubtedly the department's sharpest detective and his success was largely down to his very level-headed approach to his work. Miller smiled as he lifted the top sheet of the file and headed across to the photo-copier.

"Fair point, well put." Said the senior officer. "Okay, well if it's okay, I'll leave you to dig about in these two's backgrounds, while I pop down to the school and see if I can crack this case before you do."

"Excellent. Sounds like a plan Sir."

"Ask organised crime to apply for bank information on all of Mr Pollard's accounts. It will take about twenty-four hours to turn-around but the early bird catches the worm."

"Other clichés are available."

"When I get back, we'll compare notes and discuss whether we think we can cope, or if we need the others to jump off their work-loads and work on this."

"Okay. But let's hope that's not the case Sir, we're drowning in work. Could really do with the team staying put with their own stuff really."

Miller took the photocopy from the tray and handed the master file to Saunders.

"Noted. Okay, catch you in a bit. And if you solve this mystery before I get back, I'll have your guts for garters!"

Chapter Three

Miller arrived at the missing boy's school, Astley High in Stalybridge, and was shocked to see that there were several press reporters standing outside the main doors. As he grabbed his coat and briefcase off the back-seat of his car, he quickly worked out that any press-leak had come directly from the school. This angered Miller, as he slammed the door shut and pressed the lock on his key-fob. He walked quickly towards the school's main doors, keen to get inside before the rain started up again.

"DCI Miller! Are you treating this as an abduction scenario?" Asked a Granada Reports representative.

"Is it true that the missing pupil was recently assaulted in the school by the teacher?" Shouted a man waving a BBC Radio Manchester microphone.

"Do you have names for the missing people?"

There were several other questions but Miller avoided them all politely. From what he could gather from the questions, the press had a very vague understanding of the situation. That was good news in terms of identifying the source of the leak but the fact that they were aware of any details at all this early into the investigation was extremely frustrating.

The press had no idea how irritated Miller was, as he stepped through the barrage of questions. The only thing the well-known DCI said to them was, "good afternoon."

Once inside, Miller tapped on the glass of the office window. A rather stressed-looking lady in her fifties came across and slid the glass along its glider.

"I've already told your colleagues, we're not releasing any official statements at the present time." She looked like she wanted Miller to piss off.

"Sorry, I'm not with them. I'm DCI Miller, I've just been handed the case."

The receptionist looked embarrassed, and the expression on her face was confirmed as her cheeks turned red.

"Oh, I see. Have you an appointment?"

"Well, no... I thought, under the circumstances..."

"Sure, sure, come on through." The lady pressed a big green button, like something off a TV gameshow, and the door clicked. Miller nodded politely and headed through. She met him on the other-side of the doors.

"Sorry. Shall we start again?" She asked, extending her hand. For the first-time, Miller began to realise what a stressful morning this lady must have had. "I'm Mrs Horsfield. I'm the school secretary. We've just had the morning from hell, the phone has been non-stop, newspapers, radios, television news. And now this lot have turned up unannounced. I'm sorry, I just assumed you were with them."

"It's fine. Don't worry about it. I know how intrusive they can be."

"Well, there's intrusive, and there's down-right rude."

"Any idea how they've found out? I mean, it's not come from the police station. We have very strict rules about releasing information regarding our cases, particularly when they involve a minor."

"Oh, no, I mean, I assumed that it must have been from the police?"

"No. It must be somebody inside the school."

"Oh, I see." Mrs Horsfield looked a little embarrassed, and Miller had a sneaking suspicion that she might have leaked the story. He had an intuition for these things, he found little nuances that always gave people away. Mrs Horfield's over-genuine shock at what he'd said was a dead give-away.

"Any idea how much they know, from the questions they've been asking?"

"Er… not much from what I can gather. Just that a pupil and a teacher have been reported missing."

"Do they know the identities of the two?"

"No, no, definitely not. That's the main thing they are trying to find out. They're really stressing me out."

The secretary's response to that question made Miller revise his theory.

"If you get any more enquiries, which you will, just say that all press relations will be handled via Manchester City Police. That's the only information you are permitted to reveal.

Okay?"

She nodded, and looked relieved that she finally had something constructive to offer the media.

"We had an urgent staff briefing about it this morning, it will be a member of staff who has leaked it, probably a text message to a spouse, which has been passed on. Would explain the press not knowing very much."

Miller nodded. That made sense, and he started feeling bad for suspecting the secretary.

"Anyway, let's get down to business. Did you want to see anybody in particular?" asked Mrs Horsfield.

"Well, yes, as many people who know Mr Pollard, and Darren, as possible. I need to build up some background."

"Would you like to start with the Head?"

"Well, if it's alright with you, I'd like to start with you. I'm sure that your role as school secretary will bring you into contact with both Darren and Mr Pollard on a regular basis?"

Mrs Horsfield looked quite flattered to be the first of Miller's interviewees. "Certainly, come on into the office. I'll pull the blind on. Would you like a cup-of-tea?"

"No, no, I'm fine. Thank you. So, tell me a little bit about the two missing people, if you will." Miller sat down on the chair facing the school secretary's desk. She followed his lead and sat opposite him.

"Well, first of all, I'll place two-hundred pounds on a bet that Mr Pollard has got nothing to do with Darren Jenkins disappearance. He's one of the kindest, most professional teachers in the school. He'd have been Headmaster by now if it wasn't for the politics of modern education."

Miller smiled politely, but he didn't want a chat about internal bullshit. It was as though Mrs Horsfield read his mind, and just got on with it.

"He has worked here for thirty-something years. Half of the parents who come in on parents evening know him, he taught them. He's an old-fashioned, no-nonsense teacher with an impeccable reputation, both with staff and pupils alike. I really must impress this on you, he's the best-known personality in the whole school community."

Miller was making notes in his pad.

"Some of these questions that the press have been asking me, it's absolutely unforgivable. One asked if we knew that one of our teaching staff was a predatory paedophile!"

Miller smiled politely. He knew the press tactic of trying to gain information by upsetting the people they were quizzing.

"What about Mr Pollard's domestic situation?" asked Miller, lifting his head and making eye-contact. Mrs Horsfield seemed a little bit worked-up, and he sensed that she had the utmost respect for her colleague.

"He's recently moved out of the family-home, he has two grown up kids, Daniel and Jess. His ex-wife is… well, they are both good friends…"

"What's his ex called?"

"Sandra. She's not really… you know, I don't think they'll be separated long."

"What makes you say that," asked Miller, one eye-brow raised. This was new information, and contradicted Mr Pollard's missing person's report. Miller assumed that the school secretary might be a little behind with her gossip.

"Well, they're soul-mates at the end of the day. They've just struggled with the transition of the kids growing up and moving out. I'm sure they'll soon be back together. They got together when they were twenty and twenty-one."

"So, there are no third parties involved?"

"Oh no, God no, nothing like that. Sandra told me that they just row all the time, mainly because he's always working. If they go out for a meal, he starts talking about work. He stays up late marking, it's just a tricky time. They'll work through it."

"But Mr Pollard is…"

"Phil… please call him Phil."

"Okay, but Phil Pollard is missing. Are you not concerned about that fact?"

"Well, no I wouldn't say I'm concerned. A little curious perhaps. Like I say, he's a perfectly sensible, totally reliable man. He'll soon turn up."

"Do you have any theories about his whereabouts?"

"No."

"Any idea why he would simply take himself off somewhere during term-time?"

"Well, yes, actually." Mrs Horsfield stood, and stepped across to the door, ensuring that it was closed firmly, before turning back to face the detective. "This is strictly confidential mind, data protection and so forth…"

"Go on…"

"Well, Phil put in for early retirement at the last round of voluntary redundancy applications."

"Oh?"

"Yes, and from what I can gather, he was rejected. He's been here so long, his redundancy package would be extremely expensive. They tend to select applicants with shorter service, in order to make it economically advantageous."

"Okay, that's interesting. Have you got a phone number for Phil's ex… Sandra?"

Mrs Horsfield grabbed her handbag off the floor and found her phone. She started looking through the contacts list. "Here we are, 07584…" she read the number out to DCI Miller, who jotted the digits down.

"Thanks, and does Sandra work?"

"Yes, she works for Social Services over in Oldham."

"Thanks. That's been very interesting. I'll give her a call once I've finished here. Now, what can you tell me about the missing pupil, Darren… Jenkins?"

Mrs Horsfield's face changed. Where she had been talking affectionately about Phil and Sandra Pollard, her manner suddenly stiffened up.

"Darren is one of the school community's more challenging members. He is up here to see the Head more often than the Deputy Heads are."

"Naughty?"

"Well, we don't really use words like naughty anymore. But yes, he's what we would describe as behaviourally challenged."

"Oh right, that's a new one on me." Miller hated modern, made-up words and terms that don't even work as well as the words they were brought in to replace. What's up with just plain old 'naughty,' thought the DCI. "Would you care to explain what you mean by behaviourally challenged?"

"Well, we have certain pupils who don't want to be here. Subsequently, they make as much fuss as they can to stay outside of the classroom setting. Darren is a classic example. He's usually up here, on the corridor, in fact he's a regular feature outside this office. It has felt a bit weird without him there this week, if I'm being brutally honest."

"And tell me about Darren. Is he a nice lad, or a total head-banger?"

"He's nice. When he's on his own. But as soon as he has an audience, he's off on one. Darren is like two different people. If I'm alone in here, he can't do enough for me, he's quiet, polite, funny, kind-hearted. He'll do my errands, make me a coffee, he's even watered my plants and advised me that this one is getting too much sunlight!" The secretary pointed at a dry looking spider-plant on the window-sill and smiled. "But then, when another pupil walks in, he turns into a little monster!"

"In what way?" Miller seemed confused.

"Oh, last time, he was in here filling up the paper cupboard for me. Good as gold, just getting on with it. The next minute, a year-nine walked in here to pick up a message, and Darren turned into a different child. He was standing behind me, making funny faces, sticking the V's up behind my head, doing the curly-hair gesture. It's so annoying."

"How did you know?"

"Well, I could tell he was doing something, because the year-nine was trying not to laugh. So, I put two-and-two together, and checked the CCTV." Mrs Horsfield pointed up at the camera above Miller's head.

"So, you say he spends a lot of time here with you. What kind of things does he do wrong in the classroom?"

"Oh, I couldn't possibly say. I always ask him, and he just says he doesn't know, or says it wasn't him, or says the teacher has got it in for him. Whatever has happened, it is never his fault."

Miller was nodding, listening intently as he scribbled his notes.

"He was in a spot of trouble for bullying last year as well." Said Mrs Horsfield, almost thinking out-loud as the memory came back.

"Bullying?"

"Yes, no rough stuff, just name-calling. But it got quite bad, the boy's parents were not happy. There is a year-nine boy called Mark Arena who started getting a hard time from Darren."

"Oh right. That's interesting. Has the bullying stopped?"

"Yes, I think so. It came to a relatively quick conclusion. I think the parents were more upset with themselves for calling the boy that."

"What?"

"Mark Arena. Darren spent every day shouting 'Heeey Mark Arena!'"

Miller and the school secretary laughed at the child's unfortunate name. But the fun didn't last very long. Miller quickly pulled another question out of the bag.

"Forgive me for asking, but you don't seem particularly worried about all this. Is there a reason for that?"

Mrs Horsfield looked slightly annoyed by the question. It hadn't made her feel like she'd been made the prime suspect, but the question insinuated something that she couldn't quite put her finger on. Her cheeks were flushed again as she answered.

"Mr Miller, with respect, I've seen the comings-and-goings at this school for a long time. I imagine that you were in the second-year when I began work at this very desk."

"I left in 2007" said Miller, trying to keep the mood pleasant. The school secretary ignored his quip and continued with her point.

"In that time, I'd say we have had a pupil going walkabout once a term. I've seen the logic of teenagers up close and personal. I'd be extremely surprised if anything untoward has happened to Darren. Very surprised. This is just the latest attention-seeking stunt on a very long list, as far as I'm concerned."

"Really?"

"Really. Believe me, if I had the slightest suspicion that something untoward was going on, you'd be the first to know."

"Okay. Well I hope you're right."

"Have you spoken to Darren's peer group?"

"Peer group?" asked Miller, unfamiliar with the terminology.

"He has a small group of friends. Very small. He changes friends a lot, but he rebounds from one to the other. His long-standing friend is called Michael Donnelly. They've been going around since primary school. I think that he'd be a good person to talk to about Darren's whereabouts. If anybody is going to know the inner-workings of that child's mind, it will be Michael. I can get him up here for you, if you like."

"Yes, yes, that's a great suggestion. Thank you."

Mrs Horsfield lifted the phone off her desk and began talking a few seconds later. "Hi, it's Debbie. Can you see what lesson Michael Donnelly is in, and bring him up to the school office please?"

She placed the phone on its cradle, and looked at Miller. "He shouldn't be long. Mind you, he'll probably go for a cigarette on the way up here."

"Thanks a lot." Said Miller, as he made some additional notes on his pad.

"I'm sure this will all be settled soon enough."

"I hope you're right."

Chapter Four

"So, what's come in boss?" DC Jo Rudovsky was standing behind DI Keith Saunders, trying to see what he was doing, over his shoulder.

"Mind your nose, and pick your crows," said Saunders, without looking around.

"Well I can read the top copy. So, I know already. I'm just trying to engage you in conversation."

"And I'm busy, Jo."

"A young lad's gone missing, as well as his teacher? God, my mind's wandering already. Is it a love thing? The paedo teacher elopes with his forbidden fruit?"

Saunders carried on with his work, ignoring his best DC's attempts at distracting him.

"Oh, wait. The teacher has killed the kid, and gone Rambo on the moors?"

"Jo, off you fuck love."

"Ah, I know, the teacher has been seen going into a brothel by the kid, and the kid has tried blackmailing him. So, the teacher has thrown him down a well?"

"Jo, seriously mate. Go and jump off the roof."

"Charming!"

"Well, it's you. You're doing my head in. I don't know what's happened yet, do I? So, I don't need you talking a load of shit next to my right ear."

"Okay, the kid has been injured by the teacher, and he's hiding him away until he can work out a plausible plan that will help him to get away with it."

"Jo…"

"I'm only trying to help."

"If you want to help, go and work on your own file. If you put this much effort into your own case, you'd have it cracked by the time I've finished reading these notes."

"My case is boring. A dead prostitute with links to every drug-dealer in the city. It's making me self-harm, everyone knows what's happened, except us. This one looks well exciting though. Let me work on this please. Come on, boss. Please."

Saunders finally turned around. Rudovsky was wearing her customary charming, innocent grin.

"Jo, can I ask you a personal question?"

"How personal?"

"About you being a knob-head."

"Yes, go on then. I'm not proud."

"Were you a dickhead like this when you were at school?"

"You what?"

"Well, I'm reading notes about the missing kid, Darren Jenkins. He has a long history of doing everybody's head in. And, well, the description I'm reading, it reminds me of you."

"So, it says the missing lad is ace, basically?"

"No, not quite. It says he's really annoying. He's got a history of being a pain in the arse. But he's extremely bright, articulate and quick-witted. So, the teachers are really frustrated because he has the potential to be the brightest kid in the school. But instead he refuses to do the work, pisses about and jumps on the teacher's desk with his school-bag on his head shouting "I've got AIDS! I've got VD! I've got an itchy tit and I hope you catch it!"

Rudovsky laughed loudly, holding her hand up to her mouth to hide her embarrassment at being amused by such a stupid, childish thing.

"Is that what you were like at school?"

The DC regained her composure. "I wasn't quite like that. But I used to get into a lot of bother for talking, messing about and all that. I don't think I'm quite in the league of this one, though." Rudovsky laughed again.

"But you're like that now, aren't you? I mean, don't get me wrong Jo, it's what makes you, you. You bring a great vibe to the team. But I imagine its hard work trying to get through school with that kind of a personality?"

"Well, it was a long time ago. And I'm on nearly forty grand a year now, so it doesn't really matter, does it?"

"I remember when I was at school. There was a kid in our class who was a total throbber. Jason Parker. He used to bang his knee against the bottom of his desk in every lesson, dead loud, it made everyone jump. When the teacher had a go at him, he used to deny it, and accused the teacher of picking on him."

"What else did he do?" asked Jo.

"He was just a doughnut Jo. He wanted to be the centre of attention all the time. But the stuff he used to do, the remarks he used to shout out... it wasn't funny. Maybe once every sixty-times he'd strike lucky and get a laugh. But mostly, the rest of the class just tutted or called him a spack."

"A spack? You can't say that Sir!"

"I know, I know, but it was what we said in the eighties. He used to get crap off the teachers all day, and then he'd get beaten up off the other pupils after school, and then his parents would give him hell when he got home. I used to look at him and wonder what the hell possessed him to be such a knob. I mean, it must have been a shit existence for him. But, all the other forms in our school had a Jason Parker. I think every class has one."

"Every class except this one..." said Jo, pointing to the paperwork.

"Precisely. I need to find this kid as soon as possible. And I think that in order to do that, I need to get a better understanding of what goes on inside his head. I was always perfect at school, so it's a new world to me. But I think you might be quite useful to me for this, in your role as the resident gob-shite. So, go back to your desk, get on with your work, and if you behave well, I'll let you do something on this. If you're good."

"Bloody Norah Sir, I'm not sure I like you acting like a teacher. I might start trying to do your head in!" Rudovsky smiled widely.

"Jo, I can assure you that you do my head in every single day of the week. But I wouldn't be without you."

Chapter Five

"Hello Michael, I'm DCI Andy Miller from the police."

"Alright?" said the young lad as he threw his school-bag on the floor and stood in front of Miller.

"Take a seat, lad."

Michael sat down. He had the typical, huffy attitude of a teenager. His face was covered in acne, and his attempts at growing a beard were comical. Miller wondered if he wanted to grow the beard to cover his angry-looking zits. His black hair looked as though it had been in style several months ago, and that he was now desperately due a trip to the barbers.

"Ever been in trouble with the police, Michael?"

"No, why? What's been said?"

"Nothing."

"No, I've not done nothing."

"Good. That's great to hear. But your mate Darren has had a few brushes with the law, hasn't he?"

"I'm not sure about that. Well, maybe. A few times."

"Any idea where he is?" asked Miller, deciding to cut through the warm-up act and get straight to the point.

Michael looked down at his feet, and Miller sensed that he had stiffened up a bit. It was a reassuring gesture.

"Michael, come on, tell DCI Miller what you know…" said Mrs Horsfield, which broke Michael out of his trance.

"I don't know. Honest. He's not said nothing to me about running away or anything. I swear down."

"When did you last see Darren?"

"The other day, the day he ran off, Thursday. He knocked on for me on the way to school but it was well early. I'd only just got out of bed."

"What time?"

"Dunno, about five past eight."

"Was that unusual?"

"Yes, DCI Miller," said Mrs Horsfield. "Extremely unusual. These two usually arrive at five past nine, don't you Michael?"

The teenager grinned and looked down again. The grin

broke into a laugh, which Michael tried to conceal. It was as though the school secretary's observation had given him some kudos, which in turn gave his ego a slight boost.

"So what time would Darren usually knock at your door?" pressed Miller.

"Dunno. About quarter to..."

"And how far away do you live?"

"Not far, about twenty minutes away."

"Have you any idea why Darren was running ahead of schedule then," Miller checked his notes, "last Thursday morning?"

"He had to give something to Well'ard."

Miller looked confused.

Mrs Horsfield interjected. "I think Michael meant to say Mr Pollard, didn't you?"

"Miss."

"Is that the school nickname for Mr Pollard?" asked Miller, continuing to make notes.

"Yeah. He's been called that for years. You used to hear about Well'ard before you even started at this school." Michael seemed to be glad that he was being listened to. Miller got the impression that he rarely had this kind of opportunity.

"And why do they call him that?" asked the DCI.

"Well, I think it's because he's the teacher you don't mess with. He doesn't take any messing about."

"And what was it that Darren had to give to Well'ard?" asked Miller. It received a chuckle from Michael.

"Some essay or summat. Daz had to get it to Well'ard before assembly. If he didn't, Well'ard was going to make him get up at the front of the whole school and show him up."

Miller looked across at Mrs Horsfield, to try and gauge if she knew anything about this. He could tell that she didn't.

"Okay, you're really helping me here Michael, I really appreciate it."

"It's alright."

"So, why did Well'ard make Darren do the essay?"

"He was sent out of class or summat, he was shouting beans-on-toast, so Well'ard said he had two choices. He said Daz had to either do a two-thousand word essay, or he had to come to the front and shout beans-on-toast all the way through assembly."

"So, he chose to do the essay?"

"Yeah, well, it's like, he was really excited about it. When he came to mine, I said come in while I get ready, but he just shot off. Said he wanted to get this to Well'ard."

"Okay. So he got to school, and then there was some altercation on the corridor? Is that right?"

"I don't…"

"An altercation is an argument, Michael," said Mrs Horsfield, with an encouraging smile on her face.

"Oh, right, well I'm not sure. Like I said, I was at home."

"And you've not seen Darren since he knocked on at yours?" asked Miller.

Michael shook his head.

"Have you heard from him at all? Facebook, text message or anything?"

"No. Nothing."

"And do you think he'll be alright?"

"Yeah, yeah, definitely. He just… he hates his dad. His dad hates him. He hates school, and everyone at school hates him. So, I bet he's just done a runner."

"Has he talked about that kind of thing before?"

"Yeah, all the time. He's always on about it."

"And what does he say? What would you say is his plan for running away?"

"Well, I'm not… nothing pacific. He just always says that he's going to get away from everyone. I never take him seriously. He's just talk."

"Until now?"

"Well, probably, yeah. I think so."

"Do you know if Darren has any cash?"

"No, not really. He has his paper-round money. Gets paid Fridays. He gets about seventeen quid."

"And no savings or anything?"

"Nah. You're joking aren't you. He spends his wages on the way to school normally! Fills his bag with tosh."

"Where does he do this paper-round? I mean, which shop is it?"

"It's the paper-shop near his house, Raj's."

Miller made some more notes, before he spoke again. "And you say he has a tough-time at home?"

"Yeah, well, he's always in mither. Always grounded for summat."

"And does mum not live at the address?"

"Nah, she moved out about a year ago. She lives down in Scotland now. Daz goes there sometimes."

"Okay, well that's interesting. I might need to speak to you again, if that's alright Michael?"

The teenager shrugged.

"Well done Michael, what lesson are you supposed to be in?" asked the school secretary.

"Art, Miss."

"Right, well you go back, and tell Mr Francis that you've been here with me. Okay?"

"Miss."

Once Michael had left, Miller asked Mrs Horsfield if he could speak to the head, Mrs Houghton. He was quickly led through into the head's office, next door.

"Good afternoon," said Mrs Houghton. She was an attractive lady, roughly the same age as Miller, early forties. She looked quite relaxed, which surprised Miller as the school was in the middle of a crisis which had attracted news reporters to besiege the place.

"Ah, hello. Sorry to intrude..."

"Not at all, not at all. Please take a seat. Can I organise a drink for you? Tea, coffee?"

"No, no I'm fine, thank you. I just wanted to pick your brains about this peculiar situation we find ourselves with."

"Yes, naturally. It's very peculiar."

Mrs Horsfield left, and Miller thanked her for her help.

"She's been a great help," said Miller as the secretary closed the door.

"Excellent." Said the head.

"I've spoken to Michael Donnelly. He's been very

helpful, too."

"Oh good, I'm glad to hear that. He can be a handful at times. It's good to learn that he has been helpful. I'll give him a gold star."

"So, I was just hoping to hear your thoughts?"

"Of course. Well, as you've probably gathered already, I was the last member of staff to speak to Mr Pollard before he stormed out of school last Thursday morning."

"He stormed out, you say?"

"Yes. I gave him some constructive feedback about his handling of the incident with Darren Jenkins. He didn't take it too well, it would seem."

"And do you usually have a good relationship with Mr Pollard?"

"Well, I wouldn't say 'good.' It's quite a frosty relationship in all honesty. He doesn't really approve of the direction that the education sector has travelled in over the past decade. I think he views me as being somehow responsible."

"So, you don't get along?"

"Well, yes, professionally, we have no choice. We get along, just about, but we're not likely to meet for drinks outside of the school environment."

"Tell me about the circumstances of Mr Pollard storming out please," said Miller as he turned a fresh page in his notebook.

"Right, well Darren had been to see him, first thing on Thursday morning. Mr Pollard had sent him away, and Darren apparently snapped. He flung a door open in the corridor, smashing the glass, before running out of the school. He's not been seen or heard of by my staff since."

"And do we know why he reacted so violently to Mr Pollard?"

"Yes, well that was the reason that I had a go at, sorry, the reason why I gave the constructive feedback to Mr Pollard. Darren had written a very heart-felt letter to him, and Mr Pollard told him that he didn't have time to read it."

"Michael said that Darren seemed excited to bring the work in for Mr Pollard. Was this letter the work that he was talking about?"

"Yes, it was an essay, two-thousand words I think. It was Darren's attempt at explaining the way that he felt, describing the problems that he faced in the school community. He was really wearing his heart on his sleeve."

"You saw the letter?"

"Yes. I read it. Then I had a word with Mr Pollard, and he went off. As I understood it, he had gone to try and locate Darren and bring him back into school, and to get the situation resolved. But obviously, that hasn't happened. I instructed Mr Pollard to return to school when he phoned me, but he hung up. We've not seen or heard from Mr Pollard since."

"And what time did he go looking for Darren?"

"It would be around about 10am."

"So, a good while after Darren had broken the door?"

"Yes, the incident happened just after eight-thirty. So, there is a window of around ninety minutes."

"Do we have any concrete evidence that Mr Pollard was inside the school until 10am?" Miller was thinking of the paperwork he'd have to submit to the CPS, much further down the line, if Pollard *was* with Darren Jenkins.

"Yes, he left through the main doors, which are covered by CCTV inside and out."

Miller wrote in his pad. "Do you still have the note that Darren gave to Mr Pollard?"

"No. And I have looked in Mr Pollard's office. But it looks as though he took it with him. He still hadn't read it by the time I had. So presumably, he took it with him with the intention of reading it. It was a very good letter, very mature. Very thoughtful."

"And what was the main thrust of it?"

"Well basically, Darren was saying that he hates school, and that he hates messing about all the time, and that he can't help himself. He concluded that he wanted to leave school. I really think that he poured his heart and soul into it and was devastated when Mr Pollard just dismissed it."

Miller looked up from his paperwork and locked eyes with Mrs Houghton. "What's your theory of what's happened?"

The headteacher looked a little flummoxed by the question. It had come from nowhere and Miller could tell by her body-language that he'd caught her off-guard. He sensed that she hadn't actually come up with a theory and that she was slightly embarrassed about that. It made her appear as though she didn't really care either way. They both felt their cheeks warming up as an awkward silence hung heavily in the air.

"I'm... I mean, this is still a very new consideration. I've not actually had..."

"What's your initial reaction to the suggestion that Mr Pollard and Darren are together?"

Mrs Houghton looked stunned by the question.

"It's the angle the press are reporting. And by the way, the leaking of this story has only come from here..."

The head tried to cobble a sentence together. Her mouth was open and she looked engaged to speak. But no words came out. Eventually, she spoke, and she sounded different, her polite but patronising accent had dropped away noticeably.

"The press are involved?"

Miller raised an eye-brow. He wondered how it was possible that the person in charge of running this school could be unaware that the place had a press-pack at the main-doors.

"Well, they were when I walked in here. They're camped outside."

This announcement made the headteacher's face turn white. Miller was starting to think that this lady was out of her depth in this job. Maybe that's what Mr Pollard thought too, maybe that would explain the tension between them. Miller was thinking fast as Mrs Houghton was clearly planning her press-statement in her head. One thing was certain from this encounter, Miller didn't rate the headteacher of this school. Not in the slightest.

"Do you know if Mr Pollard has a history of any mental health issues?" asked Miller.

"No, certainly not. I know he's been having some domestic problems in recent months. But no, I'm confident that he's not ill."

"What about Darren? Do you think he might have a tendency to hurt himself?"

"No. I don't think so. Kids like him are only down for a few minutes before they bounce back up. I'm sure that his lust for life is currently just as strong as ever!" Mrs Houghton tried to make it into a sarcastic remark.

Miller had had enough of this woman's failure to grasp the enormity of the situation. He hadn't planned to put a flea in her ear, but as the words came out of his mouth, he realised that he was doing.

"Mrs Houghton. I'm becoming concerned that you seem completely oblivious of the magnitude of this situation. We have an adult and a child from this school reported as missing persons. The two people disappeared on the same day, within a very short-time frame of each other. My job is to locate them, in the quickest time possible. I'm afraid you need to sharpen yourself up a little if I'm to be successful."

Mrs Houghton looked stunned, and rather ashamed. Miller felt that he'd hit the bullseye with his assessment of her. She was way out of her depth in this job, and right now, when the chips were down, she looked like a frightened rabbit caught in the headlamps. He wondered if she was about to cry.

"Mr Miller, I…"

"Do you think that Mr Pollard might have taken Darren?"

"In what respect…"

"I don't know. To teach him a lesson for smashing the place up? He might have gone to give him a bollocking, and things got out of hand?"

"No, I don't… I really don't think that…"

"Michael told me that Mr Pollard is best known amongst the pupils as Well'ard. Can you explain that nickname?"

"No, it's meant affectionately. It's a term of endearment. No pupils have ever made any accusations against Mr Pollard. He's as straight as they come."

"But he's called Well'ard for something. He has been for decades apparently. Do you know why?"

"Well I imagine that his no-nonsense approach with the

pupils can be seen by some as 'hard' if you like. And it's a funny play on Pollard, isn't it?" Mrs Houghton seemed to be recovering from Miller's harsh questioning a little.

"As the DCI of Manchester's serious crimes unit, I've been given this job because the police force think that it is an extremely concerning case. Can you explain why you seem so relaxed about it all?" Miller was going in on the Headteacher as though she was a suspect, and he was sitting in the interview room back at HQ.

"Look, I understand if you feel slightly frustrated. But I don't know what I can say to you. I do not believe that Mr Pollard has had any involvement in this. I imagine that it is a very bizarre coincidence. Nothing more. I have every faith that Darren will walk in here any moment now, as though nothing has happened."

"What about Mr Pollard?"

"Well, I have no idea about that."

"I think you may do."

Mrs Houghton stared squarely at Miller. She looked as though she was getting tired of his aggressive interview technique. "I'm sorry. What is that supposed to mean?"

"Has Mr Pollard put in a request for voluntary redundancy?"

"Oh, I see. Well that's entirely out of my hands. I have no jurisdiction over these matters, it's the education department who oversee these human resources matters."

"Do you know if his application was successful, or unsuccessful?"

"I believe that it was unsuccessful. Three members of my staff applied for two redundancy packages. I'm aware that two members of staff were told they had been successful last week."

"Were either of them Mr Pollard?"

"No."

"And what day were these announcements made?"

"Last Wednesday."

"The day before he disappeared?"

Mrs Houghton looked as though she'd not put these

details together in her mind. Miller could see the penny begin to drop but he decided to help it on its way.

"So, Mr Pollard's marriage has just broken down, he has a pupil doing his head in on a daily basis, and has been knocked back for a redundancy package, and the next day, you give him a bollocking for not reading a letter off the kid that has probably driven him so crazy that he's applied for redundancy in the first place. And you don't think this is significant?"

"Well...I..."

"Tell you what, Miss. Remind me not to send my two to this school."

Chapter Six

"Alright Keith, it's Miller."

"Hi Sir."

"Hiya, right, interesting stuff here at the school. I'm going to go off to see Darren's dad. Something sounds a bit iffy with him."

"Okay."

"Do us a favour. Just have a quick look at the paperwork. I want to know if the constables who visited and took the initial missing person's report checked the house out?"

"One sec, Sir." The line went quiet, but for the sound of paper-shuffling. "Er, according to the reports Sir, this report was taken by phone. There hasn't been a visit."

"For fucks sake..." said Miller. The way that the government cuts were affecting the very basic standards of policing in the region was becoming unbelievable. A minor was missing for over five days and nights, and a police officer hadn't even been to the property to make the most basic checks.

"He has had a few previous runaways, Sir. Might explain it."

"Well, maybe, but if anything has happened to him Keith, there'll be an inquiry and whoever decided not to attend will be in court mate."

"Yes. Looks like a very bad call."

"Right, well, I'll need somebody with me. Is anybody at a loose-end in the office?"

Saunders laughed sarcastically. Miller knew full-well that there were no loose-ends. The department was as busy as it had ever been.

"Jo seems eager to get involved with this one," said Saunders quietly, so that she didn't hear him from across the office.

"What's she working on?"

"Agnieszka Nowacki."

"Oh, yes. Fair enough, send Jo over to meet me at Astley High School, Stalybridge, blue lights. Tell her to text me when's she's on the car park."

"Will do Sir."

Cheers. I'm nearly done here. How are your inquiries going?"

"Nothing too exciting. The teacher, Mr Pollard checks out as a perfectly normal family-man. There's no history of any wrong-doing from a criminal or professional point-of-view. He's squeaky clean, highly regarded by staff, pupils and education department employees."

"Yes, that's what I've been hearing. Over thirty-years service here, too."

"As for the boy, he's quite chaotic, he's got lots of misdemeanours and cautions to his name. Plus, he's been put forward for psychiatric tests by the school."

"Oh?"

"Yes, his report from the education authority suggests that he has undiagnosed ADHD. But he's failed to attend the two appointments that were set up for him. He's gone off their radar now, as he's approaching his final year. But I thought it was worth noting."

"Absolutely. So, who would have the responsibility for getting him to the psychiatrist? Would that be school, or parents?"

"Well most health matters fall to the parent. But I can check."

"No, its alright. I've got a very helpful school secretary stood next to me. I'll ask her."

"Okay. Well, I'll catch you later."

"Tell Jo to get a hurry on."

"Yes, okay, Sir. See you later."

*****

Miller asked Mrs Horsfield to gather all of the school's staff in the main hall for an urgent meeting. He was impressed at how quickly the teachers had managed to break away from their classrooms and unite in the school's main hall.

"How did you organise all this so quickly?" asked Miller as more and more adults filed into the school hall, filling the space in the middle very quickly.

"Just a text message to all staff. I wrote 'urgent meeting, all staff, main hall, ASAP.' We use the system quite a lot, it's much more efficient than walking around each classroom and handing a note to every teacher!"

"Great, well, it's worked out perfectly. Are they all here?" asked Miller out of the side of his mouth, once the doors had stopped opening, and new faces had stopped appearing before him.

"Yes, I think so. I'm quite confident that everybody is here."

"Great, cheers." Said Miller, before raising his voice loudly enough to be heard by the seventy or so teachers, support staff and administration employees. He addressed the sea of anxious looking faces before him.

"Good afternoon. I'm DCI Miller, and I'm leading the investigation into the missing persons enquiry. I'm sure at least one of you will know why I've asked you all to break away from your lessons. I need you all to keep a lid on the information that you learnt this morning, regarding the enquiries that I am overseeing. The press have caught on to this already, but they don't know very much. I need it to stay that way. So please, if any of you are contacted by anybody asking questions, I want you to simply state that you are not permitted to comment, and point them in the direction of the Manchester police press office. They all know the drill, but they will try it on. So, I just wanted to warn you all of the situation. Somebody stood in here did reveal information today, either directly to the press, or indirectly through a partner or friend. This could potentially hinder my enquiries. I must inform you all that you could face criminal charges if you leak any information at all, about either of the missing persons, to the press. Am I understood?"

The teachers all said "yes," in unison. Many of them looked concerned and nervous, and Miller couldn't help but wonder which one of them had been unable to keep the hot gossip quiet.

"Okay, thank you everybody and please keep your mouths shut from now on. If any of you have any information that you feel would be valuable to me, please don't hesitate to get my contact details from Mrs Horsfield. Okay, you can go back to your work, and thanks again for such a prompt response attending this meeting."

The teachers shuffled back towards the doors at either end of the large hall, unsure of whether they'd just been bollocked, or not. That had been a very intense and to-the-point encounter, and had lasted less than five minutes.

*****

Miller went back up to the school office with Mrs Horsfield, and waited for Rudovsky to arrive. He was checking the Manchester Evening News, BBC North West and the Sky News pages on his phone. He knew that he'd have to say something to the press on his way out, so had decided to see what they were reporting first. It was all very vague, but quite sensational. Sky News were reporting "Pupil and Teacher with Long History of Disputes Reported Missing." There really wasn't much more to it, other than the name of the school, and a by-line of "more to follow."

A text message popped up on the screen. It was from Rudovsky. "Hello Sir, I'm on the car park."

Miller text back. "Good stuff. I'll probably be followed by reporters so just follow my car. There in a minute."

The DCI thanked Mrs Horsfield for her help. She had been extremely helpful, especially in mentioning the redundancy issue. He left the school's main doors and walked straight into the middle of the press-pack, which had trebled in size since he'd arrived an hour or so earlier. The media staff were blocking the doors, so he had no alternative but to stay put.

"DCI Miller! What can you tell us about this enquiry?"

"DCI Miller! Can you confirm that the pupil has been abducted?"

"DCI Miller! Is there any truth in the rumour that the missing child was attacked by the missing teacher?"

Miller just stood still and let the questions wash over him. The enthusiastic shouting continued. In the end, he raised his hand, which worked in hushing them.

"Hello everyone. If you can simmer down a bit, I'll give you a brief statement."

The press-pack began shouting again, and Miller stared at the Sky News camera with a look of abject disappointment at the daft behaviour of the press. He waited for them to settle down again.

"Okay, if you're just going to shout at me, I'll not give you any information." This quietened them. "Okay, I can confirm that we are currently investigating two separate missing-persons reports. As you are currently reporting, both are members of this school's community. At this stage, I am not able to reveal the identities of either person, or whether the disappearances are linked, as this investigation is still very young, and we have no hard facts to work on at this point. But we'd like to reassure the public that we are treating this investigation with the utmost urgency. I still have a number of initial enquiries to make at this point, but I will organise a press-conference for later in the day. Hopefully, by that point, I will have a good deal more information to share. I'll ask the press-office to alert you once the press conference has been arranged. Thank you."

Miller started pushing his way through the press team and walked away from the school doors towards the car park fifty or so yards away. Several reporters followed him and continued shouting questions at the back of him. But most of the reporters knew Miller of old, and knew that once he'd finished talking, and had said thank you, that always meant that there was nothing more to come for now.

Chapter Seven

Miller and Rudovsky parked their cars outside the home of Darren Jenkins. The address was Sand Street, a row of old red-bricked terraced houses on the border of Stalybridge where it merges into Dukinfield. The missing boy's house was on a street that looked as though it had been forgotten about long ago, in much the same way that the nearby crumbling mills and decaying factories had. The street still had its old cobbles, and the run-down house had a knackered old Ford Mondeo parked outside it. It had started life as a white car, but today, it looked like the present owner was concerned that it might fall apart if it was washed.

The street was very quiet, and Miller was relieved to see that the press hadn't discovered the address details of the missing boy, yet. There wasn't a reporter in sight, and Miller knew that it was only a matter of time before this unremarkable northern street was over-run with press trucks and paparazzi cameras.

Miller got out of his car, and got into Rudovsky's once she had parked up behind him. "Alright Jo?"

"Sir."

"I'll fill you in on the background I've picked up from the school later. For now, I just want to have a few words with the lad's father, Michael Jenkins."

"Yep, no problem, Sir."

"You'll pick a lot of it up anyway, as I ask questions."

"No doubt."

"But the headline here, is that these two seem to hate each-others guts, and mum is out of the picture. I'm pretty sure that most of the answers to this mystery will be revealed here. Okay, well, we'd better go and find out. In for a penny, in for a pound."

The two detectives got out of Rudovsky's vehicle and climbed the two steep kerb-steps up from the cobbled street to the pavement, and the home of Michael and Darren Jenkins.

Miller rat-a-tat-tatted on the wooden front door. The house looked like a rented, housing association type of property as many of the doors were painted the same colour, and shared the same style of the letterboxes and door-numbers. It was the poorer end of Stalybridge, by the derelict buildings, supermarkets and factories, so it stood to reason that the missing lad's guardian wasn't a home-owner.

A man in his late thirties answered the door, he looked as though he'd just woken up.

"Alright?" he asked. His brown hair was stuck up at one side, and his stubble had passed the five o'clock stage. He was wearing a vest top, and his arms were full of shit tattoos.

"Hello, I'm DCI Andrew Miller, this is my colleague DC Jo Rudovsky. I'm afraid we need to speak to you about Darren."

"Come in." He said, swinging the door open. He looked as though he wasn't particularly happy about this unscheduled visit.

Miller's and Rudovsky's instincts told them straight away that this guy was a wrong 'un. The first clue was in the way that he gave no reaction to the introductory statement that Miller had made. The DCI had worded it in such a vague, ominous way that it should have created a look of panic on the parent's face. The sentence was so loaded with potential doom, that Miller had expected the parent to fall to his knees in tears, fearing the very worst news. But instead, the potentially devastating introduction earned nothing more than a huff.

Miller immediately placed the missing lad's father under suspicion. Rudovsky had picked up on it too. They both had one question on their minds. What did this guy know, that had prepared him for such a relaxed reception to potentially devastating news? Something wasn't right.

"Thanks," said Rudovsky as she stepped past Mike Jenkins. He just shrugged and closed the door behind her. The three were standing in a small front-room. There was very little furniture in there, just a sofa, an armchair, an enormous TV and a coffee-table which was covered in all sorts of shite, from a crusty, dirty plate which needed a good hour in soak at least, before it could be cleaned. There was other junk, from take-away cartons, over-flowing ashtrays to empty beer-cans. A greasy pizza box lay on the filthy laminate floor, by the settee.

"So, what's going on?" asked Mr Jenkins. He had his hands in the back pockets of his jeans, and relaxed wasn't the word. Miller suspected that he was a bit stoned.

"Well, we're leading the missing persons enquiry..."

"Yeah, yeah, something popped up on Facebook about it before..."

"So, we thought we'd come along and introduce ourselves."

"Well, how do you do?" asked Jenkins.

"Mr Jenkins, if we find Darren alive and well, would you prefer it if we just took him straight into care?" Rudovsky's kind and caring face often caught strangers off-guard when she suddenly pounced like this. Her warm, endearing eyes helped make her most unexpected, most vicious questions cut all the deeper.

Miller looked stunned. That was a pretty nuclear start to the chat.

"Eh, what?" asked Jenkins, with a judder.

"Well, you clearly couldn't give a fuck..."

"Hey, just a minute..."

"No, I've got a fifteen-year-old lad to look for, and I haven't got time for any arse-hole parents acting the dick."

"Alright DC Rudovsky," said Miller. "That's enough." Miller said it in a tone which Rudovsky recognised as "nice one Jo, you fucking legend." Her bombastic approach had knocked this man's sky-high confidence right down. He looked embarrassed and dazed.

"I think that my colleague has a point, Mr Jenkins. You don't seem particularly concerned about Darren's disappearance."

"You don't know about my life..." said Jenkins, sounding as though he was about to try and make all this about him. "Walk a mile in my shoes, then see what you think."

"Well, one thing that I do know about your life, is that you haven't phoned the police station once to ask how the missing person's enquiry is going. In fact, the only contact you've made was to report him missing, and the duty-log from the control-room states that you told the operator that you had to report it, otherwise you'd be liable for any absence fines from Darren's school."

"Yeah, well, that's right though innit? They've got it in for me down at that shit-hole school. Any excuse to have a fucking pop. That's what they're like. Sad bastards."

Miller and Rudovsky caught one another's eyes. They both saw what the other was thinking. They were thinking they were stood with a professional victim. One who had no interest in anybody other than himself.

"Any idea where Darren is?"

"No."

"None at all?"

"No. Why would I?"

"Okay, tell you what pal," said Miller. "If you don't sort this shitty attitude problem out, you'll be coming down the station to answer our questions, under arrest."

"Fuck's sake." Said Jenkins. "What do you want me to say? I don't know where he is, he's a little dick. How am I supposed to know where the fuck he's gone?"

The DCI exhaled a long, heavy breath and allowed a silence to follow it. "Look, shall we start again?" asked Miller, eventually.

Jenkins shrugged.

"A good start might be the offer of a seat?"

Jenkins gestured to the settee. Neither Miller or Rudovsky could stand this bloke. He really did have a chip on his shoulder the size of Blackpool Tower. They sat down, and Jenkins remained standing on the opposite side of the manky coffee-table.

"Can you sit down as well please?" asked Rudovsky, in a voice that didn't hide her irritation at this bizarre spectacle. She was setting up her dictaphone on the coffee-table, and had to move several items of rubbish to one side to create the space. Jenkins sat down in the chair opposite, leaning right back as though he was getting settled to watch a football match. He didn't look like a man who was being quizzed by police about his missing teenage son.

"I'm going to record our conversation on this," said

Rudovsky in a matter-of-fact manner.

"Is that normal?" asked Jenkins.

"Well, it's quite normal," said Miller. "My colleague is a very slow writer, so it speeds things up considerably. But if you prefer, she can take notes by hand?"

"Nah, makes no difference to me." Jenkins seemed like a man without a care in the world. It intrigued the detectives, who thought that all this was just a front. They were both eager to get going with the questions, and see what this guy was all about.

"So, Mr Jenkins, this shouldn't take long... is that recording Jo?"

Rudovsky nodded to her boss.

"So, tell me about your relationship with Darren."

"What do you want me to say? He's a little shit."

"Do you have any positive things we could say about him?"

"Well, no. Not really. He's bananas, always has been. He just wants to do your head in. Morning, noon and night. You say summat to him, like 'don't do that' and you can bet your life he'll just do it all the more. That's why his mam pissed off, and left me, stuck here with the ungrateful little bastard."

"So, you really can't find anything positive to say about Darren? I mean we'll be talking to the press later. We'll need some nice comments to say about him."

Jenkins huffed. "There's not much, like I say. He's one of life's little dickheads. He's pretty good at art, I'll give him that. Good at drawing."

"Anything else?" asked Rudovsky.

"I suppose he's pretty good at sport, he's a fast runner. I've chased him up that street a few times and he goes like shit off a shovel."

"One of the staff at the school described Darren as behaviourally challenged." Said Miller.

"Yes, that's it. Nice one. Little shit, described in posh words!" Jenkins laughed and clicked his middle-fingers three-times in appreciation of his wise-crack.

Miller and Rudovsky shared an uneasy glance at one

another. It was brief, but they both knew from that milli-second of eye-contact that they were on the same page, they were picking up the same scent from this.

Miller continued with his relaxed, gentle questioning technique, which was working brilliantly. In just a few minutes, they had the dad talking with contempt about his missing boy on numerous occasions.

"The lady at school also said that Darren is extremely funny, very kind-hearted, and charming. She also said that he can be very thoughtful." Miller let his statement hang while Jenkins mulled it over. After a few seconds, he grinned.

"Well, I wish he'd try some of that in here!"

Rudovsky had an urge to ask if Darren was that bad, but she sensed it could wait. It would only renew the tension from a little earlier.

"Tell us about the day before Darren went missing."

"In what way?"

"Well, I'm just trying to establish if there was an argument or anything?"

"There's always a fucking argument. Let me think, when was it, last Wednesday. Oh yeah, I remember now, he was acting proper weird. He sneaked in the house after school, went straight upstairs. I shouted him down and told him to make me a brew. He did, and just went upstairs. I didn't see him apart from when he came down for his tea."

"And what did he have for his tea?" asked Rudovsky.

"I can't remember now... what is this, Mastermind?"

"Try and think, please."

"I think it was a pizza. Yes, I did him a frozen pizza. He took it up to his room. The plate will still be there."

"So from finishing school, Darren stayed in his room all night?"

"Yeah. Which is good because it means he isn't outside causing any shit."

"And the following morning. Did you see Darren before school?"

"No, I was still in bed."

"Do you not work at the moment Mr Jenkins?" asked

Rudovsky.

"Yeah, yeah, course I work. But... I'm off at the minute."

"Off? On leave?"

"Leave? You mean holiday?"

"Yes."

"Well, yeah, I suppose so."

"And Darren is used to sorting himself out in the mornings is he?"

"Yes, he has his paper-round. I'll give him that, he gets up and goes with no hassle."

"Thanks. Now as you probably know, he went to school but ran out just before school was due to start. Do you have any idea what that was about?"

"No. Why would I? He's in trouble there at least once a day. I've lost interest to be honest. The more you say don't do summat, the more he'll do it. It would be easier if the school told him to piss about all day. He doesn't do what he's told. Never has."

"So, from Darren coming downstairs on the Wednesday night, to collect his pizza, you haven't seen or heard from him?"

"No. Nothing. And my blood-pressure has never been healthier."

"Are you aware that Darren has missed hospital appointments? They'd been set up by the school and the education authority to test him for ADHD?"

"Oh, for... listen, there's no such thing as ADH fucking D, yeah? I'm not taking time off work, losing pay to dick about with shrinks and do-gooders. They take the piss with all this bullshit about ADHD and all that, it's just an excuse for bad-parenting! Trust me, he's just a wrong 'un. There's no tests for that. End of."

Miller and Rudovsky let his statement hang. It was an extremely defensive and elaborate explanation for ignoring several hospital letters. He could have shared his received wisdom and expertise on the matter during a quick phone call to the staff at the hospital, but he hadn't. Both of the detectives were thinking the same thing as the silence hung like the smell of fresh cat shit.

Miller decided to go down a different route. "What do you know about Mr Pollard at the school?"

"I know that he's always on my back about Darren. Letters, phone-calls, you name it. Always mithering me to go up and have a word."

"And what does he say to you when you go?" asked Rudovsky.

Jenkins shrugged. "I don't know. Haven't been. It's not my fucking job to control Darren at school. I've got to do it all the rest of the time."

"Has Darren ever spoken about his relationship with Mr Pollard?"

"No, not really."

"Do you talk about things like this with Darren?"

"No. Like I say, we don't get on. We stay out of each others way as much as we can."

"What are your thoughts to the suggestion that Darren and Mr Pollard might be together?"

"Together how? Like poofters you mean?"

This casually dismissive comment angered Rudovsky, herself a proud, badge-wearing member of the gay community. But she handled her dissatisfaction professionally, and just sat quietly.

"Well, no, it's just that Mr Pollard has also been reported missing. He's not been seen by his family or colleagues since about an hour after Darren ran out of the school."

This comment stirred up a reaction from Jenkins.

"You what?" He leaned forward, the slouching was replaced by a stiffness. It was quite apparent that Miller's revelation had touched a nerve. But Miller was wondering how Michael Jenkins had not heard this already. It was all over the news, and after all, it was about his child.

Miller remembered that Jenkins had appeared to have been asleep when they'd arrived. He put the lack of up-to-date knowledge down to the missing boy's father having a long lie-in. But then again, he'd said that he knew that Miller was on the case when he arrived because he'd seen it on Facebook. The information wasn't stacking up.

"So we've got to look at a number of possibilities. At this moment in time, we are following a line of enquiry that they might be together."

Jenkins' attitude had changed dramatically, and his carefree, happy-go-lucky expression had turned stale. He began nibbling at a finger-nail as the gravity of Miller's announcement hit-home. He took a deep breath before speaking in a very solemn voice.

"Look, there's something I need to tell you."

Chapter Eight

The news story was one of significant interest, as would be expected. The sensational headlines were grabbing people's attention, and the public were letting their imaginations run away with them as they shared their thoughts on the pages of Facebook and Twitter.

The hashtag #AstleyHigh had started trending, but from the start, there were conflicting points of view about what was happening with the missing teacher and pupil. As had now become normal practise, the men and women of Britain aired their views on their own social media pages, or in the comments boxes underneath newspaper reports.

The story had gone national already. London resident Paul Moore wrote: "Lots of wild speculation about the events up in Manchester. But not too much from the police yet. I think we should all calm down and let the full facts emerge before we try to explain the situation."

Indeed, the public were often too fast to jump to conclusions. The majority had invented the missing blanks in their heads, and had gone live with their analysis, regardless.

"This happens all the time, time to put an age restriction on young men becoming teachers!" snarled one angry commentator on BBC News' Facebook report.

"Young girls are always throwing themselves at male teachers. Time something was done." Said one member of the Sky News online community.

"The press shouldn't be reporting on this. As soon as the teacher realises that he's been sussed out, he'll kill her."

And so it went on. The actual story, the journalists account at the top of the news-feed was too vague, too short on information. So, the public were having a good go at putting plenty of meat on the bones. For many people, particularly those in Stalybridge, the mums and dads who had children at the school, were desperate to learn more. They literally couldn't wait to learn something of substance, to receive some solid information about this extraordinary situation.

Sky News were leading on the story, and were crisscrossing their reporting between retired Met detectives in the studio, to their local reporter outside the school, Paul Mitchell, the news channel's north of England correspondent.

"The information is extremely sketchy at the present time, to say the very least. But one thing that we do know is that this situation is being treated in the most serious manner by Manchester police, a fact confirmed just over an hour ago with the arrival of DCI Miller here at the school. Many viewers will be familiar with this detective, he has worked on a number of high-profile cases in recent years, from the paedophile killings, to the hunt for Sergeant Knight, as well as investigating the disappearance of the outspoken TV celebrity Kathy Hopkirk. Most recently, DCI Miller was heading up the enquiry into the DWP attacks across Greater Manchester, so he is no stranger to high-profile cases. The one thing that we can gather from DCI Miller's appearance here today is that this must be considered as a very serious matter in the eyes of the police chiefs."

BBC News channel knew that it was going to be some time before the full story was revealed by police, so came up with a nice package to fill the meantime. The hastily prepared news report focussed on historical cases of teachers and their pupils running away together. One recent case, from just six years earlier was recounted using library footage of the hunt for the pair, and the teacher's eventual imprisonment. The married male teacher, and his fifth-year pupil had sparked an international man-hunt when they eloped to France when their love-affair had been discovered, and was about to be exposed by the school. This had been a fascinating story, and on the surface of it, the 27 year-old teacher and his 15 year-old girlfriend just looked like any other young, care-free couple on the CCTV images which had recorded them on the ferry across the channel. They had managed to stay on the run for eight days before French police caught up with them. The teacher had handed his CV in at a bar, in a bid to get work. He had his photograph on the CV, and the bar-worker had recognised him as the teacher from England who had abducted one of his pupils.

The package made interesting viewing, and served as a

five-minute break from regurgitating the very basic headline of the breaking news story in Manchester.

For the press, the next part of the story couldn't come quickly enough, and calls were being made non-stop to the police's press office, trying to gather new details, and crucially, to find out if DCI Miller had announced the time of his press conference yet.

The answer to both questions was no and no.

Chapter Nine

Mike Jenkins lit a cigarette and stared down at his bare feet. Miller and Rudovsky waited for him to speak. It seemed to take an age, but it proved to be worth the wait.

"Alright, I've not been a hundred per cent with yous, right?"

The detectives nodded as he looked up at them.

"That Mr Pollard, he came round here last Thursday morning. Banging on the fucking door, waking me up."

"What time was this?" asked Rudovsky.

"About half-ten. I was fuming mate, I'm not gonna lie. So I went down, and I never realised it before, but this Mr Pollard who's always sending me letters and text messages about our Darren… he used to be my teacher! Can you believe that?"

"Did you go to Astley?" asked Miller.

"Yeah, yeah, course I did."

"Well he's worked there for over thirty years, so it makes sense."

"So, it's like, I didn't know that this prick was the one who was giving our Darren a hard time. He made my life a fucking misery at school. And then here he is, stood at my door, bold as brass, getting in my face."

"When you say getting in your face Mr Jenkins, what exactly do you mean by that?"

"You know, he's right up in my grill, he's saying 'where's Darren, has he come back here' and all this shit."

Jenkins took a long, hard draw on his cigarette and exhaled a huge plume of smoke into the middle of the room.

"Anyway, I said to him, 'you don't remember me, do you?' and he goes all weird on me. So, I said 'Michael Jenkins, Sir' to him, and his face was a fucking picture."

"What happened?" asked Miller.

"He went all confused like, like he couldn't believe that it was me. Like I say, he was a bastard to me when I was a kid. And here he was, face to face with me, now I'm a grown man."

"Have you never seen him at parents evening or

anything?" asked Rudovsky, stunned that this man had no idea who his son's teacher was, and similarly, that the teacher had no idea who's son he was teaching.

"Nah, you're joking me aren't you? I ain't going to no school, listening to teachers telling me what a dick our Darren is. I know full well, I live with the bastard!"

"Don't they complain that you don't go?"

Jenkins shrugged. "Darren's mam used to go. But it's not my cup of tea at all."

"What happened with Mr Pollard?" Miller wanted to get back to the point.

"Well basically, I told him to fuck off, or I would be putting him to sleep."

"And did he?"

"Well yeah, obviously. Or I'd have punched his teeth so far down his throat he'd need to stick a toothbrush up his arse to brush them." Jenkins grinned at his hard-man talk, but Miller and Rudovsky weren't interested in his bullshit. The questions continued.

"So, he just went?"

"Yeah, that was it, end of chat."

"But, he was here for the sole purpose of looking for Darren? Your child?" Rudovsky wasn't keeping up with this man's sense of reason.

"Yeah, and Darren wasn't here, so I fucked him off."

"Is it possible that Darren *had* been here? I mean, you were asleep. You might not have heard him come back from the school?" suggested Miller.

"Possible I suppose, but I didn't see him after Pollard had gone."

"Did Mr Pollard have any nicknames when you were at school?"

"Yes, what was it they called him, Bollard, no, Well'ard, that was it. But he wasn't very well hard when I sent him on his merry way. Fucking nasty old cunt."

"Sorry, I'm getting a bit lost here Mr Jenkins. Were you off work last week as well?"

"Yeah, like I said, I'm off."

"How long for, may I ask?"

"What for?"

"I'm just curious. If you'd been at work, you wouldn't have known if Darren had been back. But as you were at home, there's a good chance that Darren would have known that, and avoided coming back here."

"Nah, he couldn't have known. I was only susp... I only started taking the time off the day before. And I didn't tell him."

"What have you been suspended for?" asked Rudovsky, as sharp as a razorblade, picking up on Jenkin's slip-of-the-tongue.

"What... I..."

"Come on Mr Jenkins, it's not a big deal..." said Miller.

"It's a load of bollocks. Someone blocked the loo up at work with paper towels or summat, and I've been blamed, same as always. Not complaining though, full pay, no work, and they can't prove nothing. Happy days."

Rudovsky was staring at this man, wondering if he was a full shilling. She wasn't happy with the shit that was coming out of his mouth, and there was no way she could explain that to Miller while he was sat there. Nothing that Jenkins was saying stacked up. None of it.

"So, sorry to go over this again, but I'm trying to make it clear in my head. Mr Pollard went, and you didn't hear from him again?" asked Miller.

"Nah mate, he's not that brave. He's alright picking on little kids in the playground, but he's a shit-house in the main arena, got no back-bone when he's faced with a true competitor."

Rudovsky looked down at her lap. This guy was a joke, and he really made her cringe.

Miller blew out a gust of air. He was becoming increasingly confused by this peculiar man's view of the world.

"Excuse me, is it alright if I use your bathroom?" asked Rudovsky, nice-as-pie.

"Yeah, yeah, leave 10p on the cistern though..." said Jenkins with a wide smile which exposed his pearly-yellows. What a twat, thought Rudovsky.

"Thanks a lot. Won't be a minute."

"Upstairs, middle door."

As Rudovsky walked up the stairs, she had her phone out of her pocket and was scrolling through to her text messages. As she closed the toilet door, she began typing furiously into her device.

"Sir, this guy needs to come in. Reason after reason to suspect that he's responsible for Pollard's and Darren's disappearance. Thoughts?" She pressed send and had a look around the bathroom. There was evidence of a male-only household all around the tiny, musty space. The cardboard tubes of a dozen used toilet rolls littered the filthy floor. The tiny bin was over-flowing with empty shampoo and shower-gel bottles. The toilet hadn't seen a skid-brush in years and there was no soap to wash one's hands.

"Glad I don't really need to go…" said Rudovsky under her breath, desperately fighting the overwhelming urge to scrub the tide mark off the bath and throw some bleach down the loo.

Downstairs, Miller took his phone out of his pocket very discreetly. He'd felt the vibration of a text-message, and knew it was from Rudovsky. She never used other people's toilets, so he'd been expecting it from the moment she'd asked to use the facilities. He quickly typed his reply after asking Jenkins how long he'd lived here.

"Yes, you sort the meat van. We won't tell him until its here."

"Bingo, nice one boss."

Miller listened to Jenkins boring story about when the family had moved in, while Rudovsky sent a text to Saunders, telling him to "send a custody van to Jenkins home address as soon as possible, no sirens, nice and discreet. Dad's coming in. Cheers mate."

Downstairs, Miller was asking about Darren's mum, and although this received a frosty reception at first, Miller somehow managed to get the woman's number with relative ease.

"He won't be there, though. He fucking hates her guts." Said Jenkins, although his voice lacked conviction. It sounded so phoney, so poorly delivered, that Miller suspected that the opposite was most probably true.

Upstairs, Rudovsky flushed the toilet and ran the tap at the sink for a few seconds to complete the illusion of her using the toilet. She opened the door and walked slowly down the stairs. She saw that there were two doors on either side of the bathroom door. Both doors had been damaged, one had been punched and the cardboard interior was exposed. The other was off its hinges at the bottom and there was a similar hole where it had been kicked through. Rudovsky paused a second and peered through the hole in the door as her eyes became level. It was Darren's bedroom, and it looked quite neat and tidy from what she could make out. The fact that it appeared so orderly intrigued her, as the rest of the property was a shit-tip. She was also confused by the bunk-bed, there hadn't been any mention of siblings. Rudovsky continued down the stairs and went back into the living room.

"That's better," she said. "Thanks."

"No worries. So, are we done then?" asked Jenkins.

"Not quite," said Rudovsky. "We need to have a quick look in Darren's room if that's okay?"

"What for?"

"Well, because we're looking for your son, who is missing. We might find a clue, or find that he's taken all his belongings, or that he hasn't taken anything at all." Miller was firm, and Rudovsky got the impression that his patience was wearing wafer thin with this one.

"Yeah, go on then. Seems a bit..."

"Can you come with us please?" said Miller.

"Fucks sake, tell you what..."

"Listen, Mr Jenkins. Your lad has been missing now for six days. I'm getting quite irritated by your blasé attitude towards it all. Now take us up to the lad's room, like my colleague just asked."

"Or what?"

"What do you mean, or what? Are you a glue-sniffer?"

"Funny."

Miller took his cuffs off his belt and walked the couple of steps around the coffee-table. "I'm not trying to be funny.

Michael Jenkins, I am arresting you on suspicion of obstructing police officers with their enquiries, you do not..."

Jenkins held his wrists out, demonstrating to the DCI that he was familiar with the routine. He didn't say a word. There was no struggle. There was nothing, just a subservient man who looked shocked and a little frightened by this unexpected turn-up.

"Right mate, I'm sure you'll start taking things a little more seriously now." Said Miller. Jenkins' eyes appeared to be filling up. Rudovsky looked at him, and as she glanced at the tragic, vulnerable figure before her, she wondered what the interaction with Mr Pollard had really been like last Thursday morning. Because she was pretty certain that this vulnerable looking adult hadn't said anything about knocking the teacher out. He didn't have it in him. Punching the doors upstairs, and probably Darren was all this balloon amounted to, she considered.

Jenkins just sat in his chair, his cuffed wrists between his knees. He was shaking, and it seemed quite forced and exaggerated. Jenkins looked like he was trying to play the sympathy card, the same "victim" behaviour that he had displayed at the start of the conversation was back in full view, and it wasn't working. Miller and Rudovsky had nothing but contempt for the pathetic, snivelling man.

"We'll just wait for your lift to the station Mr Jenkins, and then we'll have a look around Darren's room."

Jenkins started sobbing openly, looking down at the floor as he made no secret of his despair.

Rudovsky and Miller looked at one another and searched each-other's faces. They were desperately trying to read what the other was thinking. Did they both share the same theory about why the man was crying? Was it because he knew exactly where Pollard and Darren were? Was it because he knew he was finished? Or was it because he had absolutely no involvement, and this was just his default victim performance?

Neither of them could wait to find out.

"This is DC Rudovsky over," she said into her radio without pressing the button. "Request for a van to transport a prisoner please, over."

Jenkins began sobbing louder. Rudovsky grabbed her dictaphone off the coffee table, stopped the recording, and placed all the rubbish back in its rightful place on the table, forcing Miller to smile widely at the bizarre spectacle.

Chapter Ten

Miller and Rudovsky headed back to HQ in their CID cars, as Mike Jenkins' police van took him to the different part of the building. The custody section.

"DI Saunders! In my office please!" shouted the DCI as he entered the SCIU floor. Miller headed straight into his office and Saunders quickly followed.

Just a minute after Saunders had gone in with Miller, Rudovsky came rushing in to see the two most senior detectives in the unit.

"Shush Sir, she's here!" said Saunders quietly as she entered. It was an old joke, but Rudovsky paid it no attention. She was revved up about this case and it was plain to see that she wanted to get busy.

"Have you started?" she asked Miller.

"No. Waiting for you, Jo."

"Great, right, thanks for backing me up on the arrest Sir, I appreciate it."

"No worries."

"Right, well, you two had better start filling me in on the eventualities..." said Saunders. Miller nodded at Rudovsky, prompting her to explain why she had asked Miller to arrest the boy's father via text message from the loo.

"Okay, well, let me set the scene for you," said Rudovsky to Saunders. "This is a very dysfunctional family unit. Father and son living together in a shit-hole of a terraced house. Mum scarpered off to Scotland about twelve months ago. Darren, the son is always in hot water for something at school or around the local community. His dad hates his guts, he's quite open about it. Now, it turns out that Darren's teacher, Mr Pollard, went round to the family home shortly after Darren had stormed out of school. If what Darren's father is telling us is true, Mr Pollard was also his teacher, and he made Jenkins senior's life a misery at school as well. So, stick with me, but point one I'm trying to make is that Michael Jenkins has two people that he seems to hate going missing at a very similar time. The link to Jenkins is unmistakable, they have both been at the property that morning."

"At separate times," interjected Miller, keen as ever to insert facts where there might be some confusion.

"As far as we know at this stage Sir, but none-the-less, the fact is that Michael Jenkins has been in close proximity to the two missing individuals on the morning that they were last seen."

"Okay, point one is noted in my jotter." Said Saunders as he scribbled the details down.

"Point two, he phoned in the missing person's report the next day even though Darren has a history of disappearing for two, three, four days at a time whenever there's been a barney."

"Right?" Saunders wasn't convinced that this was a major issue.

"But if you check the duty-log, he's made long, detailed comments about how he's only ringing it in to get the school off his back about Darren's truancy, he made it clear that he wasn't concerned about Darren's welfare, and that he was simply covering his own back. However, he's told me and the boss that he ignores all the letters and communications from school. So why the hell would he say that to the control-room?"

"Fair point. Very suspicious."

"The third point, I'm sure you'll agree Sir," Rudovsky looked across the desk at Miller, "is that Jenkins was behaving extremely strangely when we questioned him. He was over-doing it to present a relaxed, laid-back attitude. But bearing in mind that his son is missing, potentially with the teacher that he alleges used to bully him, it just doesn't ring true. Add on top that Jenkins Senior has been suspended from work... well, there's not a lot to be relaxed about really, is there?"

"Anything else?" asked Saunders after a brief silence.

"Yes, Miller made it sound like he was bringing bad news when we arrived at the address. Jenkins didn't blink."

"Yeah, that got my alarm bells ringing immediately," said Miller. "Not a normal reaction by any stretch of the imagination."

"God, this guy sounds like a psychopath!" Said

Saunders.

"Nah, he's a shit-talking sociopath. Folded like a deckchair when I arrested him. Collapsed into himself and started sobbing like a small, non-gender specific child."

"He's a proper weirdo." Said Rudovsky.

"So, anything else of interest?" asked Saunders as he made more notes in his pad.

"Yes, well, I've got quite a bit to tell you both about my visit to the school." Said Miller. "Firstly, Darren is a major headache there, constantly in trouble, generally daft, stupid things. But we know about that, I just wanted to add that the school secretary and the head teacher have both told me that he is extremely bright, very articulate. He's funny, kind-hearted and can be very charming. But when he's got an audience, he turns into a pain in the arse. He was supposed to be checked for ADHD, but he missed the appointments. The other factor that has become extremely clear today is that he has a very stormy relationship with his father. I'm sure we'll hear plenty more about Darren in the forthcoming hours. But if we put his behaviour into our usual criminal perspective, my conclusion is that he is mad, rather than bad. Apart from a minor bullying issue last term centred around name-calling, he's never been in trouble for anything nasty. He's just a wally."

"A wally! Is that a psychological diagnosis?" asked Rudovsky, beaming at the old-fashioned word for a dickhead.

"A wally with a big heart, apparently – not sure what the clinical name for that is. As for Mr Pollard, well, what can I say? He's the model teacher. Kids love him, staff love him, the kid's parents all love him as he taught most of them as well. He's got all sorts of accolades for his work through the years, including winning the Tameside Teacher of the Year trophy back in the nineties."

"Sounds like a great teacher. We only remember the good ones, don't we?" said Rudovsky.

"And the useless ones, and the nasty ones!" countered Saunders.

"Oh God, how awful must it be to be a mediocre teacher. Nobody would ever talk about you!" Rudovsky was laughing.

"Anyway," said Miller with a tone that immediately closed-down the waffle. "He's got a nickname. Well'ard, and apparently, it's because he's the strictest teacher in the school. Everybody knows that he's the one teacher that you don't want to cross. Looking at recent photographs of him on his Facebook, he looks like he's a pretty strong chap, he's into his running and manages the school football team. So, I'm not having it that this Michael Jenkins threatened him. I think that he's just trying to sound a bit macho."

"Macho? God Sir, have you been watching eighties films or summat?"

"What's this?" asked Saunders, interrupting the banter. Miller nodded to Rudovsky, inviting her to recap Jenkins' "hard-man" story of Mr Pollard visiting the day they were last seen. Saunders listened intently and took lots of notes.

"Okay, so what do we think is going on here, gut feelings please." Miller noticed that Rudovsky had opened her mouth already, and waved to her to go first.

"Well, to summarise, here is my opinion on what has happened. Michael Jenkins has done something to Darren for coming home from school, then the teacher has come round and intervened, split a fight up or something, and Jenkins Senior has done something to him, I dunno, whacked him with a cricket bat or summat. Imagine it, Jenkins is battering Darren, and Mr Pollard comes round, hears all the commotion, breaks it all up, and things get out of hand. Reasons for such an over-reaction are already covered, he's worried about problems at work, his wife's walked out on him, his son is constantly stressing him out, and then a teacher who used to harass him suddenly comes around. There was plenty of evidence of alcohol consumption in the address. If this one doesn't scream 'drunken, anxious mad-man snaps' to you, I fucking resign on principal."

Miller and Saunders laughed loudly at Rudovsky's typically hysterical conclusion.

"Interesting thoughts Jo," said Miller.

"What's happening at the address?"

"Forensics are doing a deep search throughout the

house. Not expecting anything for a good few hours from that." Miller had organised this whilst waiting for a PCSO to come and guard the property, before heading back to base.

Rudovsky continued, as another thought popped into her mind. "Oh, yes, the bunk-bed. Darren has a bunk-bed in his room. Both the beds were made, both had matching Man United duvet covers. We need to know more about that, it doesn't strike me as the kind of house you'd invite your mates to sleep over, and even if it was, Michael Jenkins doesn't strike me as the kind of man who would buy an extra bed for Darren's mates to stay over. We need to find out who the other bed belongs to, and speak to them."

"Noted. So, what are your gut feelings Keith?"

Saunders looked down at the notes on his lap. "Haven't got a clue," he said without a hint of humour. "But it won't take long this one, I've a feeling there's another dimension that we don't know about yet."

"Okay, well, let's organise ourselves then, and discover what this other dimension is as soon as possible." Miller stood and ripped a page off his giant A1 Flipboard. He started writing "lines of enquiry" at the top.

"Okay, hit me..." he said, with his marker pen pointed towards Saunders and Rudovsky.

"We need to interview Jenkins under caution." Suggested Rudovsky.

"We need to talk to Darren's mother," added Saunders.

"And Pollard's estranged wife, and his two kids." Said Miller as he scribbled illegible words on the giant pad. Well, they were legible to him, and that was his main concern.

"We need a door-to-door on Sand Street, around the Jenkins' home. See if any neighbours can back-up Jenkins account of Pollard arriving and leaving, and if he was alone, and did anyone see Darren?" Suggested Rudovsky.

"Good shout Jo," said Saunders. "And what about CCTV in the area, run Pollard's registration plate through the system, see if there's any record of his car after 10.30am."

"I think it might be useful to get a better picture on Michael Jenkins," said Saunders.

"We could ask some of his colleagues about him, and some of the neighbours on his street." Said Rudovsky.

"Yes, and perhaps we should appeal for any former pupils who have been on the wrong side of Pollard, try and find out if there is a dark side to his character which is not as well known as it should be?"

Miller continued scribbling. Once he'd caught-up writing down the points, he turned to his colleagues.

"So, are we pulling the others off their cases? Or can we cope?" The DCI was talking about the rest of the SCIU team, DCs Bill Chapman, Mike Worthington, Helen Grant and Peter Kenyon, all of whom were maxed out on their own cases already.

"Are you joking Sir? We can't manage all that lot on our own. We need the others with us. It's not rocket surgery."

"Yeah. I think Jo's right, Sir. I think our priority needs to be this one, and the rest can wait. They're all cold-cases, so we can't justify focusing on those when these two might be alive somewhere."

Miller didn't look pleased. The department was busier than ever as the increase in violent crime clashed against the harsh reality of the police force being cut by one third in the face of the government cuts. After a few seconds thought, Miller realised that he had no choice.

"Okay. Keith, you tell the others they're working on this. Give them a briefing."

"Sir."

"Jo, you can give Mr Jenkins a good going over with Pete, but give it a while, the longer he's got to think stuff over, the better." Miller was talking about Rudovsky's regular partner in investigations, DC Peter Kenyon.

"Sir, I'll work out my interview questions straight away."

"Good. I'll go and brief Dixon, and I'll ask him for some constables to answer the phones after the press conference."

"You're doing a press conference, before we've grilled Jenkins?" asked Rudovsky, looking surprised that the boss seemed to be putting the cart before the horse.

"Yes, the local community in Stalybridge will be

desperate for answers. And there's not a lot to lose, we might even get some decent intelligence out of it. This decision might paint the missing boy's father in a poor light when I mention that he's in custody and he is helping us with our enquires, but quite frankly, that is at the top of the list of things I couldn't give a shit about."

Saunders and Rudovsky smiled. So what if Mike Jenkins was going to become the most talked about shit dad in Tameside? Hardies, as the locals might say.

Miller finished up. "Good work guys, lots of positive stuff to go on there." Miller stepped closer to the flip-chart and drew a circle around a few words. "What the hell does that say? Can't read my own writing!"

Chapter Eleven

DC Jo Rudovsky had gone down to her car. She was dreading this phone call, and the last thing she needed was the noise and banter of the office in the background. She couldn't put it off a second longer, and she dialled the number that Michael Jenkins had given them, the number for Darren Jenkins' mother, Dawn.

"I know this is a worrying time..." said Rudovsky, adopting her most sympathetic voice. The detective had a notebook and pen on her lap. "But I do have to ask you some difficult questions."

The mother sounded upset, and a little nervous, which made Rudovsky slightly confused.

"Yes, yes, I understand. He can be a wild bugger sometimes," said Dawn, the statement was filled with warmth.

"Yes, that's something that's coming across, but it's a very positive thing."

"Really?"

"Yes, we find that it's the kids like Darren who turn up safe and sound in cases like this. The quiet, shy ones are the ones who tend to struggle."

There was no reply, Darren's mother was waiting for the next part.

"Darren is known to go walkabout for a few days, so we're not as concerned about it as we would be if this was a boy who had no history of running away."

"Yes, but you're still looking for him, aren't you?"

"Yes, oh yes of course. I'm just trying to reassure you that we feel quite confident that everything's going to be fine. I just wanted to know, before my boss holds a press conference, if you've heard from Darren in the past six days?"

"No, I've not heard from him for at least a month. He wanted to come and live with me. I said no."

"And you've not spoken to him since?"

"No. I've tried, but his dad just starts giving me a hard time when I phone. Things are difficult between us."

Rudovsky could well imagine. She totally understood

how difficult it would be, being Michael Jenkins' ex. It had been an ordeal sitting in his presence for fifteen minutes.

"Do you think Darren might have decided to come and visit you?"

Dawn didn't speak, as she considered the question. "It's a possibility. We were really..." Dawn's voice started to break, as her emotions interrupted the call. "Sorry..."

"No, no, take your time. No rush." Rudovsky was gentle and very supportive, she was perfect for these types of jobs. Dawn sniffed and coughed, and after a few seconds, she continued.

"He's been up to see me a couple of times, he never wants to go home."

"And where are you living now?"

"I'm back at my mum and dads, in Aberdeen."

"Wow, flipping heck, that's a hell of a distance!"

"Yes, well, when you've got an abusive ex, it doesn't feel far enough."

"How had Darren got up all the way up there, to see you?"

"Train, I sent the tickets down to him."

"Oh, that's good, so he'd know how to get up there, to see you."

"Is that what you think is happening?"

"It's a strong possibility. It happens a lot, this kind of thing."

"Well, yes, he'd manage it, he's a clever lad. It scares me sometimes, how clever he is."

Each time Dawn spoke about Darren, she had a distinct affection in her voice. She clearly loved the lad, it was unmistakable. This was the polar-opposite of Michael Jenkins attitude. The fact troubled Rudovsky.

"Mrs Jenkins, I know this is difficult for you, but may I ask why you said that Darren couldn't live with you?"

"Well... it wasn't as straight forward as that. I said that he could at first, but his dad refused, he said that it will affect his education too much, swapping schools and everything. Michael said he'd fight me for custody. In the end, he said that if Darren moves out, he'll kill himself. Then he said he'd come up to Aberdeen and burn the house down while we're all asleep."

Rudovsky wanted to point out that he couldn't burn the house down, if he'd killed himself, but thought better of it, even though she could tell that Dawn would smile at the sarcastic remark.

"In the end, I promised Darren that he could come, as soon as he left school. It was all arranged, last time he was here."

"But that's not until…"

"It's a year away, roughly."

"Which is a long time for a fifteen-year-old!"

"Yeah, I tried telling him, but you know what they are like at that age." Dawn started crying down the phone, but quickly pulled herself together. "God, I miss him so much, even though he does my head in half the time!" Dawn's voice lifted at the end of the sentence. Even though she was slagging her son off, she meant it nicely.

"Well, don't worry, okay? I'm not trying to sound like a bighead, but my department, the ones who are working on this, we are the best detective team in the Manchester police. My boss, DCI Miller, he's got a brilliant record. So, you're in safe hands, there'll be no stone left unturned in the search for Darren."

"Why is it getting such a big response? I mean, that's not normal, is it?"

"Well, I'm glad you asked me that. There's either been a really weird coincidence, or there's something very peculiar going on."

Dawn didn't say anything. The expectancy in the silence hurried Rudovsky on.

"At roughly the same time that Darren went walkabout, a teacher from Darren's school did too. And they'd just had a massive argument."

"Which teacher?" asked Dawn, a sudden edge had sharpened her voice.

"Mr Pollard. Do you know him?"

"Yes, yes, course I do. He's been Darren's head of year

since he started, in year seven. He's gone missing?"

"Yes, I'm afraid so, that's what we're investigating. What do you think of Mr Pollard?"

"Honestly?"

"Yes?"

"I love him, he's the nicest bloke I've ever known. He's so calm, so kind, never judges you. I'm not exaggerating, but once or twice, when I've had to go in and see him about Darren, I've quite looked forward to it!"

"Really? Your ex has a different opinion entirely."

"Oh, well, there's a surprise."

"We've actually got Michael in custody at the moment, we need to ask him some questions about all this. I just wondered if you thought that there might be some possibility that Michael might have caused some harm to Mr Pollard?"

Dawn was fast in her reply. "No. There's no way. He's good at hitting women, and his kids, but he's a total shit-bag with other blokes. I'd bet my next week's wages that he'd run for the hills if Mr Pollard asked him for a fight."

"Yes, that's kind of the impression I got as well."

"It is very weird though, like you say."

"Well, we're throwing everything at it, we'll have more to update you with soon, I'm sure. I'll give you a buzz with any developments."

"Please, if you don't mind?"

"Certainly. And, just so you know, this is going to be going on the six o'clock news. I just wanted to give you some notice to ring family and friends."

"Thank you. You've been so kind. Thanks very much, what was your name again?"

"Jo. Jo Rudovsky. Save my number, and don't hesitate to call if you want anything, or if you hear from Darren."

"Okay. Thank you."

"I know it sounds stupid but try not to worry. We'll get this sorted."

Chapter Twelve

Miller was sitting in his office, feeling a familiar sense of dread and nervousness. His press conference was scheduled for 6pm, and he never looked forward to them.

A lot of intelligence had come to light in the six or so hours since he had first heard about this mystery. DCS Dixon, Miller's boss, had been pleased by the amount of information Miller had managed to gather in such a short time-frame. On the face of it, this was all looking like a very basic job, and both Miller and Dixon were quietly confident that Rudovsky and Kenyon's good-cop, bad-cop routine would break Michael Jenkins down in no time. And then the mystery would be unravelled, quite possibly in record time.

But, there was no room for complacency. Miller explained his plan for the press conference to Dixon, who approved the information which was to be released. Matters were usually complicated where a minor was involved. But as there was a very real concern regarding the boy's welfare, Dixon agreed to the details which Miller was planning to reveal. The DCS also granted Miller's wish for five constables to join the team for admin duties such as taking the calls from the public and logging details. It had been a very positive visit to Dixon's office, as things didn't always go Miller's way so easily, particularly where the question of extra staff was concerned.

Miller checked his watch. It was ten to six. He decided to go over the details again, quickly, before heading downstairs and into the Manchester City Police media-centre.

*****

"Good evening ladies and gentlemen," said Miller as he sat down in his seat, in front of the familiar Manchester City Police motif. The media-centre was packed, dozens of familiar faces from the area's radio, TV and online new agencies, as well as reporters from all of the local newspapers. There were a number of national news networks in attendance too. Sky News were dropping their six o'clock headlines, and were taking the conference live. This was a big story, and the realisation that Miller was going live on national TV made his nervousness return, despite him having done these broadcasts countless times previously without any real problems.

"Okay, lots to get through, so we'll get cracking." Miller waited a few seconds, allowing the media staff chance to hit their "record" or "on air" buttons. A hush suddenly spread throughout the room as Miller began reading his statement.

"Good evening, and thank you for coming along tonight. As you will be aware, this is a very fresh inquiry which was only launched this morning, for a variety of complex reasons. But the reason you are here, is because a young lad, and his teacher have both disappeared, at approximately the same time, last Thursday morning."

There were gasps and muffled sounds of chattering and whispering. Miller knew that the press had all assumed that it was a female pupil who'd gone off with a male teacher. He allowed them a few seconds to get over the realisation that they'd been wrong. He could see that they were now imagining a female teacher, with the boy.

"Alright, now, as I've mentioned, this is a very complex enquiry, and I've invited you along here today in the hope that you can help us to get the information out into the community. We are extremely concerned about the welfare of both missing persons."

Once again, there was the sound of muttering. This was turning out to be a bit different from what the press had been alluding to all day. But how different?

"The teacher is 56 year-old Mr Phillip Pollard, he is a very well-known individual in the Stalybridge and Tameside area. He has been a teacher at Astley High School since the nineteen-eighties, and I know that many viewers and listeners in that community will instantly know who I am talking about, he is described as a 'larger-than-life' character, and is considered an extremely popular member of the school community. The pupil, is 15-year-old Darren Jenkins. Darren has a history of problems at school and at home, and has had some involvement in matters that have required police intervention. Darren has also been reported missing on several occasions previously."

This brief sentence painted a very negative picture of Darren Jenkins, and Miller was well-aware of the fact. But it was deliberate. It was supposed to provoke a reaction in any former troubled pupils who may have witnessed another side to Mr Pollard.

"Now, in a very conscious attempt to give out the most accurate information, it is important that I point out that these two individuals are extremely well-known to one another, and that the relationship between them is often quite volatile."

It could be seen on the faces of the press that this story had just grown arms and legs and had started sprinting onto the next day's front pages.

"Mr Pollard and Darren had a heated exchange in the school grounds last Thursday morning, and a short time later, they both disappeared. Our initial inquiries have found that there have been no sightings of either individual since that time, which was approximately 10.00am on Thursday the 16th May. So, as I have already pointed out, we are extremely concerned."

Miller took a pause and lifted his glass of water to his lips. He took a sip and glanced around the room, feeling pleased that the press appeared to be taking this information extremely seriously. The DCI pressed a button on the table-top and the projector screen to Miller's right suddenly lit up with the faces of the two-missing people. Mr Pollard's photograph was his staff mug-shot, which was used for his security fob and on the school's website. Darren's picture was his most recent school photo. His long, mousy brown hair looked as though he'd combed it with his fingers, and his tie was loose. It wasn't a very impressive school photo, and Darren appeared every bit the trouble-maker. Mr Pollard's however looked very warm and endearing. He looked confident, happy, and very smart. Most of all, he looked like a very nice, kind man.

"These are the people that we are desperate to make contact with. We will of course release a press-statement which will include these photographs, and will contain all of this information, just as soon as we all leave here. I am urging you all to please put this at the top of your news agenda, and help us to try and make sense of what's gone on."

Miller took another sip of his water, and let that ominous remark hang in the air a moment.

"Now, we have made some progress in this enquiry, and we do have a male in custody, and we believe that this person may have some vital information which will help us with our investigation. But we want to hear from anybody who may have seen Phillip Pollard, or Darren Jenkins anywhere since last Thursday morning. The telephone number for our major incident room is on the screen now," said Miller as he pressed the button again. "Please, even if you're not one hundred per cent sure it was either of them, we really need to speak to you. Last time Darren was seen, he was wearing the Astley school uniform which consists of black pants, white shirt, black blazer and green and yellow tie. Phillip was wearing a dark grey suit, white shirt and a bright pink, or magenta coloured tie."

The press were lapping this up. This was a major story, made all the more interesting by the sinister element to the missing pair's relationship. Miller could see that they couldn't wait to get out of here and start writing their first copies.

"Now, I'm extremely concerned about this situation, as I have said. I won't be taking any questions today..."

There was the familiar sound of disappointment from the media people. "Alright, let me finish..." Miller smiled at the press people, many of whom he knew very well. "...I have literally given you all the information that I have. So, there's no point in asking me questions, because I'm just going to be saying 'I don't know' to everything."

Despite what Miller had just said, a few questions were shouted out.

"Who have you got in custody?" shouted one.

"Do you think they are alive?" shouted another, without any consideration for the thoughts and feelings of the missing people's loved ones.

"DCI Miller, do you think that Mr Pollard has done something to Darren?"

Miller held his hand up and waited for the silence to return. Eventually, it did.

"Okay, thanks everybody. I'll update you all tomorrow at some stage. Thank you for your support."

The DCI stood and walked off the small stage, and headed past all of the journalists and camera operators, and out of the media centre as the TV reporters began talking excitedly into their camera lenses. They may have been disappointed that there were no questions and answers today, but they were happy enough. They all knew that they had a nice, big, sensational story on their hands with this one.

Chapter Thirteen

Miller was back in his office, and on the phone to Clare, his wife, within minutes of his press conference ending so abruptly.

"Hiya love, listen, got a big one in. I'm going to be late home."

"Hi, yes, I know, I just saw you on Granada Reports."

"So... I'm apologising in advance..."

"Yes, its fine, don't worry about it. What do you think's gone on?" Clare was always keen to hear the real news, not the bullshit that Miller leaked to the press.

"Not sure. Very complex one this."

"Who've you got in custody?"

"The boy's father. He's a right balloon."

"Shit. You think he's done something to them?"

"Jo does. I'm not so sure. I don't think he could break the skin on a rice-pudding!"

"Well, Jo's not often wrong."

"No, that's true. But Keith reckons there's another element to all this, and we're just hoping that the phones are going to start ringing in a minute, and a few clues will start coming in. I'm just feeling gutted that I'm not going to see your pretty face for a few hours, at least."

"Oh my God, can you hear me cringing down the phone?"

"Yes."

"Want a quick word with the twins?"

"Please."

"No worries. Leo! Molly! Dad's on the phone."

Miller laughed as he heard his six-year olds running through the kitchen and into the living room.

"Hiya dad!" said Leo. He'd beaten his sister to the phone.

"Hiya mate, are you alright?"

"Yeah, dad, Luke Parkinson has got a puppy, he's called Archie. His mum brought him to pick him up!"

"Wow! Really? Is he cute?"

"Yeah."

"And are you now going to ask for a puppy?"

"Yeah."

"And have you asked your mum?"

"Yeah."

"What did she say?"

"Ask dad."

Miller laughed. "Well, we'll see. Alright?"

"Yeah."

"Listen mate, I'm not going to be home for bedtime story tonight. Got a crook to catch!"

"I know."

"How did you know?"

"Because you're phoning up. Mum says if dad phones when he should be here, it means he's going to be a Larry let-down."

Miller laughed again. "Right well, I'm sorry."

"It's alright."

"Can you put Molly on?"

"Yeah."

"Alright then mate. Na night. Love you."

"Thanks."

There was a ruffle and a click, and then Molly spoke.

"Hello dad."

"Hello gorgeous. Are you alright?"

"Yeah."

"Did you see the puppy?"

"Yeah."

"Did you like him?"

"Yeah. He licked my face!" Molly laughed down the phone, and Miller felt his cheeks raise up high as he imagined her beautiful little face laughing.

"I'm sorry Molly, but I'm going to be working late. So, I can't do your story."

"Will you do a bigger one tomorrow?"

"Yes, of course I will."

"Alright."

"Alright. Well I'm sorry. Love you."

"Thanks."

"See you tomorrow."

"See you. Do you want mum?"

"Yes please."

There was another muffle and a click, and Clare was back on the line. "Hiya," she said.

"Hiya. Well, I'll have to get on. Just wanted to thank you for putting the puppy decision on me!"

"You're very welcome. It's a lot easier than saying no!"

"Ha! You devious cow. Right, I'm going. Love you."

"Love you too."

"I thought you were just going to say thanks, like the kids do."

"Ha ha, is that what they were thanking you for?"

"Yes. They're funny. See ya."

Miller ended the call, delighted that his kids had made him so happy, and that Clare had been so understanding about the late night. He clapped his hands together. "Right, let's find these two!" he said, still beaming from ear-to-ear from his brief chat with the kids.

Chapter Fourteen

"Right, what's happening?" asked Miller of Saunders, who was standing at the end of the desk which was being manned by five police constables who were taking the incident room calls. Saunders was reading the reports as they stacked up. All five lines were busy, and as one call ended, the phone started ringing again. That was a very promising sign.

"Nowt much. Nothing that has made me jump in the car and race down to speak to the caller." Saunders checked his watch. "But it's early doors yet."

"Okay, first positive call that comes in, I want to know. The first sighting of Darren, or Mr Pollard outside the school last Thursday morning, I need to speak to them. Cheers." Miller headed back into his office and opened Google on his laptop. He typed into the search engine "missing teacher schoolboy" and was pleased to see that the first page of results all related to this investigation. The Sun, The Mirror, The Mail Online, The Express and The Metro were all carrying the story as their top news item. Miller looked through them all, and was delighted to see that all of the papers were covering it as a top priority story.

He then put the Sky News feed on, and began watching the channel's output on his laptop. They too were making as much of the story as they could, and a reporter who had been outside the school earlier was talking to camera, emphasising the points that Miller had made half an hour earlier in the press conference.

"Sir!" shouted Saunders, from the main office floor. Miller looked up, out of the window which separated his work-space from the others. Saunders was gesturing him by hand.

"Here we go," said Miller triumphantly as he raced through to where the constables were taking calls. "What's come in?"

"Darren's paper-round, he went into the shop at about quarter past ten on Thursday, asking for his wages early."

Miller raised his eyebrows as he grabbed the phone from a young PC.

"Hello, this is DCI Miller," he said, the enthusiasm in his

voice was unmistakable. Miller gestured to Saunders for a pen.

"Yes, hello, I was just telling your officer, Darren works for us,"

"Where?"

"It's the Raja Brothers Express, on Cheetham Hill Road."

"In Stalybridge?"

"Well, no, it's Dukinfield, it's just like, it's near the sign that says welcome to Stalybridge. The border, that's the word I'm…"

"And was it you that spoke to him?"

"No, no, it was Kelly, the manager. I just heard about it when I came in at dinner-time. She said he was dead upset."

"Did she give him his wages?"

"I don't know, she didn't say."

"What's her surname, please?"

"Fisher."

"Mobile number?" Miller felt there wasn't a second to waste, and was pounding this lady with questions.

"Yeah, hang about…"

Miller felt his heartbeat quicken as he realised that he had his first sighting of Darren outside the school. His mind was racing, filled with possibilities now that he had a trail to start from.

"07783…"

"Yeah,"

"871607"

"And its Kelly Fisher?"

"Yes."

Miller finished taking notes from the shop worker, and thanked her for her call, making sure she knew how significant it was to the enquiry. As soon as he ended the call, he handed the phone back to the constable who'd been made temporarily redundant for the past few minutes. He took his mobile out of his pocket and started pressing the numbers. It connected and a ring tone was heard as Miller put it to his ear.

"Hello?"

"Hi, is that Kelly Fisher?"

"Yeah. Who's that?" She sounded nice, friendly, but a

little unnerved by this unfamiliar voice. Miller introduced himself and gave a brief overview of the call he'd just had with Kelly's member of staff.

"So, I was just wondering what happened on Thursday morning?"

"Well, he came in, he looked right upset so I asked him what was up. He seemed really worked up. He wouldn't tell me what was wrong, he just said he's in trouble again at school."

"And he asked for his wages?"

"Yeah, he promised to do Sunday if I paid him early."

"And you did?"

"Well, yeah. I didn't want to, but he looked so sad, and, well I do need someone for the Sunday papers. No-one ever wants to do it because the bags are dead heavy."

"How do you find him, generally I mean?"

"Darren? He's a great lad, one of my best. He'll never say no to a double-round. He even looked after the shop once when my mum was taken ill, stayed until another member of staff could get down."

"Are you surprised to hear that he's gone missing?"

"Honestly, yes, after he said he'd work Sunday. It's not like him to let me down. But apart from that, I know he's not a happy lad really, his dad and him don't see eye-to-eye. He's been in more than once with a black eye and a swollen cheek."

"You think his dad did that to him?"

"Yeah, without a doubt. He'd just look embarrassed if I asked him what had happened. Having kids of my own, I know that usually, there's a story to be told, a big drama about a fight or whatever. So yeah, I'd bet money on it."

"Is there any CCTV in the shop, which might have recorded Darren's visit last Thursday morning?"

"Yes, there's loads of cameras, they will have it all."

"Brilliant. Where are you now?"

"I'm at home."

"Is it near the shop?"

"Yeah, well, about five minutes drive."

"Any chance you could meet me at the shop in the next thirty minutes?"

"Yeah, if you think it's going to help?"

"Yes, it really is. Your shop is now the start of the search for him, it's really, really useful."

*****

DCs Jo Rudovsky and Peter Kenyon were in interview room 5 with Michael Jenkins. He'd dropped the victim routine again now. He was more annoyed than consumed with self-pity.

"Listen, I know it might have come across that I was being a dick before, but I just can't be doing with dibble at my door."

"Is that an apology?" asked Rudovsky.

"Well, yeah, suppose so. All I'm saying is, I've got fuck all to do with this, I swear on my mum's life."

"And is your mum still alive?"

"Yes, course she is... what..."

"Hi Mr Jenkins, I'm Peter Kenyon, we haven't met before." Pete was warming up his good-cop patter, ready to counter his partner's bad-cop.

"Alright?"

"Yes, so, as you'll be aware, all this is new to me. What exactly is it that you've been brought in for this afternoon?"

"Well, I don't know. Our Darren's gone missing, yeah, and I don't know if these have got some stupid ideas that I've done summat to him."

Kenyon was nodding sympathetically, as Rudovsky smiled inwardly at his silky skills of befriending the missing boy's father.

Kenyon turned to Rudovsky. "What have you got to go on?" he asked, his tone was quite harsh. The only person who didn't know that this was a play-act was Jenkins.

"What? We haven't... we were trying to talk to him and he was just messing us about..." Rudovsky looked angry at her colleague. Kenyon looked at Rudovsky as though she was a pain in the arse.

"Alright mate, sorry about this. I wish this had been sorted out at your house to be honest. We won't keep you long."

"Yeah, well, blame her. It's her!"

"Don't worry, We'll be having words later. But for now, can we just go through some questions with you, and I'll organise a police car to take you back home."

Bingo. The deal was done. DC Kenyon had a new best mate, and Rudovsky sat there sulking, letting Jenkins believe that she was genuinely humiliated by that harsh rebuff from her colleague. But the joke was on Jenkins, little did he know.

"Right, I'm so sorry that you have to go over this again, but please just tell me what's gone on." Kenyon kept his eyes on Darren's father, laying it on thick about how much he cared, and how annoyed he was that Mr Jenkins had been brought down here in the first place.

Jenkins told the story, all of it, from the beginning, starting with Darren's strange behaviour the night before he disappeared, and ending with his phone call to report his child missing. He'd covered Mr Pollard's visit too, and had kept his story, about threatening the teacher, as it was.

Once he was done, Kenyon looked sympathetic. "God, this must be an awful time for you, mate. Last thing you need is being dragged down here. We'll get you on your way in a few minutes," said Kenyon in a soft, friendly voice.

"Can you tell me why Darren has a bunk-bed in his room, please?" said Rudovsky. Her voice sounded cold.

Jenkins looked at her, and then at his new mate, DC Kenyon. His eyes seemed to be filling up. And it didn't look like a play-act this time. Rudovsky sat up slightly in her chair.

"That... that was Johnny's bed." A tear broke free from Michael Jenkins eye, and created a tiny puddle on the table-top as it landed. It was quickly followed by another.

"Johnny?" asked Kenyon, softly.

"My other son. He died last year."

* * * * *

Miller arrived in Dukinfield, at the Raja Bros shop within twenty minutes of ending the call to Kelly. She was standing outside the busy convenience store, waiting for him.

"Hiya, are you Kelly?" he asked of the black-haired lady with thick-rimmed designer glasses.

"Yes, hiya, alright?" she said, extending her hand for a shake.

"Yeah, well, I will be when I've got this lot sorted out. Shall we go in?"

The pair walked into the store and Kelly led Miller past the alcohol aisle and through to the office. The CCTV was impressive, twelve cameras covered the small store. She started messing with the computer and found last Thursday's recordings. She selected 10am and started fast forwarding through the footage. Within a minute, she presented Miller with his first visual footage of the missing child.

"Wow! These are in HD!" He usually encountered really grainy images from CCTV, most of the time they were useless, as though margarine had been smeared all over the lens. The images that Kelly was providing looked as though they were TV broadcast quality.

Miller spent a couple of minutes watching the footage of Darren Jenkins pleading for his pay. Once Kelly had been in the till and given him his money, he walked around the shop and bought several items, before returning to the till to pay for them.

"What's he buying?"

"He got a loaf, a couple of tubs of salmon paste, and four Double Deckers, the tiny ones that are a quid."

Miller looked troubled. "I don't mind Double Deckers, but what's with the salmon paste?"

"What's wrong with Salmon paste?" asked Kelly.

Darren made to leave the shop. Miller was moved to see that Kelly came around from the counter and gave him a hug as he went. They clearly got on well.

"What are you saying to him there?" asked the DCI.

"Oh, I just said cheer up, school isn't everything."

"How much did you give him?"

"Seventeen pounds, fifty."

"And what did he spend?"

"Honestly?"

"Well, yes."

"Nowt. I rung it through as spoiled stock." Kelly put her wrists out for the hand-cuffs. Miller laughed at the joke, but was touched by the gesture. He was starting to think that Darren wasn't quite the arse-hole that contemporary opinion held him in. He certainly wasn't behaving like an arse-hole on the CCTV footage. He looked very sad, and vulnerable.

"Did he say anything, you know, about plans to run away or anything like that?" asked Miller as he watched Darren leave the store, turning right onto Cheetham Hill Road.

"No. Honest to God. Nothing like that. I'd have sorted his head out if he had. I just assumed that he was going home. I'm really sorry if my actions have had any effect on the situation."

"No, no, bloody hell. Don't start thinking like that. It's nowt to do with you."

"Well, it is. We're a strong community round here. We stick together."

"I know, I know. But listen, there's a lot more to this. It's nowt to do with you." Miller pulled his USB memory stick out of his pocket. "Are you any good at saving these things to USBs?"

"Yeah, God, we have police officers in here every week asking for it. Hang about." Kelly took the USB, inserted it into the machine and began doing something with the mouse. A minute later, she handed the tiny memory stick back to Miller.

"Cheers, so, he turned right when he left here. That's the direction of his house, isn't it?"

"Yes, it's about two-hundred and fifty yards down the road, on the right."

"Brilliant, okay, thank you Kelly, you've been a massive help."

Miller left, got into his car and followed the road down towards Sand street, the little terraced street where Darren and his father lived. He was looking for CCTV cameras as he drove, but was disappointed that there were none.

The fact that Darren had left the shop at twenty past

ten, and Mr Pollard had visited the family home, just five minutes walk away, at half-past, troubled the DCI. He felt that the answer to the mystery lay here, somewhere between that shop, and the old Victorian cobbles of Sand street.

Miller pulled his car over and reached for his notebook. He wrote "door-to-doors, Cheetham Hill Road to Sand Street and surrounding."

Miller threw the note-pad and pen onto his passenger seat, pulled his phone out of his pocket, then rang Saunders.

"Sir?"

"Hiya Keith. I've got Darren at the shop, twenty past ten, CCTV footage is brilliant. I'm guessing he's run away from home from the clues. At least, that seems to have been his intention."

"What makes you say that?"

"Oh, a couple of things, I'll tell you in detail when I get back. I just want to do a recce of Mr Pollard's house while I'm over here. What's the address Keith?"

Saunders was lightning fast in his reply. "We've had a call in from a neighbour of Pollard's. Apparently, he's renting a flat at the minute, but we've got his address as the family home. It is listed as 563 Mottram Road, Stalybridge, Sir. Hang on a sec, and I'll find the flat address." A moment later, Saunders continued. "He's renting a flat at 17b Grey Street, Stalybridge."

"Great, okay, I'll go and have a nosey around. Back in about an hour."

*****

In interview room 5 back at HQ, Rudovsky and Kenyon were learning all about Johnny Jenkins.

Darren's elder brother had committed suicide the previous year, during his second-year at a young-offenders institution up in Carlisle.

Johnny had been sentenced to three years for repeated TWOC offences, better known as nicking cars. He'd been doing it for years, and the last time he'd been caught, the Judge had decided to teach him a lesson. It was a lesson that Johnny

Jenkins couldn't handle, and his parents had been informed by phone call, that their son had hanged himself in his room.

Johnny Jenkins was laid to rest at Dukinfield Cemetry, with hundreds of mourners there to pay their last respects. He had been a well-known character in the area, a lovable rogue, always up-to-no-good, but funny with it. He was only 19 years old when he died.

Rudovsky felt remarkably sad, as she heard Michael Jenkins' story about his eldest son. Her sadness came from that neat, tidy bunk-bed in that awful house which just screamed of bad-vibes and depression.

This was a very interesting development as far as Rudovsky was concerned, and she felt that Johnny's death was beginning to explain why Jenkins seemed so cold towards Darren. It was a natural coping mechanism, to reject your surviving children whilst grieving, a trick your brain plays on you, in an attempt to try and shield you from ever feeling that pain, that sorrow, that complete and utter heart-breaking loss, ever again. Rudovsky had seen this before, a form of PTSD, crucially, a mental-health problem brought on by extreme emotional trauma. It explained the strange attitude that Jenkins had been displaying regarding his son's disappearance. A behaviour which had earlier seemed completely inexplicable.

She was starting to rethink her theory about Jenkins being responsible for the disappearance of Darren and Mr Pollard, and she was starting to feel a little bit bad, too. The man was obviously ill, and she felt disappointed in herself for not having picked up on this earlier, after all, the signs had been there.

*****

Mottram Road is one of the main arterial roads out of Stalybridge, linking it to the main routes across the Pennines. It didn't take Miller long to work out that this was the posh end of town. The further up Mottram Road he travelled, the further away the council houses and the two-up, two-down terraces felt. The homes up here were very nice, and definitely expensive. Some were bordering on mansions, great old Victorian houses, of sizes that could easily be renovated into an old folks home or create a block of flats. Miller was impressed that a couple on a teacher's and a social services salary could afford to buy one of these impressive homes, but quickly reminded himself that they would have been much more affordable twenty, or thirty years ago. But today, he guessed that you'd not get much change out of £500,000 for one.

He arrived at the address and parked across the road. The lights were on, and a lady was standing near the front window, she was talking on the phone. It looked as though she was crying. She wasn't paying Miller any attention, she was wrapped up in her phone conversation.

Miller saw that a car was headed in his direction, going towards Stalybridge from Mottram. He leant over the passenger seat to avoid the headlights illuminating him, and potentially alerting Mrs Pollard to his presence. The car passed, and Miller looked back across the road, and into the window. She was still there, and visibly upset. Miller checked his watch, it was almost 9pm. He decided that it was too late to pay a visit, especially as Mrs Pollard was clearly in a poor emotional state. Besides, it would be unannounced, and nobody gave any useful information when they'd been surprised, they were usually on the defensive. He typed the other address into his Sat Nav, and it told him that the address was only a mile away, straight down the road, near the town centre.

A couple of minutes later, Miller pulled up outside the address. It was a row of terraced houses, not dissimilar to the home that Darren Jenkins had disappeared from.

"Bloody hell, you've come down in the world, living here." Said Miller, to himself - shocked at the stark differences between the two properties.

Miller decided to have a look around. He went around the back of the properties, and found Pollard's flat was up a steel staircase, "17b" was painted on the wall in white emulsion, with an arrow pointing up. He went up the steps, taking care not to make much noise. He pressed his shoulder against the door and felt that there was plenty of give in between the door-frame and the lock. It was a Yale lock, three quarters of the way up the door. Miller thought that all doors had a good mortice bolt in the middle section these days, but he wasn't complaining as he knew that he'd be in here in a second.

With a heavy push of his leg and his hip against the bottom of the door, Miller heard the Yale lock submit as the force of the door being twisted below released the catch.

"Easy!" said Miller as he stepped inside and felt for a light switch. His heart was racing, as a sudden excitement filled his veins. This was bang out of order, and wholly unprofessional. Just how he liked it.

As he flicked the light-switch, Miller was surprised by the sight which greeted him.

Chapter Fifteen

DI Saunders was impressed, the televised appeal for information was yielding some amazing calls from the community around Stalybridge.

Dozens of calls had come in, some of which were trivial, but there were a handful of extremely positive ones.

A bank clerk at Natwest in Ashton had called to say that Mr Pollard had been in on Friday morning, and had withdrawn £5,000 in twenty-pound notes. This had been the first positive sighting of Mr Pollard, since the last-time anybody had heard from him, which was almost 24 hours earlier, when he'd left the school at around 10am the previous day.

That wasn't all. A shop worker at JD Sports had called. He said that Mr Pollard had been into the store and had spent several hundred pounds in cash on clothing for a male teenager, including an Adidas tracksuit, a pair of Nike Air Max trainers in a size eight, a North Face jacket and a couple of t-shirts. He'd asked the assistant if these were definitely popular for a fifteen year-old lad.

Then, a call came in which had made Saunders punch the air. Donna Moran, the owner of Tameside Camper Hire had telephoned to inform the officers that Mr Pollard had been in on Friday morning, and had hired a Motor-Home, paying in cash for a week's rental. It had cost over two-thousand pounds. The best news of all was that the Motor-Home had a tracker on it, so that the company could see exactly where their vehicles were at all times.

It was an unforgettable call, and Saunders was waiting for them to call back again, once the manager had gone down to the office to check her vehicle tracking software, and hopefully provide a location for the vehicle. This was looking very much like case closed, and Saunders loved the feeling, it never got boring.

"Wait 'til the Gaffer hears about this little lot," he kept saying, over and over again, rubbing his hands together.

*****

Miller was inside Mr Pollard's flat. There was evidence that Darren had been there, lots of evidence. Most telling was the dirty-looking school uniform which had been thrown onto the double-bed. There was evidence that new clothes had been bought, and a Nike shoebox was on the kitchen work-top. Miller looked at the sticker. The trainers were size 8. He went into the bedroom and looked through Pollard's wardrobe. His shoes and trainers were sized 10.

An i-phone had been left by the bedside table, it was plugged into the mains. Miller desperately wanted to pick it up and have a look at it, but that would have to wait until the forensics examinations had been carried out. Miller scanned the rest of the room, there was no clear evidence that Pollard had packed anything, plenty of underpants and socks were in the drawer, and a suitcase was covered with shoes, belts and ties at the bottom of the wardrobe. Miller walked through into the kitchen. Several empty JD sports bags lay on the breakfast bar, and several tags had been cut off new items of clothing. North Face, Nike, Adidas and Fred Perry tags lay all over the work-top.

"What the..." muttered Miller as he found tags from Puma socks, and a box which had contained new boxer shorts, priced at £24.99. They were sized medium.

Suddenly, Miller felt a very peculiar sensation. He was relieved that these clues suggested that Darren and Mr Pollard were together, and apparently in rather pleasant circumstances. But the sense of relief at this thought, brought with it a very sinister under-current. As far as Miller was concerned, the evidence of these new clothes, alongside those dirty, scruffy looking uniform garments made the DCI think that something rather unsavoury was going on. Classic grooming, he thought. Why would you buy a kid the latest clothes, at significant expense? Especially bearing in mind the fact that the kid in question was the biggest pain in Mr Pollard's neck. It all had an underlying, ominous suggestion about it.

In the small bathroom, there was evidence that Darren had taken a bath, or a shower here. A pair of filthy socks and a childish pair of underpants were lay on the floor near the sink, a towel had been used and thrown down beside them. Miller went back to the bedroom, and lifted the quilt, trying to find evidence of sexual activity. There was nothing obvious to the naked eye. He went back through into the kitchen. A large, 16-inch takeaway pizza box lay on the draining board. It had a delivery note stuck to it with Sellotape. It had been ordered at 20:43 on Thursday 16th May, the customer name was Phil. This was good information, it gave proof of life evidence for Mr Pollard, 10 hours after he'd last been seen. Miller lifted the pizza box lid and saw that a couple of dried up, congealed slices had been left.

Miller looked in the bin, there was a microwave lasagne wrapper and its plastic container, along with a few used tea-bags. There was no evidence of any alcohol being consumed, which relieved him. He had another quick look around the flat. It was a mess, but it was all surface mess. It looked as though the two had left in a hurry, as behind the clutter, the place looked as though it was usually kept very clean and tidy. Miller rang the CSI duty sergeant and requested a forensics team to attend urgently. It was clear to Miller that this flat, and the items within it contained valuable information which would be crucial to the investigation, especially the phone. Miller rang the local Inspector at Tameside and requested for a police officer to come immediately and guard the address until further notice.

In the back of Miller's mind, a thought was troubling him. It had been Pollard's estranged wife who had reported him missing, on Monday. Officers had been round to the couple's home on Mottram Road and had taken a statement, and had done the mandatory search of the house, including the attic, garage and shed. Mrs Pollard had not made any reference to the fact that they were estranged, and that Mr Pollard was living at a separate address, down the road. It smelt funny, and Miller now wanted to know what the smell was. As soon as the PC arrived to keep the flat secure, he decided to drive back up Mottram Road, and have it out with Mrs Pollard.

Miller pulled up, in the same spot he'd parked at half an hour previous, and put his phone on airplane mode so that he wouldn't be disturbed. His earlier intentions of showing good manners and compassion at this address were the last things on his mind now, as he walked across the road, and up to the front door. He tapped out a CID knock on the door, and heard activity inside the house, somebody talking, as they walked towards the front door. Miller checked his watch. It was 9.30pm.

*****

Donna Moran, the owner of Tameside Camper Hire had kept her word, and had been back on to Saunders. She had gone back to the office and checked the tracker status for the mobile home which Mr Pollard had hired the previous Friday.

She had a location, and her excitement was clear as she read the Satellite co-ordinate details to Saunders. He couldn't tell if she was more excited about being involved in a major police operation, or to get the vehicle back in one-piece. These motor-homes cost over a hundred thousand pounds and insurance companies always wanted to pay a largely reduced figure on the true value.

Saunders jotted down the numbers. "Thanks so much Donna, if I need any more details, I'll give you a buzz back, is it okay if you stay there so that if the vehicle starts moving, you can guide us?"

"Yeah, no worries. But it looks like its parked up for the night, it's a nice spot on the coast."

"Great, well that would be perfect. Stay there, hopefully I'll ring you to tell you that you can have your motor-home back in one piece within the hour!"

As soon as the call ended Saunders typed the co-ordinates into Google Maps. Instantly, the location appeared on the screen. The motor-home was eighty-five miles away, on the coast in North Wales. Saunders zoomed in to the specific location and recognised it immediately as Llandudno, just two hours drive away. He felt his heart racing in his throat and grabbed his phone, and called Miller. It didn't connect.

"You've reached DCI Andrew Miller, sorry I can't take..."

"Fuck's sake." He tried it again. It didn't connect. He left a voice-mail. "Sir, its Saunders, urgent call, I've got a location for... long story, but I've got a location for Philip Pollard. Call me back asap."

Five minutes passed where Saunders did nothing other than pace between the office window, his Google map of Llandudno, with its big red flag on the location of the vehicle and called Miller again.

"What the fuck?" He said, time and time again as the familiar "You've reached DCI Andrew Miller, sorry I can't take your call right now. Please leave a message and I'll get back to you as soon as humanly possible" message.

"Yes, but you never do, Sir!" said Saunders to the voicemail recorder. The DI was fuming, he put his phone in his pocket, realising that Miller must be doing something pretty important if he'd switched his phone off.

Saunders decided that there was no time to waste, he needed to alert the local police to this unexpected and extraordinary development. The police in Llandudno would have to get involved with the business end of this major missing persons inquiry.

Zooming right in on the map, so that he knew exactly what he was talking about, Saunders opened another window and opened the national police service contact database. He found the nearest operational police station at this time was 6 miles away in Colwyn Bay, a sixteen-minute car drive away, if no local officers were available.

Saunders was stressed. He didn't know if he should wait for Miller to call the shots, or just get on with the job and get this handed over to North Wales Police. He was tapping his pen against his hand as he tried Miller's phone a final time. It went straight to answer machine.

"Fuck it," he said, as he dialled the Inspector's number for Colwyn Bay Police Station. Saunders introduced himself, explained the situation and then hastily relayed the information regarding the vehicle, and most importantly, its last known location.

"Ah, yes, I have it here, see, that's on the Orme, that is."

"Sorry, I don't speak Welsh. What are you saying?"

"I'm just saying, that location is on the Orme boyo,

bloody big rock on the edge of Llandudno, that is."

"Right, and the two most famous missing people in the UK are there, right now."

"Yes, I appreciate you saying that, but like I say, it's a bloody big rock sticking out into the Irish Sea, so it not going to be difficult to find them, is it?"

"I don't know it." Said Saunders, his enthusiasm fading a little. It was as though the most mellow police Inspector he'd ever encountered was talking about a missing cat.

"Well, see, there's a great big rock that sticks out of the end of Llandudno, it's a mile wide, and it has a single track, one-way road which goes all around it. If these people are in a vehicle, then there's only one place they're going to come off there. Now, this location you've given me, it's the car park of the café half-way round."

"Yes."

"Well, that's a great spot for a motor-home. Providing it's not windy mind! If it is windy, a good gust could throw you down to your death in the sea from there."

"And is it windy there now?"

The Inspector thought about the question. "No, not particularly."

Saunders was beginning to get annoyed with this Inspector, he was either taking the piss, or he was as thick as Theresa May on a walking holiday. The Manchester DI couldn't decide which of the two depressing options was better.

"Okay, I've despatched our undercover patrol car, it's not too far away, so they'll be up there in the next five to ten minutes. My officers will be able to assess the situation without arousing any suspicion. And we can take it from there."

"So, what, are you going to ring me back?"

"Yes, I'll give you a call as soon as I know what's occurring. Don't worry Detective Inspector, you're in safe hands with us."

Saunders thanked him and hung up. "I'd rather have Benny from Crossroads in charge, mate," he said under his breath, as he started nibbling at a finger-nail.

Chapter Sixteen

The huge front door opened slowly, and a nervous-looking face peeped around the small gap. It was the woman that Miller had been watching earlier, through the living-room window.

"Hello, my name is DCI Andrew Miller, Manchester City Police, can I come in?"

The door swung open, and Miller stepped up the couple of steps into the house. Normally, Miller would engage in a couple of minutes of exchanging pleasantries and setting up a relaxed mood. But tonight, he couldn't be arsed with all that. Sandra Pollard showed the DCI through to the lounge, and he started his interrogation as he was still walking.

"I've just come from your husband's flat. I'm not being funny, but why haven't you told us about this vital detail?"

Boom! That instant, unforgiving line of enquiry went off like a firework, and Mrs Pollard looked shocked, frightened almost.

"I'm... we're..."

"When I looked through the missing person report this morning, it had this address as Philip's home. But as the day has gone on, I've learnt that he hasn't lived here for several months." Miller wasn't being aggressive, but he was certainly demonstrating his most assertive manner. "I've wasted several hours today, missed vital information. Can you explain that to me please?"

Mrs Pollard sat down. She was an attractive, mid-fifties, professional looking woman. She looked ashamed, and embarrassed. "I'm just... I've been worried about him. I didn't think it mattered about his flat... I knew he wasn't there, I've been round, several times over the weekend."

"You've been in the flat?"

"Yes." She started crying.

"So, you've seen what is in there?"

She started nodding, and more tears came flowing.

"Can you describe what you saw in the flat, please?"

"Darren's stuff."

"And can you please explain to me why you failed to mention this when you reported Philip missing?" Miller wasn't happy with this, it didn't make sense.

Mrs Pollard looked stressed, she tried answering, but she was worked up, and it was never a productive scenario to have a witness feeling so stressed out. Miller decided to soften his approach.

"Listen, calm down, alright," he pulled a small packet of tissues out of his jacket pocket and handed them to Mrs Pollard. Her hands were trembling as she reached over to Miller and took them. He sat down on the couch and gave her a couple of minutes to get herself together. Eventually, she began to talk.

"We've not been getting on. My fault. He's obsessed with his work, and, well... I gave him an ultimatum. I said that he needs to choose me, or his bloody job." She started crying again, and took another tissue out of Miller's packet.

A young woman suddenly appeared by the doorway. She was a plump, but attractive, dark haired lady in her late twenties, early thirties. She looked concerned.

"Are you alright, mum?"

"Yes, I'm, I'll be fine..."

"And you must be Jess?" said Miller.

"Yes, that's right."

"Okay, well if you can just leave me and your mum alone for a bit, please." Miller didn't want any distractions. He needed to understand what was going on here.

Jess gave him an icy stare before turning to her mother. "I'll just be through there if you need me, mum."

Miller walked across to the door and closed it behind the missing man's daughter. He didn't feel bad about it, he was still annoyed that Mrs Pollard had failed to alert the police officers to his real address, and was further incensed that she had known about Darren's presence at the flat, and had said nothing. It was dodgy as hell.

Miller sat back down, facing the sad, nervous looking lady.

"So, come on, you might as well explain it to me. You knew that Darren had been there, yet you didn't mention it to the police officers... and you failed to even mention that he was living at a separate address."

"I didn't know anything about Darren being missing until today!"

"But you knew that a pupil from your husband's school had been staying at his flat?"

She looked down at her lap. Her hand tensed around the tissue that she was holding.

"I thought..."

Miller let the pause hang.

"I don't know what's going on, okay? There, although I'm aware of all this weird stuff, yes, I should have said. I accept that. But I'm just embarrassed?"

"Embarrassed about what?"

Mrs Pollard shot Miller a threatening stare. "Don't make me say it!" she hissed at him.

"I need to hear your thoughts, Mrs Pollard, as difficult as they may be to talk about. At this moment in time, it looks as though a minor has been abducted by your husband, and the evidence so far suggests that you've been covering this crime up."

This brutal statement of fact sent Mrs Pollard over the edge, and her trembling seemed to get worse as she jerked forward in her chair, sobbing uncontrollably.

"As things stand, I have two options. The first is to lock you up and let you have a night in the cells at Ashton, and then interview you under caution in the morning."

A long, uncomfortable minute of sniffing, nose-blowing and eye-wiping passed before she spoke.

"And what's the second option?"

"You tell me what the hell is going on, and without any edited highlights. I need the full story."

Another pregnant paused filled the room. Finally, Mrs Pollard began to explain what she knew to the frustrated, tired looking DCI.

"Okay, first of all, the first I knew about Darren disappearing was today. That's the God's honest truth. I've been genuinely concerned about Phil. I'd not been able to contact him since I last saw him on Wednesday night. We had a blazing row, and he left here at about, I don't know, ten o'clock. I tried to phone him, after school on Thursday to apologise. It was ringing at first, but I think he switched his phone off. I kept trying, but it just wouldn't connect. I had a really bad feeling..."

"What sort of bad feeling?"

"I thought he might have done something stupid..."

"Killed himself?"

Mrs Pollard had a wobble at the sheer harshness of Miller's question, but fought on, speaking through her emotion. "Yes, I said some terrible things to him that night." It was obvious that Mrs Pollard was still very close to her husband. It didn't quite ring-true that they were separated. Why separate, when you're as close as these two seem to be? Thought Miller, his mind racing with possibilities.

"So, you went round to the flat, when was this?"

"Saturday morning, first. Then I went back on Saturday afternoon, and again on Saturday evening. I did the same thing throughout Sunday, I was convinced that he'd have turned up. I rang school on Monday to see if he'd been in. That's when Debbie told me that he wasn't in, and hadn't been in on Friday, either."

"And then you phoned the police?"

"Yes, and... well, I wanted to know if anybody matching his description had, you know..."

Miller shrugged.

"...been found dead or something..."

"Seriously? You really thought that he'd killed himself?"

She broke down again. "Yes, I really did."

Miller decided to change the topic slightly. He could come back to this later. "So, what was the row about?"

"He'd applied for a redundancy package at school. I promised him that we'd make a go of things if he didn't have that bloody school at the forefront of his mind all the time. He came round on Wednesday night, after tea."

"Did he have tea here?"

"No, he came round after he'd had his tea, and had done his marking. He had the letter with him, from the education authority. He asked me to open it. His hand was shaking as he handed it to me."

"Go on."

"So, I opened it, and saw a jumble of words 'sorry to inform you' and then 'regrettably' and 'unsuccessful.' I threw it at him and called him useless. I said you can't even get a redundancy deal!" Mrs Pollard started dabbing at her eyes with a fresh tissue. "He looked really sad, and he just left."

"And that's the last you saw or heard of him?"

"Yes. Although if you look at my phone, I've tried to call him a hundred times."

"So, you reported him missing, because you thought that he'd killed himself. You wanted confirmation, or hope."

"Well, yes, I guess so."

"But none of this explains the scene at your husband's flat. Pizza, new clothes, dirty underwear in the bathroom."

Mrs Pollard just sat nodding.

"Any idea what that's all about?"

"No, no. No, genuinely. I truly cannot explain that. But… well, it's obvious what it looks like."

"Have you ever had any doubts about your husband, you know… that he might be interested in young lads?"

This was too much, and Miller could see immediately that he'd crossed the line. He'd taken this too far and knew that another couple of minutes of emotional turmoil were about to disrupt his progress. He waited for her to settle down. Eventually, she spoke.

"No. I've never thought that. Not once in thirty-five years of marriage."

"And what about now?"

"Well, I've… I just don't know. Can't explain it."

Miller was satisfied with the story, it matched up to the information that he'd gained from the school. The row also added authenticity to Miller's view that this could be some kind of a mental breakdown scenario. The wife kicks him out, because he works too hard, he tries to put it right by applying to leave his job, and was rejected. Miller was seriously beginning to sympathise with Mr Pollard's circumstances.

"How did you get into the flat?"

"I have a key."

"Can I have it please?"

Mrs Pollard stood and walked across to her handbag which was on the side-board. She started jangling a big bunch of keys, and then separated one from the rest. She walked back to Miller.

"There you go."

"Thanks. Okay, well, I know this is difficult. But, I hope you understand that I have to ask these questions?"

Mrs Pollard nodded quickly. As a social worker, she was fully aware of the reality of these situations.

"Okay, I'll leave you in peace for now. Thanks for all your help."

"Thanks for... well, you know, not arresting me. I'm sorry about... but I wasn't trying to cover anything up, honestly."

Miller nodded politely as he stood and headed to the living-room door which he had closed in Jess Pollard's face. He opened it quickly and headed straight for the front door and left. He crossed the road, grabbing his phone and switching off the airplane mode. As he did so, the phone began vibrating incessantly, as the screen lit up, telling Miller that he had 18 missed calls from DI Saunders.

"What the..."

Chapter Seventeen

Llandudno is a unique British seaside town, mainly due to its unenviable record of having successfully competed against the past forty years of cheap, overseas package holidays. Where dozens of other, once-popular seaside resorts have now decayed and become areas of high deprivation, Llandudno has managed to hold its own, and maintain a strong trade.

Situated at the edge of North Wales, nestled in between Anglesey to the west, and Colwyn Bay to the East, Llandudno still attracts British holiday-makers in huge numbers, year in, year out.

Its pleasant, well-kept promenade, clean beaches and the famous pier, which protrudes half a mile into the sea from beneath the Grand Hotel, makes this a lovely place for a day out, or a long weekend, attracting people from all across the north-west and central England. The stunning views around this part of the world can make visitors feel a million miles away from the hustle and bustle of everyday life in the urban metropolises of Manchester, Liverpool and Stoke, and the tourists come flocking back, every year.

The Great Orme is one of Llandudno's best-known landmarks, a giant limestone headland on the edge of town, with a coastal road named Marine Drive circling it, offers breath-taking views of the town, the coast, and of course the Irish Sea. The summit of the Orme has several tourist attractions, from cable-cars, a tram-way, visitor's centres and a ski slope, as well as ancient churches and bronze mines.

This is a very special place, attracting not only human visitors, but many species of wild-life too, including endangered butterflies and moths attracted to the limestone flowers and grasses. The dozens of colonies of sea-bird within the cliffs, and most famously, a herd of 200 Kashmir goats live up here. The herd, which has roamed the Orme since the middle of the 19th century, is descended from a pair of goats which were presented by the Shah of Persia to Queen Victoria shortly after her coronation in 1837.

But tonight, police officers from nearby Colwyn Bay

were not here looking for endangered species, or to enjoy the pleasant views. They were looking for a white, Eldiss Autoquest 6 berth motor-home, registration PN67 WYN.

The unmarked, silver Astra police car had done a full lap of the Orme, all the way around Marine Drive. There was no motor-home at the location that Manchester police had enquired about, which was listed as the car park of the Rest And Be Thankful café, close to the light-house. The officers had proceeded with caution, posing as members of the public out for a night drive. But when it became clear that there was nothing on the car-park, the officers had parked their unmarked car, got out and had a quick look around using their torches. There was literally nothing there, just an empty, gravel car park and the thunderous sound of waves crashing against the rocks below.

It wasn't beyond the realms of possibility that the motor-home had moved on, away from Llandudno, or to higher-ground, at the top of the Great Orme. Following instruction from their Inspector over radio, the officers were told to climb the steep road to the summit, and check the roads up there.

Five minutes later, they were back on the radio, to instruct their Inspector, Colin Myers, that there was a no sign of the vehicle anywhere on the giant rock.

Inspector Myers called DI Saunders in Manchester.

"Hello, Detective Inspector, this is Inspector Myers from North Wales."

"Hi, yes, anything?" Saunders sounded worked up.

"I'm afraid not. Nothing doing, my officers have searched the whole area. They've driven along every road and bridleway. There is no motor-home on the Orme."

"Okay, thanks, just hold the line a moment." Saunders picked up a landline phone from a nearby desk and started dialling the number that he had scribbled on his post-it pad. It was the manager of the motor-home hire company.

"Donna, hi, it's DI Saunders. Are you still with the tracking software?"

"Hi, yes, still here. The van's still there, too."

"In the same location?"

"Yes."

"Okay, hold the line."

Saunders picked his mobile phone up from the desk, the connection was still there. "Hello, Inspector Myers. The vehicle is still there. It's showing up from its tracking device as being parked exactly where I gave you the co-ordinates. Can I just check them again with you?"

"Yes, go ahead."

Saunders read the long, GPS address number to the Inspector.

"Yes, that's exactly what I have. My officers have searched the entire area, there are no vehicles at that location, the car park is deserted."

"It can't be!" Saunders hadn't meant to snap, but he knew that he had done. The Inspector took it in good humour.

"No, DI Saunders, trust me. There are no vehicles there this evening. It must be a blip on the software."

Saunders talked into the other phone. "Donna, can you refresh the software?"

"In what way?"

"The officers searching are saying it's not there. It looks like a software blip at your end."

"There's no blip. Look, I'll close it down, and relaunch it. Okay, just a sec... right, its back on. I can see a map of the UK, and seven red lights in different locations, each red light corresponds to one of my vehicles. The Autoquest which Mr Pollard hired is still situated at that location, same co-ordinates that I gave you earlier."

"Aw for... what's going on?" Saunders was trying to think. This made no sense, none at all. How could the police in Wales not see a fucking big massive white camper-van on a perfectly specified car park which normally accommodated no more than fifteen vehicles?

"Okay, Inspector, the software has been reloaded, its showing the same location."

"Well... I can assure you, it's not there. My officers have checked, by car, and on foot."

"Well, can you offer me any other explanation?"

"Possibly, these trackers are only true to a distance of

ten metres, usually."

"Yes..." there was an unmistakable tone of expectation present in Saunders' voice.

Well, I'm just thinking, it could have been driven over the edge of the cliff..."

Chapter Eighteen

"Hi Sir,"

"Hi Keith, I've had eighteen missed calls. What's happened?"

"Oh God, where do I start?" Saunders sounded totally stressed as he gave his boss an update on everything, from the call from Tameside Camper Hire, to the latest, unbelievable development, that it looked like the motor-home could have been driven off the cliff.

"You okay, mate?" asked Miller, unhappy with how stressed his colleague sounded.

"Nah, not really, the Inspector I've been dealing with over there sounds as thick as two short planks, and like he's had too many Valium."

"Alright, well, I'm on my way back now, lots of interesting stuff to tell you. I'll be about twenty minutes. Phone air support, and request India 99, tell them DCI Miller has raised a code-one priority on it, travelling to North Wales. Tell them to make sure its fuelled up and ready to leave in twenty minutes."

Miller hung up, and squeezed his foot hard against the accelerator, switching on his blues and twos as the car exceeded the speed limit.

India 99 is the Manchester force's helicopter, and although it is extremely hit-and-miss as to whether it would be available for a random job under normal circumstances, the fact that Miller had put in a code-one meant that even if it was out on a shout now, it had to return to base and prepare for a new flight.

"Hello, this is DI Saunders in the SCIU."

"Hi, how are you doing tonight?" asked the shift manager.

"Pretty stressed actually. DCI Miller has asked me to issue a code-one on India 99."

"Oh, anything interesting?"

"Yes, we need to get to North Wales, sharpish. Llandudno. Is the chopper home?"

"Yes, it's been dead quiet today, not been out yet. So

this is welcome news."

"Can you have her ready in fifteen minutes?"

"Yes, she's ready now, scramble time is around four minutes."

"Excellent, okay, that's brilliant news, he's coming over from Stalybridge now on the hurry-up, so we'll be about fifteen minutes."

"Yes, that's not a problem. See you soon."

*****

The flight from HQ to Llandudno took just twenty minutes, the distance in a straight line was only 65 miles, compared to almost 90 miles by road. India 99 managed to cruise at a steady speed of 160 miles per hour. It was just enough time for Miller and Saunders, and Rudovsky who had tagged along, to compare notes.

Miller updated the officers about Mrs Pollard's disingenuous missing person's report, as well as the scene at the flat. Saunders managed to confirm the information was accurate as he relayed the phone conversation with the JD sports worker who had served Pollard.

Rudovsky revealed the information that she had managed to get from Dawn Jenkins, including her glowing reference for Mr Pollard, and the circumstances around Darren not living with her in Aberdeen. She went on to update her colleagues about Michael Jenkins, and explained the situation regarding Johnny, information which, coupled with the latest developments, effectively took the suspect badge off Michael Jenkins.

They also discussed the bank withdrawal, and of course, the hire of the motor-home. All in all, it had been a superb reaction from the public, one which had very quickly provided plenty of clues as to what was going on, and had really brought this mystery to life.

But now, as the helicopter hugged the North Wales coast, past Rhyl, Abergely and Colwyn Bay, the mood changed. All three detectives knew that there was every chance that they were about to face a most distressing and tragic conclusion to this investigation. The mood became tense as India 99 approached the Great Orme and engaged its powerful search light. The blinding white beam began illuminating the rocks at the foot of the huge cliffs which surrounded the gigantic limestone rock which made up the Great Orme.

The waves were crashing violently against the base of the rock, and it was instantly obvious that if the motor-home had indeed been driven off the cliff 100 metres above, there was no way the occupants would have survived.

After several minutes of searching, the helicopter officers, as well as Miller and his colleagues agreed that there was no evidence of any vehicle having crashed down the cliff face. They would have expected at least one item of debris to be lapping up and bashing back into the rocks.

"Can you check the car park?" asked Miller, into the microphone that he was wearing in front of his mouth. The deafening roar of the helicopters engines and rotor blades above made it impossible to communicate without the headsets. The air observer officer retrained the giant torch onto the area that Miller had requested.

The area was a car park, next to a café called "Rest and Be Thankful." It was surrounded by a stone-built wall, although there was a section where the wall was missing. There was the opportunity to drive off the edge, but it looked as though the railings were still intact.

Sure enough, there was no sign of the motor-home on the car park. The helicopter hovered above the spot, while Miller and his officers assessed the location. There was nothing here, just a deserted café, and an empty car park.

"Will you be able to land her here?" asked Miller.

The pilot was quick to reply. "No problem. Do you want to do that now?"

"Yes, I think so. We'll have a quick look on the ground, and then give the entire area the once over."

"Okay, prepare for landing."

Within seconds, India 99 was down, and parked at one of the nation's favourite beauty spots.

Miller was the first to alight the chopper, just as soon as the rotor blades had stopped rotating. The force of the down drought could have easily blown one of the detectives off the car park, and down to their deaths in the Irish Sea had they attempted to alight with them still spinning.

"Keith, give your contact a call, see if her software is still showing this site. And if it is, tell her from me that it's just cost tens of thousands of pounds to prove her software is shite!"

"Sir." Saunders followed his orders, and rang Donna. She answered on the second ring.

"Hi," she said.

"Hiya, we're here now. The motor-home is definitely not here."

"Bloody hell, how did…"

"We're in the helicopter. We've had a good look around. There's no sign of your vehicle, I'm sorry to say."

Donna sounded gutted. "Well, it's still there, according to my tracker. And all of my other vehicles have either moved since we last spoke, or are stationary. I've phoned the people that haven't moved, and they've confirmed the locations are what my computer is saying."

Saunders was shocked. This didn't make any sense.

"Sir!" shouted Rudovsky. She was crouched down by some bushes. Miller and Saunders walked across to her. She was shining her phone's torch at the bush.

Miller and Saunders saw it instantly. The tracker device was there, a little black box, no bigger than a CD case. A little red light on its side was flashing intermittently.

"Oh, Donna, I think we've found your tracker."

"It's not the tracker that's shite." Said Rudovsky. "It's taken me twenty seconds to find it. Why the fuck couldn't the bobbies who came up here have had a quick look?"

"Keith, keep her on the phone mate." Miller returned to the aircraft, and came back a few seconds later with an evidence bag and a pair of rubber gloves. He put the gloves on and placed the small device inside the clear, plastic bag. He began walking out of the car park, and onto Marine Drive, heading down the hill in the direction of the town. "Come on," he said to Saunders and Rudovsky.

After walking for a minute, he asked Saunders to find out if the motor-home was moving on Donna's computer screen.

"Yes, its showing the vehicle heading south-east on Marine Drive."

"Okay, thanks Donna. We've got your tracker, anyway."

"Tell her we'll get her motor-home as well." Said Miller, who had a weird expression on his face. He looked relieved that they hadn't located the motor-home and retrieved two dead bodies from the sea, but at the same time he was gutted that he had fallen for this crafty plan and scrambled the helicopter to pick up a £200 tracker device from North Wales.

"Let's head back. It's bed-time."

Chapter Nineteen
Thursday

Miller was first in the office, beating Saunders for a change. He was still fuming about the tracker device but deep-down, he knew that this stupid prank had only empowered his desire to catch Philip Pollard at the earliest opportunity.

He turned his computer on and headed straight to the Google Maps website, looking at the road system around Llandudno, looking at the options that Pollard had available to get away.

Due to the fact that he had no idea how long the tracker had been on the Great Orme, he realised that this was a futile exercise. His first task needed to be a nationwide request for ANPR details on the motor-home. ANPR is an abbreviation of "automatic number plate recognition" technology. The ANPR cameras automatically log all number-plates going past. The cameras are on police vehicles, city-centre CCTV and motorway and town centre speed cameras, and hundreds of new ANPR cameras are added to the nation's road network every week.

Miller started a list. Number 1 was to contact the National Crime Agency and ask them to pull in all ANPR logs of the motor-home from every Constabulary in the UK. Pollard could sling the tracker in bushes all he wanted, but he couldn't evade the power of automatic number-plate recognition technology.

Number 2 on the list was a further press conference. Knowing what he now did, following the first press conference, just over 12 hours ago, Miller was sure that the developments in the story would be of huge interest to the press, and as a result would bring in lots of fresh information.

Number 3 was to organise a team briefing and bring the other detectives of the SCIU up-to-speed with the developments of the investigation so that they were freshly equipped with all of the latest information and fully prepped for a day of none-stop investigation work, and organising door-to-doors all around the Jenkins house to try and discover exactly what had happened at the door when Mr Pollard called around the previous Thursday morning, seven days earlier.

Although he hated to admit it, this stunt with the tracker device had really got under Miller's skin. For a variety of reasons, he was extremely annoyed by this attempt to throw the police off Pollard's scent. The fact that the North Wales police couldn't even be arsed to have a quick look around at the site and save them a trip in the helicopter really bugged him. After all, it had taken Rudovsky less than a minute to locate the bloody thing. But more than that, this now felt quite personal. Miller didn't like to take things personally, but he felt genuinely angry about the wild-goose chase the previous night, and he felt pissed off that Pollard's own wife had been messing him about, too.

Saunders arrived soon after Miller had begun writing the 4th task on his to-do-list. He could see that Saunders wasn't happy as he walked into the office.

"Morning Sir," he said, without his usual warmth.

"What's up with you, did Helen make you clean the bath again?" asked Miller, trying to get a smile from his DI.

"Not, nowt... what do you mean?"

"You just look uncharacteristically pissed off. Everything alright?"

"Do I, oh, sorry. It wasn't intentional. Just feeling a bit narked by that performance last night."

"Yeah, I know what you mean. But don't let it get you down. We'll still get the silly bastard."

"Oh, there was a parcel for you at reception." Saunders stepped into Miller's office and handed him the folded, brown A4 envelope which was addressed simply to "DCI Miller."

Miller took the parcel and opened it. He laughed humourlessly when he saw what was inside. It contained three chocolate-chip cereal bars, and a Manchester City Police Air Support compliments slip, which read "For Andy and co, just in case you get hungry LOL." The cereal bars were called "Trackers."

"Knob heads!" said Miller as he opened one and threw another to Saunders, who found the joke a lot more amusing than his boss did.

"Well, that's cheered you up. If only I knew a free breakfast was the answer! Right, go and get a brew, I'm working on today's priorities. I want Pollard in our custody today, I'm not messing about now."

"Do you want one?" asked Saunders.

"You know me, Keith. Never say no to a brew."

*****

The morning briefing had gone well, and all of the SCIU officers were geared up, ready for a busy day.

Miller had arrived back at his desk to good news. The Forensics department had managed to find finger-prints for Pollard on the tracker device, taken from finger-prints taken from around his flat and his i-phone.

Darren's finger-prints were already on file, and positive matches had been found in several locations around the flat. The positive news kept coming too, as Miller read through the report. No signs of violence or sexual activity had been discovered within the flat, and the evidence pointed to Darren having slept on the sofa on the night that he stayed at the flat. This was all good news, and Miller hoped that this was just the start. He had a really positive feeling that there was plenty more to come throughout the day.

The morning-shift of constables had arrived, pumping the team's strength up slightly. But Miller needed more help on man-power, particularly for the door-to-doors in Stalybridge. He and Saunders felt certain that something would come up, something of value, so Miller had asked his boss, DCS Dixon to call in a few favours from Tameside police, and try and get some bodies to help with this operation. The sooner it was done, the better.

With his team all aware of their tasks, and what the day's plan was, Miller set them off, and retreated into his office to organise his own activities for the day.

*****

Ashton CID, along with several bobbies and PCSO's had been drafted in to assist with the door-to-doors around Sand Street, and all the way up Cheetham Hill Road, to the Raj Bros shop. DI Saunders was heading this operation, and had prepared a questionnaire that he wanted each police officer to fill out at every address on Sand Street initially, and then the neighbouring streets and roads.

"Hello, I'm from Manchester City Police, just wondered if we could ask you a few questions about the young lad that's gone missing from this street?" asked one police officer.

"Darren? Yeah, I heard about that. He's not a bad lad. Bit of a gob-shite but weren't we all at that age?" The neighbour, a fat man in his late fifties looked as though he couldn't decide if he needed to shave or if he wanted to grow a beard. "His mum was a nice woman, do out for anyone, she would, and Johnny weren't a bad lad either. Shame what happened to him really. The dad's a fucking bell-end though, so I imagine Darren's run away so he can get away from that useless fucker!"

The response was similar at each door on Sand Street. One or two neighbours had a few choice words about Darren, and some of the activities that he'd been caught up in, but it was Darren's father who most of the community had issues with. The message was unmistakable, Michael Jenkins was a fucking knob.

The street was filled with police officers, their cars, vans and smart, unmarked CID cars. The officers were all wearing MCP high vis jackets, even the detectives. Most doors were unanswered as the occupants were out at work, so officers posted through a note which had already been printed on MCP letterhead, asking the householder to contact the number below, if they saw anything of Darren, or Mr Pollard, on Thursday of last week.

Some of the neighbours were quite excited by all this activity on their quiet, unremarkable little street, and one in particular had been filming the police activities on his mobile phone, and had uploaded the footage to the BBC North West Tonight Facebook page, along with the comment "Police presence right now on Darren Jenkins street."

The video footage showed officers knocking on doors,

chatting with neighbours and looking in wheelie bins. The mood was very sombre, and the officers looked as though they weren't expecting a happy ending to this unusual case.

Eventually, a couple of officers arrived at a house across the road from the Jenkins household, whose owner said that she had seen Mr Pollard arguing with Michael Jenkins on the morning in question. When asked what time this argument had occurred, the lady in question, Mrs Aspinall said, "it was about half past ten, because This Morning had just started and I had to mute it to hear what was going on."

DI Saunders, who has out on the street, knocking on doors was quickly called to the address.

"Hi, I'm Detective Inspector Saunders. Do you mind if I sit down?"

"No, no, you get yourself comfy. Would you like a cup of tea?" Mrs Aspinall was a nice old lady. Her walls were covered with photos, and Saunders quickly assessed that she was a great grandmother, following the generations of faces that adorned the walls and shelves.

"No, thank you, I'm fine. So, what happened, what did you see?"

Mrs Aspinall sat down opposite Saunders, in her comfy chair by the window.

"Well, Mr Pollard came along, he parked his car outside. I didn't realise it was him until it was on the news last night. He taught my grand-kids, he's supposed to be a lovely man, so it makes you think…"

"And what happened?" Saunders gently steered her back to the point.

"I heard all this shouting."

"And was this on the street?"

"Yes…"

"Did Mr Pollard go inside the property at any point?"

"No, not when I was watching. He stood arguing outside, on the street, then stormed off, got in his car and drove away."

"He definitely didn't go inside the house?"

"No, he wasn't welcome. That much was clear. Michael

shouted something after him, I can't... it was... do-gooder! Or something like that. Then he went in his house and slammed the front door shut. He always does that, gives me the fright of my life!"

"Did you see Darren at all?"

"No, no, just Mr Pollard, and his dad. I thought Mr Pollard was going to go for him at one point, Michael backed off and went in the house for a few seconds, but he came back out as Mr Pollard returned to his car."

"Mr Pollard definitely didn't go inside?"

"No. How many times? I might be a little old biddy, but I'm not retarded."

"Sorry, and he drove away you say?"

"Yes, he looked annoyed, upset even. He just drove down the hill." Mrs Aspinall demonstrated which way the car had travelled.

"Can you describe the vehicle?"

"Yes, it was a black car, newish. It was a nice car, posh looking, it definitely looked out of place around here."

"Thank you, Mrs Aspinall. You've been really helpful. I will leave you my card, please give me a call if you remember anything else."

"Okay, just leave it next to the phone for me."

The door-to-doors continued, but there was hardly any decent intelligence coming in, just lots of anecdotes of things Darren or Michael had done in the past. As the inquiries on Sand Street drew to a close, Saunders was grateful for the information Mrs Aspinall had provided, but he was disappointed that not a single other neighbour had provided anything. It's common to encounter a wall of silence in certain cases for fear of repercussions or community smears about "grassing", but Saunders was always disappointed when the public stayed quiet on cases involving kids.

"Right, I think we're done here, thanks very much everyone. Stand down," said Saunders into his radio.

Chapter Twenty

Miller's press conference had been advertised as "brief" on the official invitation, which had been sent out to all local and national media outlets on the press office's database. To stress the point about how brief it was intended to be, the invitation stated that the press conference was to be held outside the MCP headquarters main entrance.

The press knew this tactic, it meant that Miller was literally only going to speak for a couple of minutes, tops. And they were right. The press release did include all of the key developments, though, and contained the CCTV footage of Philip Pollard withdrawing a large sum of money from his bank, along with footage of him inside JD Sports. These clips were accompanied by photographs of the items which Pollard had purchased and Darren Jenkins was now presumably wearing. There was also a photograph of the mobile home that he had hired. The press release also contained excellent footage of Darren Jenkins, from the paper-shop he worked at on the morning that he had disappeared. This up-to-the-minute footage was invaluable for letting the public know exactly who they were keeping an eye out for.

At 12 noon precisely, DCI Miller stepped out of the huge, glass fronted building, and walked straight towards the press. He made sure that the building's giant red, blue and silver police motif was in shot of the cameras, before he began reading his short, prepared statement.

"Hello, thank you all for attending this lunchtime. As you will all appreciate, this is a very fast-moving inquiry and I have lots to get on with, so this briefing will be very short. I hope that you have all received the press release, and the information attached, and have begun broadcasting and sharing the information on your networks. I know that Sky News have been quick to put it on the air, so thank you for that, Paul."

Miller nodded his appreciation to Sky's north of England correspondent, who was standing before him.

"As the press-release states, we have learnt a lot through the night, and I would like to take this opportunity to thank all of the members of the public who have supported us. Thanks to you, we have made significant progress already, and continue to do so, as we search for Philip Pollard and Darren Jenkins."

Miller paused momentarily to catch his breath. "I can confirm that the person who was helping us with our enquiries yesterday has been extremely helpful and has given us several interesting leads to follow up and is now back home. We have eliminated this individual from our enquiries."

This was news. Miller hadn't said it, but the press all knew that he was talking about the boy's father.

"Now, I'm appealing to everybody who Mr Pollard has taught through the years. We really need to speak to you if you have any information about this teacher. It might be information that you are embarrassed to speak about, but we can help you with any of these concerns, we have specially trained officers who are able to support you. If Mr Pollard ever did anything that you were uncomfortable with, anything that you thought was inappropriate, anything at all, I'm urging you to contact us, and get it off your chest. You could have information that might lead us to Mr Pollard, and Darren Jenkins."

"What do you mean by inappropriate?" shouted one reporter. Miller was glad that he she did.

"Well, not to put too fine a point on it, Mr Pollard has had lots of unsupervised one-to-one interactions with pupils over many years. Our inquiries have found that he has demonstrated an unusual amount of interest in Darren Jenkins, and I'm trying to ascertain if this is a common behaviour? If you were a student of Astley High School, did you spend a lot of time alone with Mr Pollard, and did he ever do anything, or say anything which you found peculiar? Did he ever buy you gifts, or arrange to meet with you outside the school community? If the answer is yes to any of those questions, I'd really like to hear from you as soon as possible. I know that this is shocking, and very disturbing for many people in the Stalybridge area, and I also acknowledge that Mr Pollard has previously enjoyed a very good reputation among pupils, staff and parents. However, as you are reporting, there does appear to be another side to Mr

Pollard's character, and it is crucial that I hear all of the details of that, at the very earliest opportunity, in order to find a swift and positive outcome from this case. Thank you."

With that, Miller turned and walked back towards the police HQ, as lots of different questions were shouted at his back. Miller was happy with that, he'd said just enough, but not too much. He'd painted Pollard as a weirdo creep, which was precisely the angle he'd aimed for. It would be excellent if the phone started ringing, with calls from ex-pupils. But, that wasn't his number one objective.

Miller had wanted to get inside Pollard's head, and he knew that this was the fastest way. Insinuate that he's a creepy weirdo paedophile teacher with an unhealthy interest in his pupils. Miller didn't actually believe that, deep down. The evidence just didn't point to that, so far. But this was going to be the fastest way of changing that, as well as undermining all of Mr Pollard's excellent achievements through the years.

Saunders greeted Miller as he walked back into the SCIU department.

"Ooh, I think that will have really pissed him off, Sir."

"Good."

"Do you not think it might push him over the edge though? His mental state seems pretty fragile already." Saunders looked concerned.

"I doubt it will push him over the edge mate, he went over the edge last Friday when he hired that motor-home and emptied his savings account."

"Yeah, but, I mean, you've made him out as a right weirdo in that statement."

"I know mate. But, he started it."

*****

"Not being funny, but this copper is barking up the wrong tree! As if Well'ard is a wrong'un!" Said Pete Gregory, commenting on the Manchester Evening News' Facebook story.

"I hope Well'ard is going to kick this copper's arse!" wrote another commentator on the page.

"This DCI Miller is going to get his phone confiscated until end of term if he doesn't stop slagging Well'ard off!"

It just went to show that even under the weight of these dark, mysterious circumstances, the people of Stalybridge still held the well-known teacher in high regard. Those that knew Mr Pollard were quite happy to rubbish any suggestions that he was upto anything untoward. It was quite a powerful message which was coming back from the local community.

The comments were appearing everywhere on social media, on the local, and national news feeds, and they were all painting Mr Pollard in a very positive light. It was encouraging to see, as the remarks really did suggest that whatever it was that was happening with Darren Jenkins, there was a good chance that the boy wasn't in any real danger. That was the hope that casual observers took from the comments, anyway.

But there were plenty of other comments from people who did not know anything about Mr Pollard, and these comments were classic "judge, jury and executioner" type statements made by people who were quite happy to present a version of the story which simply did not exist, in order to try and appear clever.

"This teacher will have been grooming the lad for years, and now, he's finally given in to his desires. They should bring back the death penalty." Said one.

"This kind of thing happens all the time," said another. "Blokes shouldn't be allowed to teach in schools, its unnatural. What the fuck do they want to be around kids for all day anyway? Go on, ask yourselves that!"

The idiotic, stupid comments attracted plenty of replies, especially from the very people they were aimed at. Teachers. And it was a very large target audience, since the UK has almost half a million teachers, employed to teach the nation's eight-million plus kids.

"That is the single-most stupid comment I have ever read in my entire life!" said one of the half a million teachers, 43 year-old Daniel Ganitski. "I have been a teacher for twenty-one years, and I joined the profession because I love it. I love taking kids in at eleven, guiding them through the most important years of their lives, and then watching them open their exam results five years later, seeing the grades they earned, knowing that I played an integral part of their future success in life. How dare you suggest that there is some sinister reason for wanting to work in the greatest profession that there is. My advice for you is to explore the darkness of your own mind, which is capable of conjuring up such a disturbing thought and seek help."

There was no reply to Mr Ganitski's comment, but there were over 2000 likes. It was obviously an internet troll who'd left the statement, hoping to cause offence and gain a reaction. It wasn't quite the reaction that the troll had aimed for.

This story was now at the awkward phase where everybody's imagination was running away with them, and some of the less-bright people were making comments that made them appear stupid. They were all there, cracking the case as they sat on the bus, or waited for their drying at the launderette.

"It seems pretty obvious to me that this teacher has snapped. He's done the kid in, and now he's done himself in. Good luck finding the bodies is all I can say."

The amateur comedians were there too, in amongst the comments from people who were genuinely concerned about both parties in this unusual case.

"I feel sorry for the lad, imagine how much extra maths he's having to do!"

"I've just heard that a teacher has run off with one of his pupils, and I am totally disgusted. The kid's a little chav with a lazy eye, apparently."

It wasn't all rash opinions and jokes though. Hundreds, if not thousands of simple, to-the-point comments filled up the comment sections underneath each news story.

"Praying for a happy ending."

"Sending positive thoughts to Mr Pollard. #ItsOkayToNotBeOkay"

"Hoping all ends well."

One thing was abundantly clear, though. This story was massive, and there was an enormous appetite to hear the next detail, and hopefully, to learn that Mr Pollard, and Darren

Jenkins had been found safe and well.

Chapter Twenty-One

22 year-old Kieron Davis was watching the news report, lay on his bed. He'd been locked in his cell for most of the day, as usual, and his daily routine of TV watching had been unaltered. He was now filling in the time between Doctors, and A Place in the Sun, with his regular catch-up of Sky News.

He was shocked by the story that the news channel was reporting. He'd never seen anybody that he knew on the news before. But here it was, his old teacher, Well'ard on the screen. The channel was showing CCTV footage of him withdrawing five thousand pounds in cash at the bank in Ashton. Kieron was shocked at how little Well'ard had changed over the six years since he had left Astley High School.

The news report was unbelievable, and Kieron really couldn't believe that Mr Pollard was being accused of the crime that they were talking about on the news. The thing that the copper had said, asking if any former pupils had ever been approached in an inappropriate way by Mr Pollard was bang out of order.

Kieron sat up and moved his face closer to the tiny TV screen as the picture changed from Mr Pollard, to a shot of the school. It brought back a lot of great memories, seeing his old school again. Despite the fact that he'd felt that he hated every moment there, while he was a pupil. But as time had gone on, like every other kid in the world, Kieron knew that the old saying was true. School days really are the best days of your life.

After leaving school, in 2011, with no qualifications, Kieron had learnt very quickly that the little bubble he'd been contained in, with all of its safety nets, simply didn't exist in the real world. It hadn't taken long for him to realise that when you've got no qualifications, the world can be a very cold, very hard place.

He'd tried to get on training courses and apprenticeships but had no luck. He tried a different path and signed up at college to try again with his GCSEs. But after just a few weeks at the sixth form, his old behaviour traits had returned. His bad attitude, his disruptive behaviour, his non-attendance to certain lessons had all caught up with him again.

He soon found that at college, there wasn't a teacher like Well'ard, who's office you could sit and doss in all day, having a laugh and talking about random things instead of doing boring lessons. At college, it soon became apparent, nobody gives a shit, not like they do at school. If you can't be arsed, they can't. One college teacher told Kieron that he has two choices; "Fit in, or fuck off."

Kieron did the latter. But he had the last word and told his teacher that the college was bollocks. The teacher didn't look remotely interested in the 16 year-old's observation. Kieron stepped out of there, into a biting wind, and for the first time in his young life, he had no idea what to do now.

He couldn't go home. He'd caused so much shit at home that his mum had told him that if he doesn't make a go of things at college, she would kick him out. She wasn't joking either. The amount of stress, worry and anger that Kieron had created during his short life had brought his mum to the edge of her sanity, and to the end of her patience.

Two days after Kieron had given the college tutor his opinion of the place, his mother received a letter from the college, advising that her son had left, and if she tries to apply for tax credits in respect to his further-education, she would be liable to prosecution.

Life changed very quickly for Kieron. His mother was as good as her word and kicked him out that day.

"How many fucking times can I say this shit?" She asked, as she slammed the door behind him. He waltzed down the street as though the victory was his. He was homeless, he was unemployable, he'd screwed up his second chance at the college, all before he was seventeen-years-old. And he walked down the street like he owned the place.

After a spell of crashing at mates' houses, their mums and dads were becoming a little irritated that the cocky kid that they didn't even approve of their child hanging around with, seemed to have moved in. Kieron spent a couple of weeks of this chaotic existence, before one of his friend's mums rang Social Services, and explained the situation.

A car arrived, and Kieron was led out to it by two youth team social workers and driven away. Kieron had a shock, as he realised that his new-found freedom was not all that it seemed. He was taken to a house which looked like a cross between a children's home, and a prison.

"We've spoken to your mum, and she says that she doesn't want you back at home. She says that you cause too much trouble, she says you're lazy, that you're cheeky, that you won't do anything you're asked. She's reached the end of her tether with you Kieron." The Social worker guy was alright, he'd seemed pretty sound as he explained what was happening. "But this presents you with a problem. Because you're still a child in the eyes of the law, you have to be looked after by us, until you're eighteen."

Kieron shrugged, as if to say he wasn't bothered.

But he soon discovered that he *was* bothered. He was sharing the house with seven other lads, all of whom had similar problems to Kieron's. A few of them were alright, but, most of them were not. Kieron had entered a strange, scary new world, where just looking at one of the other lads in the wrong way earned him a punch in the face at best, a severe beating at worst. The tiny amount of belongings that he'd been allowed in his dorm were stolen, and the staff, well, they didn't want to get involved.

Within days, Kieron was starting to realise that life was nothing like he'd imagined it to be. Life was turning out to be pretty shit. He ran away from the home a few times, but never got too far. And when he was returned, usually by police officers, he had the few "liberties" that he'd been afforded, removed. This meant that he had no free-time and had to spend all of his time in the house, watching TV, trying not to piss anybody off. It was miserable, and Kieron longed for home.

In his regular meetings with the social workers, Kieron would tell them that he wanted out.

"Okay, so let's say that I phone your mum now, and tell her that you're sorry. Do you think that's enough?"

"Yes," said Kieron, shrugging.

"The problem we have here Kieron, is that you just

don't understand how much unhappiness your behaviour causes other people. Your mum has tried everything with you, and she can't cope. And your answer is to just say sorry and carry on."

"Yeah, and I'll tell her I'll stop being a dick."

"But will you stop being a dick?"

"Yeah, course."

"But you had the chance to stop being a dick when you were at college. And you..."

"That was different."

"It wasn't Kieron. This is the problem, you don't seem to have any kind of awareness of your own actions, and how they result badly for you. Until you start to make that connection, I'm afraid there's no way I can ring your mum."

"Yeah, well, you're on her side aren't you? This is fucking bullshit. I want to go to my room."

"But we need to discuss this. We need to work out a strategy, agree trigger points."

Kieron would get stressed and angry when it wasn't going his way. "The only trigger I can think of is going to be pulled in your wobbly face IF YOU DON'T FUCK OFF NOW!"

At the heart of Kieron's problems was a lack of self-awareness. The way that Kieron was, seemed perfectly natural to him. This was just how he was, and he didn't see what the big fuss was about. It wasn't as though he was a child-killer, or an arsonist or anything. He just wanted a laugh, he just wanted to do the things that he wanted to do. He really didn't understand why it was such a big deal, and to be fair, he didn't spend too much time thinking about it. He didn't see the point. Everyone had it in for him, and that was it.

Kieron managed to do just enough to stay out of trouble in the home, he'd learnt how to get through each day without getting his face punched, or his things nicked. He attended the daft lessons and courses that the home put on for the residents but it was just like school, and none of the information seemed to make sense. It was as though he was watching TV with the sound down, with a road drill banging away outside. He simply couldn't get his head into it whenever he tried to concentrate and learn whatever it was that the person was saying.

Admittedly, Kieron didn't feel the need to be so disruptive in this setting, though. The main reason was his peer group. In Kieron's view, they were knob-heads, and he just couldn't be bothered trying to compete. Besides, he'd get a kicking off the other lads for being a bell-end if he did say anything.

Things changed dramatically once Kieron reached his 18th birthday. Practically overnight, he was moved from the care of social services, and placed in a one-bedroom flat on a rough estate near Manchester. At first, Kieron was delighted, he was so happy to be out of that shitty home, buzzing to be away from the arsehole lads in there. Most of all, he was happy because he felt that finally, he was a man now. He didn't have any stupid social services people doing his head in every five minutes. He didn't have to go to bed at half-ten anymore or get up at eight o'clock in the morning. Best of all, the omnipresent threat of a kicking was gone.

But it didn't take long before Kieron realised that once again, the safety nets had been removed, and he was on his own. His life very quickly went off the rails, as he met new people, and mixed in new social circles. The council estate where he'd been given his flat was used to rehome troubled individuals and families. The place was full of ex-cons and anti-social families. Kieron had only been living in the area for a few weeks when his flat was burgled. All he had in there was a telly, a toaster and a kettle, which his mum had brought round for him. They'd been nicked, and somebody had done a shit in his bath.

Kieron sat down on the cold, hard floor of his empty, soulless flat, and realised that everything that he had ever believed about life was wrong. He'd gone through school, and life, with a smile on his face and the view that life was going to be good to him. He'd imagined that he'd have a nice car, the best clothes, and all the latest Xbox games, on the day they came out, maybe a girlfriend one day. It was sobering to realise just how wrong he'd imagined it, despite thousands of hours of teacher's, parent's and social worker's time explaining that it was inevitable that this was where he'd end up if he carried on.

But it was worse than that. Within 6 months of getting his flat, Kieron had ended up in Forest Bank prison, for stealing a car and crashing it into a set of traffic lights. He'd been back out, and back in, three times in four years since then. This latest sentence he was serving was for two years, for multiple burglaries.

Prison had become the safety net, now. It was a lot easier in prison than it had been in the real world, and Kieron knew that he always had this place to fall back on. Three good meals, warm bed, his own TV and some good lads to knock around with and have a laugh with during association time.

Kieron couldn't wait for exercise period to come around, so he could ask one of the screws to get the Governor to contact DCI Miller. He had some important information that he wanted to share about Mr Pollard. Kieron wanted to set the record straight, he owed Well'ard that.

Chapter Twenty-Two

"Hello, Mrs Pollard?"

"Yes?"

"Hi, it's DCI Miller. We met last night..."

"Oh, hi, what's..."

"Oh, sorry, I've not got any information. Nothing of major significance anyway."

There was a long silence. Miller felt bad. It was obvious that for Sandra Pollard, every minute felt as though it was lasting an hour. She was desperate for something. Her disappointment was silent, but unmistakable down the phone.

"So, what's new?"

"Well, I wanted to invite you down here for a chat, let you meet my team, let you see where our investigations are up to... and, well, I wanted to explore the possibility of doing a news conference with you?"

"A news conference... for TV you mean?" She didn't sound overly keen.

"Yes, well, in my experience, the best method of connecting with somebody, is through their loved one."

Another thick, heavy silence hung on the line.

"I'm just a bit... it's a bit embarrassing."

Miller held the phone away from his ear and stared at it. He wasn't expecting to hear such a strange response.

"Sorry, I don't follow. How do you mean embarrassing?"

"Yes, sorry DCI Miller, that must sound so shallow. What I mean is, I'm quite ashamed that we've split up. And, well, I'm quite ashamed about what's happening, with Darren I mean."

Miller thought for a second. It was understandable, to a certain degree, maybe a little humiliating. But this was a serious matter. He wasn't sure what to say, but it didn't matter.

"Oh, what am I saying? Of course I will do it. Sorry, I'm just all over the place at the minute."

That was a relief. "Oh, no, don't apologise Mrs Pollard, I can't imagine what you're going through."

"Thank you. What time would you like me?"

"Oh, well, what time is it now? One o'clock... what do you think about five?"

"Yes, that's fine. Is it the police head-quarters where you are based?"

"That's right, on Hyde Road. Just ask for me at reception. I'm sure I'll have a lot more to tell you by then."

"Would it be alright if I brought my daughter along, Jess?"

"Yes, yes, I can't see why not. Okay, I'll see you at five, and we can discuss the press conference as well."

"Okay, thank you. And, obviously, if you hear anything beforehand..."

"Rest assured Mrs Pollard, you'll be the first to hear any news. Okay, talk later."

Miller ended the call, and began writing an e-mail to the press office, asking them to organise a full press conference for 6pm.

*****

Kieron Davis jumped as he heard his cell door being unlocked. Once it was open, he was shocked by what he saw. It was the Governor of HMP Forest Bank, standing right outside his cell.

"Hello, Sir." Said Kieron.

"Hiya Kieron, can I come in a minute please?"

"Yes Sir, of course."

The Governor was a nice man, and the entire prison population respected him. It was very rare to get a visit from him though, it was usually the other way round. Cons visit the Governor in normal circumstances.

"Nice place you've got here," said the Governor. Kieron laughed at the stupid joke and imagined that he said it to every prisoner in the jail.

Kieron's "place" was a single occupancy cell which contained a toilet, a small sink, a bed and a window made up of four-inch panes of glass set in a steel window frame. The only access to fresh air was from a small hatch at the bottom of the window. The view outside was one of the best in the prison, looking out across the railway, the express trains whizzing past on their way into, or out of Manchester every five minutes. It was just a shame that previous occupants of the cell had scratched the tiny glass panes so badly over the years, it made the view very foggy.

There was a tiny walkway beside the bed, and a shelf opposite it for a small TV and a few belongings, such as soap, toilet roll, a razor and a flannel. There was a plastic cup next to the TV, and that was about it. It was a very modest place that Kieron had here, but he liked it.

"So, sorry to intrude but Mr Gelsthorpe told me that you need to contact DCI Miller, about the missing school kid?" Mr Gelsthorpe was the screw that Kieron had spoken to earlier, during social.

"Yes, that's right Sir. Mr Pollard, the teacher who's missing, well me and him go way back. And that copper was saying he wanted to hear from anyone who had information about him."

"And do you have information?" asked the Governer.

"Yes Sir." Kieron looked pleased with himself.

"It's just, this kind of thing happens a lot. And I'm not saying that you would, but there are quite a few people who waste the police's time with things like this, just for the hell of it. I have to check its all above board, before I can make the call to the police."

"Yeah, yeah, totally Sir. Look," Kieron stepped forward towards his unexpected visitor and opened his drawer beneath the TV. He pulled out a stack of hand-written letters and began rummaging through them. Eventually, he pulled one from the pile, and offered it to the Governor.

It was a letter from Mr Pollard, to Kieron, written two months earlier. After a quick scan through, the Governor was happy with everything.

"That's perfect Kieron, good lad. I'll contact DCI Miller and I'm sure he'll want to speak to you. May I borrow this letter, for the time-being?"

"Yes Sir, of course, no problem about that."

"Okay. I'll probably see you later then. Good lad Kieron."

"Thank you, Sir."

*****

The incident room phone had been ringing non-stop all day, as the public rang in to offer their sightings and anecdotes about Darren and Mr Pollard. There was some good stuff coming in. The best one so far, potentially, was a call from a filling station at Gisburn, on the A59 in between Yorkshire and Lancashire. According to the owner, they had CCTV footage of a motor-home filling up a few days earlier, and the owner was sure it had been Mr Pollard, who'd paid seventy pounds in cash. The owner had checked his CCTV and was convinced that it had been Pollard. There was no sign of Darren, however, and he had reversed the footage, and checked it several times, replaying the footage as the motor-home entered, and left the forecourt. As far as the garage owner was concerned, there was definitely no passenger on board in the cab. Lancashire officers based at Clitheroe police station had agreed to go to the garage and retrieve the footage. Miller and his team were still waiting for an e-mail with the clip attached, so they could see if this had legs. It would be an excellent turn-up, if it was right. So far, this was the hottest lead they'd had since the motor-home call had come in the previous evening.

And then a call came in from the Governor of Forest Bank Prison, just three miles outside of Manchester city centre. This call sounded very promising, and Miller was handed the phone straight away.

"Yes, hi, I'm the Governor at Forest Bank, we have met before, a few years ago, you probably won't remember?"

"Yeah, yeah, I do remember, course I do. How's it going?"

"Very well. Actually, I think I may have a prisoner that you'll want to speak with. He's asked me to get in touch, he's a former pupil of Mr Pollard, the missing teacher."

"That sounds good. Is it legit?"

"Yes, it seems so, I have a letter here, addressed to him, from Mr Pollard."

"What does it say?" asked Miller. He was definitely intrigued by this unexpected turn-up.

"What, you want me to read it?"

"Would you not mind?"

"No, that's fine. It reads, Dear Kieron, thank you for your letter and your kind words about me, although when I read it, I thought you must have got me mixed up with somebody else. I always thought that you hated my guts!

Sorry to read that you're having a tough time, and I hope that things are going well in prison. What plans do you have for when you are released? I hope that you can get yourself on one of the courses they run there, Forest Bank are really good at offering new skills and opportunities to their inmates. I'll be keeping my fingers crossed for you young man, and please write to me again and let me know how you are getting on. If you ever want one of my long lectures, or just a chat, send me a visitor pass, preferably weekend if you can.

I'll never forget the day you sneaked under my desk in English and tied my shoelaces together. It's a good job I couldn't chase you that day, or you'd have been in a cemetery now, not a flipping prison! Classic joke that was, I'd have been a lot angrier if it had been anybody else who'd done it.

Keep smiling lad and keep believing in yourself. I've always believed in you.

Best Wishes

Well'ard. (Phil Pollard)"

"Wow, flipping heck. I think I'll definitely come and see him. Did he say anything about what he wanted to speak to me about?"

"No, nothing like that, and I didn't want to pry. I was just satisfied that he did have an authentic connection to Mr Pollard."

"Brilliant, this sounds interesting. I can come now, if you like? Fifteen minutes?"

"Yes, no problem. See you soon."

Chapter Twenty-Three

It took Miller fifteen minutes to get through the security checks at HMP Forest Bank. There are no favours in prison security, not even for one of the city's best-known police detectives.

HMP Forest Bank is a modern prison, which was built in the late 1990's on the former Agecroft Power Station site, on the edge of Salford. This facility has made the news many times, most notably for several escapes which involved armed gangs stopping ambulances which were transporting inmates to hospital. The escape plans had been made possible thanks to the number of contraband mobile phones inside the 8-wing prison, which accommodates over 1400 prisoners, the majority of whom are young men from the Greater Manchester area.

The smell of the prison hit Miller as soon as he stepped beyond the security entrance. It was a smell which only exists in prison, and youth centres. A smell of stale sweat, cheap deodorant and roll-up cigarettes. As Miller finally completed his signing in, it was reassuring to know that the prison took security so seriously, but it was bloody frustrating for Miller, knowing that this was dead time. He was also aware that Forest Bank prison was well known for its security vulnerabilities overhead. It didn't matter how many metal detectors, scanners and frisks were taking place at the doors, when crime gangs were piloting drones packed with drugs, mobile phones and cash into the prison's grounds every night, from the opposite side of the railway tracks.

"Ah, so you must be Kieron?" asked Miller, when he finally reached the Governor's office.

"Yes, Sir."

"What are you in for, son?" asked Miller.

"Oh, just daft stuff Sir, TWOCing, burglary, stupid stuff Sir, trying to get by."

"On the wrong side of the tracks are you, mate?"

"Yes, Sir. But I'm trying to sort my head out. I've got to."

"And you went to Astley, did you?"

"Yes Sir."

"And I hear you were close with Mr Pollard?"

"That's right, Sir. Although I must admit, at the time we didn't get on that well. But he was always good with me."

"What do you think is going on?"

"Me, Sir?"

Miller nodded.

Kieron shrugged. "Haven't got the first clue, I'm sorry to say."

"Same here!" Miller laughed, which forced Kieron to laugh loudly too.

"Seriously though, I've never met the guy, but I've heard all these great stories about him..."

"Yeah, definitely. He is a proper top bloke, shit, the stuff I used to get up to with him, winding him up, stressing him out. He never got sick of me. I proper missed him after I left, he was like a dad to me."

"In what way?"

"Well, loads of ways really. He was just proper supportive and stuff."

"Did he ever give you any gifts?"

"Gifts, what like Myhr? Frankinsense?"

Millier laughed enthusiastically. That gag had come from nowhere, lightning quick. Kieron reminded him of Rudovsky, that's the kind of thing she'd say.

"No, I'm kidding, he never gave me any gifts like, you know, obvious, but once, there was this school trip down London. It was about two-hundred quid. He was really keen for me to go, but there was no way my mam could afford it. Besides, I was always in a load of trouble anyway, so even if she did have the cash, there's no way she'd have let me."

"So, what happened?"

"Well'ard paid for me. He went round and seen my mum, spoke to her and that. He reckoned that because it was about six months away, that he'd be able to blackmail me into behaving until the trip."

"And he paid it, out of his own pocket?"

"Yeah, like I say, top, top bloke."

"Well, it sounds like it, on the face of it. The only problem is, usually this type of thing arouses suspicion, you know, grooming and all that."

"Yeah, sure, I get that. But that's not what Well'ard was about. No way Sir, never. He told me that I'd get a lot out of it, he told me that I have to see other things, apart from Stalybridge and Ashton. He said that if I came down to London and saw all the cool stuff, like Tower Bridge, and Buckingham Palace, and Big Ben and all that, he said it would open my mind up, show me that there's more to life than the estate I live on and the school I go to."

"And did it?"

"Yes and no really. I liked it, but I got into trouble for something, can't remember what it was now. Well'ard was proper pissed off with me. I really felt like I'd let him down."

"And I have to ask you this, Kieron. Did Well'ard ever touch you, you know, in a sexual way?"

"Nah, seriously man, this is why I asked the Governor to phone you. That's not what this shit is about, I guarantee you."

"You're confident?"

"One hundred per cent Sir. Whatever is going down, it isn't to do with sex, I'm totally confident about that."

"The lad who's gone missing stayed at Pollard's flat the night before they disappeared. And Mr Pollard had bought him hundreds of pounds worth of clothes from JD."

"Well, yeah, I can see how that shit would look, to somebody that doesn't know Well'ard. But trust me, if that was what he was about, then I'd know. I spent nearly every day in his office, four, five, six hours a day, for five years. Just me and him. He never did nothing, never said nothing about sex. And look at me, I'm a very bonny lad!" Kieron grinned, and Miller laughed.

"Modest, too."

"Trust me though. This isn't about Well'ard being a perv. Absolutely no way."

"If I rang your mum, would she remember Mr Pollard?"

"Yeah, definitely. God, I bet the neighbours thought they were going out, he was round our house that much."

"And she'll remember the London trip?"

"Yeah, you're joking aren't you? A full weekend off from me. Course she'll remember it Sir!" Kieron smiled. He wasn't in denial that he had his problems and was quite happy to take the piss out of himself despite them. To Miller, that was a very endearing quality.

Miller really liked this young lad. He'd met thousands like him, and most of the time, they were just young blokes that had fallen through the cracks of the system. They weren't supposed to be involved in crime, it wasn't a plan they'd set out with. Usually, it was circumstances, bad luck, and poor decision making that had led them to this depressing place, and once they were in, it was hard to escape the revolving door. Most didn't.

"I read the letter that Mr Pollard sent you. Did you send him a visitor pass?"

Kieron looked down at the floor. "No Sir."

"Why not, if you don't mind me asking?"

"I dunno. I was just so buzzing to get a letter back off him. I didn't want to come across as a pain in the arse."

"Well, from what I can gather from the letter, I don't get the impression that he would have thought of you as a pain in the arse. I mean, he could have just left that line out, if he didn't want to see you."

"Well, okay, I just didn't want to hear the lecture."

*****

Upon leaving the prison, Miller sat in his car and rang Kieron's mum, after getting the number from the Governor.

"Hello, is that Kieron's mum?"

There was a sudden frostiness on the line, the sound of panic.

"Yes, who... who's this?"

"Hiya, it's nothing to worry about." Miller sensed that Kieron's mum's first instinct was concern about her son's welfare.

"Oh, right..."

"My name is DCI Miller, I've just been in Forest Bank, to

see Kieron. It was about his former teacher, Mr Pollard."

"Oh, right, aw God, you had my heart going then, thought something was wrong."

"No, no, not at all. Kieron contacted us, wanted to put his side of the story across regarding Mr Pollard. He feels that we're barking up the wrong tree, insinuating that Mr Pollard is…"

"Yeah, I've seen you on the news. He's right, its way off, what you've been suggesting about Mr Pollard."

"Well, I'm starting to see that. He's a nice lad, Kieron."

"Yes, well, he's a nice lad, but he's a lot of work. Always has been."

"He says that he was quite close with Mr Pollard. Would you agree with that statement?"

"Yes, I would actually. Mr Pollard really cared about him, tried really hard with him. It was all for nothing, mind."

"That's pretty much what he told me. But he wanted me to know that he really doesn't think that Mr Pollard has any sexual interest in the missing lad. Would you agree with that, based on your knowledge of him?"

"Yes. In a heart-beat. That's not what Mr Pollard's about. Not at all."

"Okay, well, that does present a problem. We can't seem to find another reason for him to take off with this young lad."

"Well, I'm sorry, I can't help you with that. But I'd never have let Kieron anywhere near Mr Pollard if I'd had the slightest doubt about him. Honestly, he's just a really good guy."

"Kieron told me that he paid for a trip to London, out of his own pocket?"

"Yes, he did. I tried arguing with him, saying that firstly, it was too generous, and secondly, Kieron didn't deserve it anyway! But he insisted, he said that Kieron would get a lot from it."

"And did he?" asked Miller.

"No, he got arrested for knocking a policeman's helmet off. Mr Pollard had to spend the afternoon in the police station with him!"

"Right, yes, he did elude to that, but said he couldn't remember what he'd done."

"Yes, that's Kieron. Claims that he can never remember what he's done wrong but can remember the name of every Man United player since George Best played for them."

"Okay, well, like I say, he's a nice lad. I hope things work out for him when he gets out."

"Thank you. That's really kind of you to say."

Miller hung up and felt like he wanted to nip home and change his shirt. He could still smell the stale, lingering odour of despair from the jail as he headed back towards Manchester.

"Sod it," he said, as he reached the A6. The traffic was light. He could be home in ten minutes, and back at work in half an hour. Plus, he would win brownie points off the wife for making an unexpected trip home.

Miller indicated right, rather than left, and pressed his foot on the accelerator, switching on his blues and twos so he could race along the East Lancs road towards Worsley, without picking up a speeding ticket.

Ten minutes later, he was home. Clare looked pleased to see him.

"Hello stranger!" she said.

"Hiya, alright?" said Miller as he kissed his wife.

"Yeah, not bad, just having this sandwich, then doing some washing before I pick the twins up."

"Oh, cool, you can chuck these in. Been in Forest Bank, I smell like an inmate!" Miller started stripping off, and Clare pretended to gag as she chewed her sandwich.

"What?"

"Nowt. Just playing. What were you doing in prison, anyway?"

"Some young lad that Mr Pollard used to teach had some information. Good kid."

"Can't be that good, if he's in jail."

"Yeah, true." Miller didn't have time to discuss modern criminal philosophy, so agreed with his wife's rather sweeping statement. "Interesting chat though. The more I hear about this missing teacher, the more intrigued I am about him."

"Have you forgiven him for dumping that tracker device then?"

Miller was stood in his boxer shorts. "No." He said, his eyes bulging out in a very camp and over-the-top way, which made his wife laugh loudly.

"Right anyway, I'd better get back. I've got Pollard's wife coming in, going to try and get her to do an emotional plea."

"Well, I suggest that you put some clothes on first, or it won't be an emotional plea, it will be a mercy plea!"

Chapter Twenty-Four

Miller was back in the incident room, and happy to see that all of his team were in the office, all busy working on their various tasks.

"Right guys, any chance we can break off from what we are doing? I think we need a team-talk." Miller walked across to the incident room wall and waited for his colleagues to finish the calls they were making, the research they were carrying out, and the notes and reports they were working on. They knew the drill when Miller made a request like this; carry on until it's a sensible time to stop, and then join him. One thing that really annoyed the DCI was sloppy work, and experience had taught him that disrupting his team when they were in the middle of something only encouraged mistakes and problems further down the line. It made sense to let them finish what they were doing, or make notes of where they were up to.

Five minutes later, the team were all sat around their DCI, who was still altering things on the incident room wall. The huge space only had a quarter, less even, filled with information. The other three quarters of the wall were brilliant white. Just huge sheets of paper which were yet to be written on, or to have photos, or maps or pictures of evidence pinned on. The wall didn't look as busy as it probably should, considering the amount of intelligence that had been pouring in over the past twenty-four hours or so.

Once he realised that everybody was ready, he turned around and faced the officers, his regular team of detectives, Saunders, Rudovsky, Kenyon, Worthington, Chapman and Grant. The five police constables who'd been drafted in for the early shift on the incident-room phones had also joined the meeting, their phones had been taken off the hook for now.

"Alright everyone, sorry to break you away from your duties, I'm sure you've all been having a very productive time?"

There were plenty of enthusiastic nods and shouts of "yes, Sir."

"Good, it's a pretty good case this, I'm quite enjoying it. I've got Philip Pollard's estranged wife coming in at five, so I thought we should touch-base. I'm going to try and get her to do a press conference with me. It's all booked for six in the media-centre. So, if you can all please be as lovely as ever, put her at ease, make her feel at home, that will be a massive help. Okay?"

"Sir!"

"Yes, no problem Sir."

"Cheers, I appreciate your support. Whether she does it or not, I still have to present some information to the press and do a fresh appeal for eye-witnesses. The opinion that I set out with at roughly this time yesterday has been scrapped and as each hour passes, I seem to be revising my opinions about everything!"

The team smiled, or laughed. They too recognised what an unusual investigation this had been so far, one with lots of strange stops and starts.

"Alright, this morning when we met, the general consensus was that our earliest theory was based around dad," Miller walked a few feet, to the picture of Michael Jenkins and patted it, "was a non-runner. I want us to revise that and put him back in the race. He's not odds-on favourite but I feel it would be foolish to eliminate him entirely at this stage. I've just come back from visiting one of Mr Pollard's former pupils, another disruptive lad who spent a great deal of time with Mr Pollard. He says that there is absolutely no way that the motivation behind this incident is romantic."

"Can we trust him though?" asked DC Bill Chapman.

"I think so. I can't think of any reason why he would go to the trouble of having his Governor ring us to tell us that. Why would he?"

"To get out of his cell for half an hour?" countered Chapman.

"Yes, it's a fair point. But he laid it on very thick, he was furious that we're slagging Pollard off, genuinely gutted at how he is being portrayed in the news. Also, he said that his mum would back him up and I've phoned her. Same story."

"Yes, Sir, we are getting a number of calls along those lines from ex-pupils." It was one of the PCs who'd been answering the phones all morning.

"Well I think we need to think outside the box, then." Suggested DC Rudovsky. "If its not a love affair, pervy old teacher and infatuated kid, then what is it?"

"Exactly, Jo. We need to give this some consideration. We need to work out a reason why a well-respected, highly-regarded teacher would ruin his reputation to run off with a kid from his school, wreck his entire career, end his troubled marriage, all for a kid who does his head in." Miller had a very serious, thoughtful look on his face. It was obvious to all of his officers that he was stuck.

"Sir," said DC Chapman, going in for round two. "I'm of the opinion that he has harmed or intends to harm Darren. It's the only explanation for this if it's not sexual or romantic."

Miller didn't give it a second's thought. "No, I reject that Bill. If that *was* his intention, which would be wildly out of character anyway, but if it was, why would he go and sort Darren out with all that nice new clobber?"

It was a good question. Why would he? It wasn't even the mid-price range stuff. It was all the best and latest sportswear from JD Sports, the premier shop for kids that age. Pollard had even asked the staff if this was the best stuff for a fifteen-year-old. It had been a treat, that was Miller's first instinct, and he still felt it was the case. Chapman looked pissed off that his suggestion had been binned so quickly. But then again, Chapman always looked pissed off, so nobody could really tell the difference.

"Don't worry about it Bill, I've been wrong about several theories on this so far, at least, that's how it looks. But I'm confident that Pollard doesn't wish any harm on Darren. I just don't have a clue what he's up to."

"Sir," said Saunders. Miller took his eyes off Chapman and focused on his number two in the department. Miller looked relieved that Saunders had something to say. It was always good stuff from his DI.

"Go ahead Keith."

"I've been chasing up ANPR logs for the mobile home. It's not been past a single camera since it arrived in Llandudno."

"And when did it arrive in Llandudno?"

"Sunday. I've been onto Donna, and she's generated the GPS log on that vehicle since Pollard hired it. It travelled across to Scarborough on the first day, and stayed overnight on the promenade, that was Friday."

"The Scarborough on the opposite side of the country?"

"Yes, Sir, the one on the east coast, two hundred miles away from Llandudno on the west coast. He's then headed back in the direction of the north-west and stayed near Harrogate on Saturday night. Then, on Sunday, they arrived at Llandudno. We've got ANPR data which confirms this, as well as CCTV of the mobile-home at a garage close to the Yorkshire Lancashire border. It clearly shows Pollard filling up and paying, but there is no sign of Darren on the footage."

"Then what?"

"Then, according to the GPS tracker, the motor-home stayed put in Llandudno, until we arrived on Wednesday night."

"In other words, we know that Pollard got to Llandudno, but we have no idea when he left?"

"Precisely. There is absolutely no record of the motor-home's registration plate going through ANPR since Sunday."

"And no proof of life for Darren Jenkins since the CCTV footage at the shop on Thursday." This comment from DC Helen Grant lowered the mood significantly.

Miller walked across to another wall in the incident room, where a gigantic map of Great Britain was displayed. He began putting red pins on the map, one in Scarborough, one in Harrogate, and one in Llandudno.

He tapped the map, about four inches westerly of Llandudno. "Look over here, Holyhead, what's that, half-an-hour's drive? Less?" The team nodded. "How hard would it be to get on a ferry to Ireland? It could explain the lack of ANPR pings."

"Possible, Sir, assuming that Darren is actually with Pollard, and that he had his passport with him."

"I doubt he's got a passport somehow, they don't strike me as the kind of family that jet-off to Benidorm every summer. But even if Darren *has* got a passport, I doubt that he'd have taken it to school with him last Thursday morning!" Rudovsky was right. It was a bit of a stretch of the imagination.

"No, wait," said Kenyon. "How stringent are the checks on the English, Irish border? A motor-home has got plenty of places for Darren to hide. Under the bed, in the toilet... I dunno, in a quilt."

The team looked at Kenyon and they considered this suggestion. It was true, the border wasn't as intensive as the major borders at airports.

"Yes, you've got a point Pete," said Miller. "Me and Clare went to Dublin for a romantic weekend a few years ago, didn't get asked for passports once, on either side."

"Okay, this is good. But, I'm not happy that there isn't a single ANPR camera between Llandudno and Holyhead. There's got to have been one." Saunders pulled his phone out of his pocket, and Googled "ANPR Anglesey."

Anglesey is the island on the very edge of north-west Wales, where the famous Holyhead ferry terminal has daily departures and arrivals to and from Dublin. It is a major terminal which deals with over a million passengers per year.

"Ah, here we go," said Saunders. There are several ANPR cameras on Anglesey, the most prominent ones are on the Menai suspension bridge, and the Britannia bridge, the only two road links between the island and the Welsh mainland. They've got the island locked down, all traffic coming in, or going out, is covered by cameras. There's no way around it."

"Well, its very good news. It means that they didn't go that way. So, we can scrub a search of Ireland off our list!" Miller smiled.

"No, Sir. It means that when Pollard removed that tracking device off the motor-home, he very probably changed the number-plates, too."

"Shit." Miller hadn't considered this. And as soon as he deliberated it, it made perfect sense. And it also meant that trying to find a white motor-home with unspecified registration plates was going to be a hell of a challenge, to say the very least.

"For God's sake." This was the last thing Miller needed to hear.

Sandra Pollard arrived at the reception desk a few minutes before five. She was joined by her daughter, Jess, a voluptuous, attractive, professional looking woman in her late twenties, or early thirties. She was linking her mother tightly.

The receptionist phoned Miller, and he came down to greet Pollard's wife of thirty-five years, and Pollard's daughter, in more pleasant and cordial circumstances than last time they had all met, at the Pollard home the previous night.

"Hello, hello, thanks for coming, I'll take you upstairs and show you both around." Miller was warm, charming. Mrs Pollard seemed receptive, she was still grateful for Miller's kindness in not arresting her, he'd been well within his rights.

Jess Pollard however didn't seem so keen on the DCI and made no secret of her hostility. He had been quite rude to her the previous night, closing the door in her face. He decided to fall on his sword and apologise, even though he didn't mean it.

"Look, Jess, isn't it?"

"That's right," she said, brushing her long, wavy black hair behind her ear.

"I'm sorry about last night, if I came across as ill-mannered."

"Well, you did, actually. My mum's going through hell right now. We both are. I didn't expect to be made to feel like a suspect!" Miller nodded sympathetically and apologised again. He didn't mean it, he didn't like this young woman much. Miller suspected that Mrs Pollard hadn't explained to her daughter that she'd had a close-call the previous night and that she could have very easily been banged up for numerous offences, such as providing false statements, aiding and abetting an offender, and perverting the course of justice. As such, this young woman's frosty greeting was a bit much but Miller did appear genuinely sorry to her. All he wanted was her mother on the 6 'clock news. Jess's bullshit was a mere distraction.

"Look, can we start again?"

"Yes, for my mother's sake." Said Jess, feeling

empowered and vindicated by Miller's response. Little did she know that he thought she was coming across as a bit of a diva and that this wasn't about her. He smiled charmingly and touched her shoulder gently.

"Thank you. Okay, well, let's go upstairs, and I'll introduce you to my team, and let you see what's happening."

Miller led them up the stairs and started his boring introductory speech about his department as they made their way towards the SCIU offices on the first floor. Once they arrived the DCI held open the door and welcomed them through.

"Right, first things first, would you like a drink? Tea, coffee?"

"No, no, I'm fine thank you," said Sandra Pollard.

"Jess?"

She shook her head.

"Okay, well, if you would like to follow me, I'll introduce you to the team who are currently trying to find out where Philip is."

Miller walked around the department and told the two visitors who everybody was as they continued talking on phones, or writing reports, or discussing matters amongst themselves. Eventually, Miller took Jess and Sandra across to the incident room wall and explained the situation as it was understood, described the lines of enquiry and tried as hard as he could to make it sound as though his greatest motivation was to help Philip Pollard.

It took a while and Miller glanced at his watch, it was 5.25pm. He felt a sudden nervousness, as he realised how little time he had to firstly convince Sandra to do the press conference, and secondly, prep her for it.

"So, that's where we are up to. As I'm sure you'll agree, we've got lots of quality information and as you may have noticed, the whole time you've been here, those phone lines have been constantly busy. We have plenty of good intelligence coming in."

Sandra looked pleased with just how much effort was going into trying to find her estranged-husband. Jess just looked like a sulky teenager despite that fact that she should have been at least a decade beyond that phase. Miller saw his chance for the segue into the press conference.

"My next task is to update the press. Specifically, I want to appeal to the people of Llandudno and any holidaymakers who were there on Sunday." Miller had set it up and now needed to create some panic. "The thing is, we really need proof of life for Darren Jenkins."

Boom. That devastating remark had worked beautifully. Sandra Pollard looked as though her legs were about to give way. She reached out to hold onto the back of Saunders' chair. Jess grabbed her mother's arm.

"Are you alright, mum?" she asked.

Sandra had turned a funny colour, as though all the blood had drained from her.

"Hey, hey, sorry. That's just technical police talk. Here, take a seat." Miller shoved Saunders in the arm, and the DI gave up his chair. Sandra sat down, her eyes were filled with tears.

"For God's sake!" snapped Jess. "Mum, are you okay?" She shot Miller an icy stare. He wasn't bothered.

"What I meant was," Miller crouched down slightly so he was talking at the same level as Sandra Pollard. "We literally have no evidence that Darren is safe. I'm sure its just a matter of time before we get it, and once we do, we can relax a little. But I want you to do an appeal to your husband."

Sandra was worked up, understandably. This was the best time to get her to agree to his demands.

"In our experience, it's the person's closest family who can get through to them."

"Mum, are you alright?" repeated Jess, interrupting Miller.

"I'm fine, I'm fine," said Sandra, although she still looked a little shook up. "What would I need to say?" she asked, looking in Miller's direction for the first time since she'd been helped into the seat.

"That's entirely up to you. Jess, you could join your mum, to give her a little moral support." Miller made it sound less of a suggestion, more of an instruction. Her mother was quick to pounce on the opportunity.

"Would you, love?"

"Well, I'm, I'm just not sure mum…"

"It's embarrassing," said Sandra, looking back at Miller.

"In what way?" he asked, taking a sly glance at his watch.

"Well, all this, everybody talking about Phil in this way. People are pointing the finger…"

"That's all the more reason to say your piece. You know Phil, the media don't, the public don't. You could start off talking about the row you had. Maybe apologise for the things you said?"

"I'm not sure, mum…" said Jess, interrupting again. Miller was getting sick of this young woman now, she was becoming a proper pain in the arse.

"Your mum's right Jess. If you want everybody to stop saying all these things about your dad, this is the best opportunity."

Jess looked at Miller, her contempt for him was undeniable. "How, how is it?"

Miller was quick in his reply. "Well I'll guarantee you that you'll be better off getting the first word in, because if I know the press, they'll have spent all day trying to dig things up. They'll have phoned all your family, friends, neighbours, ex-boyfriends."

"What?"

"Seriously, they are ruthless. And they'll have their stories written already, just waiting for tomorrow's papers. You have a golden opportunity to kill off any bad publicity here, before its even printed."

"You're really keen for this to happen, aren't you Mr Miller?" Jess looked suspiciously at the DCI.

"No, it makes no difference to me. But it might be what your dad needs to hear, and it might prompt him to give us some indication that Darren is okay. Without trying to sugar-coat it, as things stand, your dad is in a lot of trouble. I want to help him out of it as best I can."

"Are you saying that you don't think that dad's taken Darren away for some disgusting purpose?"

"Do you think he has?" asked Miller.

Jess looked furious. She spat the words as she snapped, "No, of course not. Don't be so ridiculous!"

"I agree." Said Miller. "I'm absolutely convinced that whatever is going on here, it has got nothing to do with anything sexual."

"Why? What's made you arrive at that conclusion?" asked Jess. She really didn't like the DCI at all, and she certainly didn't trust him.

"Well, earlier today, I visited Forest Bank prison and spoke to an ex-pupil of your father's. Kieron Davis. Does that name ring any bells?"

Jess shook her head.

Sandra nodded.

"Yes, I know about Kieron. He was one of your dad's project pupils, Jess. Your dad tried everything with him." Sandra looked as though she'd got over the initial shock of Miller's dramatic announcement a few minutes earlier.

"That's right. And he was furious to hear that we were linking this case to a sexual motivation. So much so, he had me drive over to the prison to tell me, in no uncertain terms, that there is no way that your dad is involved in anything to do with sex. He convinced me, that's for sure. Plus, we haven't had a single telephone call from anybody who has a bad word to say about Mr Pollard. That's why I don't think this is about sex, or a love affair, or anything of that nature."

"Are you going to say that in the press conference?" asked Jess.

"Yes, I can do. I haven't got a problem with that."

"Right, it's okay, we'll do it." Said Sandra. Miller smiled warmly. Jess shot Miller yet another icy stare. She wasn't impressed.

Chapter Twenty-Five

The news agency reaction to this extraordinary case was reaching fever-pitch. It was the main headline on radio, TV news, as well as all of the newspaper websites. The amount of press staff crammed into the media-centre confirmed that this was the nation's BREAKING NEWS story and it was so big, this place was standing room only.

The noise in the media-centre at Manchester City Police HQ was deafening, particularly when Miller appeared, walking next to the missing teacher's wife and daughter. The opportunity of an appeal from a relative made this an even more enthralling story.

The drama, the emotion, the intimacy of a public appeal to the missing man was brilliant content for turning a news item into a soap opera. The media were filled with excitement and the photographer's bulbs were flashing as the two relatives of Philip Pollard walked towards the stage area.

Miller led them through the press representatives and helped them both up the steps onto the raised platform, which had three chairs out and three glasses of water. After helping Mrs Pollard into her seat and directing Jess Pollard to sit on the end, beside her mother, Miller sat down on the other side of Sandra Pollard, a pretty, mature, delicately-featured professional woman who looked utterly broken and ashamed.

The well-known DCI seemed downbeat as he began talking to the sea of faces from the media.

"Good evening ladies and gentlemen. Thank you for attending. I will move on to a full update on this case so far and there will be an opportunity for questions later. But I'd like us to start with a few words from Philip Pollard's wife, Sandra Pollard, and the couple's daughter, Jess."

The camera bulbs were strobing and the TV cameras and radio recorders were all pointed in the two women's direction, leaving Miller out of the frame. Mrs Pollard looked shaky and emotional. Jess grabbed her mum's hand on the table-top and the gesture of support seemed to upset Mr Pollard's wife, as a fresh wave of emotion crashed against her, forcing her to break-down. Miller began to comfort her, trying to calm her down, he was whispering something as he rubbed her back gently.

Jess decided that she would speak first to give her mum a bit of time to recover. She looked as though she'd surprised herself as she started speaking.

"Hello, my name is Jess, Jess Pollard, I'm Philip Pollard's daughter and I'm here to support my mum through this ordeal. Obviously, you have all jumped to your own conclusions as to what's happening with my dad and Darren. Well, I'd just like to say, that if you think that my dad has done anything, anything wrong towards this young lad, then you really don't know my dad." She looked accusingly around the faces, before finding a TV camera to stare at. "Dad, if you're watching this, I just want to say that I love you, and... well, I don't know what's going on, I know you and mum have been having a tough time. But please, I can't stand this, I can't stand strangers saying all kinds of awful things about you. Come home, dad. We all love you..." Jess had delivered her impromptu, unrehearsed speech brilliantly, there was no sign of nerves, no pauses, no hesitation.

Miller smiled warmly at the missing man's daughter. "Thank you Jess. Okay, so, as I was saying, Sandra Pollard would like to say a few words." Miller whispered something softly in Mrs Pollard's direction. She coughed quietly, before she started to speak. Her hands were still trembling visibly on the table-top.

"Phil, if you are watching this, I am begging you to get in touch and let me know that you're okay, and that Darren is okay as well. I've been going out of my mind with worry and at the same time, I've been telling myself that I'm silly, that I don't need to worry, because in thirty-five years of marriage, you've never once let me down. You've never done anything that should make me worry. You have been a perfect husband to me, a perfect father to your children. I don't know what's wrong but I do know that we can fix it, together. Please Phil, like Jess said, please just come home. I'm sorry about what I said to you last Wednesday night. I didn't mean it, I was just upset and disappointed that our plans had to change again. But you know I didn't mean what I said. Please, Phil, you must know that I love you, and I need you home, here with me. Come on love, even if you don't want to come home yet, I understand, but you have to let me know you're okay, and let Darren's parents know that he's okay too. I love you."

Sandra Pollard had done remarkably well, as had Jess. Miller was really pleased with how they had handled the scary and intimidating situation. The press were happy, they'd managed to get some excellent content out of this, and a couple of extra layers of intrigue too.

"Okay, ladies and gentlemen, if we can just pause for a few minutes. I'm going to escort Philip Pollard's relatives out and I'll be back in a few moments to continue." Miller stood, and waited for Sandra and Jess to follow his lead. Despite looking slightly humiliated and sheepish on their way in, they both looked much more confident and dignified now as they followed Miller out of the hot, noisy, crowded room in silence.

Once they were outside the media-centre doors, Miller thanked them both, and pointed them in the direction of the main reception area, promising to phone Sandra later on for a catch up. As they walked away, Miller went back into the press conference, walking quickly to try and minimise this delay to proceedings.

"Okay, thank you everybody for your patience. Right, let's get on with it..."

Chapter Twenty-Six

Within minutes of concluding business in the media-centre, Miller arrived at the incident room, looking quite chipper. He hated press conferences, so it was always a relief to get one done. Saunders was waiting for him. He had "the look" on his face.

"What's up?" asked Miller. He knew that look. It meant there was a problem.

"Can I speak to you in private please, Sir?"

"Sure," Miller turned, and headed back towards his office, with Saunders hot on his heels.

The DI closed the door and sat down facing Miller.

"What's up?"

"What are your thoughts about Jess Pollard?" Saunders looked troubled.

"I'm not a fan. She strikes me as a bit of a spoilt-brat."

"She doesn't like you!" said Saunders.

"Oh, you noticed?"

"Couldn't miss it. It was awkward to witness."

"I gave her the cold shoulder last night, when I was quizzing her mum. I think she holds a grudge."

"Well, I doubt its that. I imagine it's you suggesting that her dad is a wrong 'un on the news this lunch-time."

Miller nodded. "Possibly. But I'm not trying to win a popularity contest, I'm trying to locate Darren Jenkins, and his teacher."

"Yes, I get that. But…"

"What's up Keith?"

"I've got a really dodgy feeling about Jess Pollard."

"Oh?" Miller looked surprised.

"Yes, something's not right. She's not remotely concerned about her father. Or Darren for that matter. She was more concerned about winning ego points against you."

Miller thought about Saunders' observation. He was right, thinking about it. It hadn't occurred to him at the time, but yes, on reflection, Jess didn't seem remotely concerned. She didn't appear particularly interested in Miller's update on the investigation, either.

"I noticed it when you gave Mrs Pollard a fright up here, about Darren's safety. But, it really struck me when you were doing the press conference, that she knows something. It's almost as though she knows her dad's fine. She knows that Darren is fine. Why else would she act like a diva towards the cop who's working on the case? Why wouldn't she be absolutely terrified of what might be coming down the line, like her mum clearly is? And, well that opens up a whole new world of questions. Top of the list, why would she be so relaxed about her dad disappearing in a motorhome, abducting a fifteen-year old pupil and trashing his career?"

"Yes, shit, you're on to something. I was just concentrating on Mrs Pollard."

"I know. And from Mrs Pollard's demeanour, her nerves, her body-language, it looks to me that she hasn't got a clue what's going on. Jess Pollard is another kettle of fish altogether."

"Interesting observations. Hard to prove, though."

"Have either Jess or Sandra Pollard mentioned Daniel?"

"Daniel. The brother?"

"Yes. Mr Pollard's son."

"No, I don't think so."

"Well, I'm not happy with this. I've been looking into him. He's married, two-kids, runs a garage over in Filey."

"Filey. Near Scarborough?"

"The very same. And from what I understand, he hasn't been over to see his mum since this hit the news. I rang his garage up pretending to be a punter. I started explaining an issue with my car, and he sounded perfectly relaxed, told me what the problem was."

"And what was it?"

"Head-gasket."

"It always is."

"So the mystery deepens. Jess is too busy trying to be the alpha around you and Daniel is carrying on with his work on the north Yorkshire coast, despite the fact that his dad's being made out as a paedo child-snatcher and his mum is breaking her heart on the tea-time news."

"Fucking hell. This isn't adding up, is it?"

"Well one thing that does make sense now, is the rather confusing drive over to Scarborough on Friday."

Miller smiled widely and nodded. "Yes, suddenly that does start to make sense."

"And if a bloke who runs a garage can't advise you how to remove a tracking device, or knock you up some fake registration plates, well, I don't know who can."

"Jesus, Keith. You're on it. What do you suggest we do?"

"Well, I've already asked North Yorkshire police to go and arrest him. I've a good feeling that he'll know what this new number plate is."

"Fucking hell! You were a slow starter on this one, I was thinking of telling uniform to take you on, but you've come up with the good stuff now."

"He's going to be taken to Scarborough police station. Local officers are going to search his house, his business premises and his phone records have been requested from his providers. While all this is going on, I suggest he stays the night and one of us lot can go over and interview him in the morning."

"And what about Jess?"

"I think she needs a night in the cells as well. Do you want the honours?" asked Saunders.

"Er, no. I'm a bit scared of her, to be honest."

"Okay, I'll ask the Inspector at Tameside to send a couple of uniforms round. I think we're going to have this mystery solved by tomorrow dinner."

Both Miller and Saunders jumped, as a sudden rat-a-tat-tat resounded from the glass of the office door. It was one of the constables from the phones. Miller gestured her in.

"Bloody hell, scared the life out of me then!" said Miller, looking stressed, but mildly amused by the sudden fright.

"Sir, just had a call. It was the manager of the Wetherspoons in Llandudno. The Palladium. He says Darren and Pollard were there on Sunday, they both had an Aberdeen Angus steak and he's got CCTV footage too."

"Proof of life!" said Miller. "Finally!" The DCI clapped his hands together.

"He said he was going to ring in about it last night, said that he felt sure it was them but said he'd feel daft if it wasn't so he didn't ring. But when you mentioned Llandudno in your press conference before, he definitely knew it was right." The PC looked absolutely thrilled, as did Saunders who'd been just as desperate as Miller to hear that Darren had been sighted with Pollard. This was the first time.

"Well done Constable! Fantastic work!"

Chapter Twenty-Seven

The Palladium is one of Llandudno's best-known bars. Part of the Wetherspoons chain of cheap and cheerful gastro-pubs, this particular one is extremely unusual in that it started out as a theatre.

Built in the 1920's, The Palladium was the number one entertainment venue in the tiny sea-side resort, presenting shows which featured the biggest stars of the day, the best known regular was Gracie Fields. But as time went on, the magic of live theatre slowly but surely gave way to the excitement of cinema, then television, followed by home video players, and eventually satellite TV.

Struggling to make ends meet during the 1970's, the theatre converted into a dual-purpose entertainment venue. During the daytime, The Palladium introduced a bingo-hall on the ground floor, using the space that the stalls had previously occupied, but retained the upper seating circles, which were used for cinema screenings in the evenings.

But in 1999, the tired, worn-out looking building closed its doors to its bingo and cinema fans for the last time and was sold to JD Wetherspoon. Two years later, the beautiful Baroque style building opened its doors once again, following a major refurbishment and modernisation into a pub. Typically of Wetherspoons, they were keen to preserve as much of the building's heritage as possible. Many visitors are amazed to see that most of the original features remain, including the seating circles up above their heads.

It was this fascination into the building's history which had first aroused the attention of The Palladium's manager. Philip Pollard had been ordering food at the bar, when he'd struck up a conversation with the bar-tender.

The young man behind the bar didn't know too much about the building's history, but promised to send his manager across to speak to the bloke who'd been asking all the questions.

The manager, Lee Travis, wasn't impressed. He had two staff off sick, a late delivery, and he didn't know much about the building's history anyway. But, customer service training kicked in and he did a quick Google search, before heading across to speak to the geeky bloke, who was sitting with a young lad, who he'd automatically assumed was his son.

They talked for several minutes and Lee admitted that he wasn't as knowledgeable about The Palladium as he ought to be.

Since the news had broke on Wednesday tea-time, Lee had been considering that the missing teacher was the same man that had been asking questions and the pupil was the kid that he'd assumed was his son. Now that DCI Miller had made a direct plea for information in the Llandudno area, he knew 100% that his instincts had been correct.

Miller was on the phone to Lee, quizzing him about the encounter.

"How did he seem, was he calm, nervous?"

"He seemed perfectly fine. Calm, relaxed, he said that he'd fallen in love with the building, said he'd never been in a pub like it before."

"And what about the lad?"

"Yeah, fine, like I say, I just thought they were father and son. The young lad went off to the toilets for most of the time I was talking to the man, so I didn't really speak to him. But he seemed fine, there was absolutely no reason to suspect them of anything. They just blended into the background."

"Except Pollard made a big deal of grabbing your attention?"

"Yes, well, I mean he seemed totally genuine. He really was fascinated by the place. I showed him over to the wall that has all the old photographs and history and everything, and as I went back to the bar, the young lad was coming down the stairs from the toilet. I told him where his dad was, and he just laughed and said, 'keep him there, he's boring me to death.' Or something along those lines."

"Right, so let me get this straight, Darren went off to the toilet, by himself, and came back, and waited for Philip Pollard to return from whatever it was he was looking at?" Miller's mind was doing over-time. This information was sensational in terms of figuring out the mind-set of both missing people.

"Yeah, well, shortly afterwards, their food came out. And the man returned to the table."

"I don't suppose you can remember what they were drinking?"

"Yes, the young lad had a Coke, and his... and the man had a coffee."

"And then what happened?"

"I don't know, I returned to what I was doing, and that was the end of that."

"And you have CCTV, is that right?"

"Yes, absolutely, I've just been watching it. I was going to stick it on a memory stick and post it."

"No, no, forget that. I'll get a taxi to pick it up. Put it in an envelope for me, but do me a favour, once you've taken it off your recorder, and onto the memory stick, just check its on there, stick it in another computer. You wouldn't believe how many empty memory-sticks we get!"

"Yes, of course, no problem. I just wish I'd contacted you earlier."

"Well, don't worry about it. This is the best news I've had so far, it's the first sighting of the two of them together, and the first indication that Darren is safe and well since Thursday morning, its dynamite information. So, I owe you a pint some time."

"Oh, well, I don't drink. Working in here, you see what alcohol does to people! It puts you off."

"Well, I'll call in for a brew and to shake your hand. Thank you, Lee."

*****

Miller was home and in bed by the time the taxi had delivered the small envelope to police HQ in Manchester. It had been a nice job for the taxi driver, apart from the fact that it would take at least six weeks for him to get paid for the 180-mile round-trip.

As Miller snored, blissfully unaware of the fact that his

wife Clare wanted to smother him for keeping her awake, two other people were wide awake, too. Jess Pollard and Daniel Pollard.

Jess was in the custody cells of Ashton police station, while Daniel was spending the night at Scarborough.

It was going to be a long night for both of them. Neither had any idea why they'd been arrested, other than it being in relation to their father's disappearance. Nor did either know that their sibling had also been taken into custody.

Things were really starting to get going now.

Chapter Twenty-Eight
Friday

"Good morning and welcome to BBC Radio Five Live, I'm Steve Moger. The top story this morning surrounds the continuing search for the missing school teacher Philip Pollard and his fifteen-year-old pupil Darren Jenkins. It has emerged overnight that Mr Pollard's son and daughter have been taken into police custody, following raids at two separate addresses last night. At this stage, we have no further information about these arrests, but we are expecting a news conference later this morning."

The news presenter stopped to catch a breath before continuing. "Our reporter is outside Mr Pollard's son's home in North Yorkshire. Sally, this is an extremely shocking development this morning, can you offer any explanation about this unexpected direction the police enquiry has taken today?"

"Good morning Steve, yes, you're absolutely right, this development has certainly taken this local community in Filey, on the east coast, quite literally by surprise. I'm standing on a very normal looking street of semi-detached houses, not far from the sea-front here, in this tiny seaside resort between Scarborough and Bridlington."

"Yes, we can definitely tell that you are by the sea, the sound of those sea-gulls is coming through loud and clear Sally! I do hope its not too annoying for our listeners."

"Yes, they are in fine voice this morning, Steve. I've been here since around five o'clock this morning, and several neighbours have been coming over to ask me what is going on."

"And, what is going on, as you understand it?"

"Well, there is not a great deal of information at this stage but we do know that Daniel Pollard, the thirty-two-year old son of Philip Pollard was taken away from this address by police last night at around eight pm. Since that time, police have been at this address, and many officers have been coming and going with various items from the house sealed in evidence bags. Those items that we know of include a couple of mobile phones, a laptop and a desktop computer system."

"And no clues as to what the police think is Daniel's involvement in his father's disappearance, Sally?"

"No, there's no word on that and officers here are remaining very tight-lipped about everything. The only thing that I have managed to find out is that officers from Manchester are on their way over the Pennines, and they are coming to interview Daniel Pollard under caution."

"Thank you Sally, these are certainly very dramatic developments. Overnight, we heard that Daniel's sister, Jessica Pollard was also taken away by police officers, from the family home in Stalybridge. This arrest happened just a couple of hours after last night's press conference with DCI Miller, which Jess Pollard was a part of. Do you have any information about that Sally?"

"Nothing concrete at present, but what we do know is that Jess was arrested at roughly the same time as Daniel, at approximately eight pm last night. So, this does look like a co-ordinated operation between the two police forces. At this stage though, all we can do is speculate as to why Mr Pollard's son and daughter have been taken into police custody. We can assume that it is not simply to assist police with their enquiries, as there is a much politer way to go about that. And the fact that Daniel Pollard's items have been taken away suggests that the police must have some very serious suspicions that Daniel Pollard either knows something about his father's disappearance, or that there may be some suspicion that he is involved in some way."

"Tell us a little bit about Daniel Pollard, Sally."

"Well Daniel is thirty-two, he is married and has two children. His wife is a local lady, and Daniel settled here shortly after leaving college. He runs a local MOT testing station and garage, and by all accounts, he is a very well-regarded member of this small, close-knit community in Filey."

"And can you confirm the rumours that Daniel's garage and business premises have also been searched by the police overnight?"

"Yes, I can confirm that there has been a very visual presence by local police at both addresses."

"There is a lot of speculation this morning that Jess Pollard's appearance in last night's press conference in Manchester has aroused police suspicions, and subsequently prompted these arrests. Several commentators are suggesting that she appeared quite cold and not particularly concerned about her father's welfare in the televised briefing. Have you been hearing any similar comments?"

"Well, yes, in a word. But I'm not in a position to offer conjecture on these wild, speculative opinions myself. The fact of the matter is that the story still centres around the disappearance of a fifteen-year-old boy, allegedly at the hands of his teacher. This speculation and gossip is not helping to keep that important detail in the spotlight."

"No, that's a very good point Sally."

"But obviously, this is a very fast-moving news story, the disappearance of Darren Jenkins and Philip Pollard was only reported two days ago, so it's very hard to keep track of all of these emerging threads to the investigation. I think we will just have to sit tight for now and wait to see what this morning's press conference brings."

"Any word on when that will be?"

"Manchester Police press office have indicated that it will be early, but other than that, we have no further information."

*****

"This is Sunrise on Sky News, and we're joined this morning by retired Metropolitan Police detective Joanne Dewhurst. Good morning."

"Good morning." Said the red-haired former detective, smartly dressed in a grey suit.

"Well, quite a night, it looks like things are beginning to move at quite a pace now in the missing teacher and pupil inquiry. What do you think is the significance of the two arrests which were made last night?"

"Oh, I think it is hugely significant. The officers working on this case will have had good reason to make those arrests, especially as they were both made at the same time, on opposite sides of the country."

"And the thing that is most extraordinary is that Jess Pollard, the missing man's daughter was seen on this channel, and is on the front of many of this morning's newspapers, following that live press conference from Manchester yesterday tea-time. In fact, Jess Pollard must have only just got home when the police arrived to arrest her. What do you think must have happened to prompt such a swift course of action?"

The detective smiled. "Well, I can't answer that. The only people who really know what is happening, and who are aware of the information which led them to the conclusion that they had to make these arrests, are the officers dealing with this investigation."

"Police officers have been seen throughout the night removing belongings from the two home addresses, as well as Daniel Pollard's business premises. Can you tell us any more about this?"

"Yes, well, its quite normal for police officers to seize items which they feel may hold valuable evidence. Typically, these days, those items tend to be communication tools, such as phones, computers, laptops. I would imagine that the technical investigators are now scanning these items, looking for whatever information it is that they suspect is contained."

"Obviously, this is pure speculation at this stage, and we are expecting a press conference within the hour, which should shed some light on these developments. But I want to ask you, in your experience Joanne, would police normally arrest two relatives in these dramatic circumstances, or could they have simply asked the son and daughter, Daniel and Jess Pollard to come along to the station to help with their enquiries?"

"Well, I think what you are asking me is whether Daniel and Jess are being viewed as suspects in this inquiry. The short answer is yes. The methods used in the arrests, and the subsequent removal of personal belongings from both addresses tells me that they are certainly under a great deal of suspicion. Quite what they are suspected of at this stage is anybody's guess."

"In reality, the suggestion is that they are either suspected of being involved in the disappearance of Philip Pollard and Darren Jenkins, or they are suspected of being responsible for the disappearance. There doesn't seem to be many other possibilities. Does that sound about right?"

"In theory, yes, that is what it is looking like at this moment in time, but as I say, it's just the officers in Manchester, and in North Yorkshire who will know exactly what is going on right now. But as I understand it, the search for Darren and Mr Pollard continues, and finding them is still the top priority job for every single police constabulary in the UK."

"Okay, Joanne Dewhurst, retired Met detective, thank you. Please stay with us, and we will talk to you again after the press conference."

Chapter Twenty-Nine

Miller was driving into work, listening to the news report. He felt great, he hadn't been anticipating getting such a good night's sleep until this case was closed. But the previous night's developments were so positive, he'd decided that it was common sense to turn in and get an early night so that his battery was fully charged for today. Normally, during a high-profile case, he would snatch a few hours sleep here and there, whenever the opportunity arose. It was rare for him to get a full seven hours in when the stakes were as high as they were in this investigation.

It was 6.30, and the Manchester rush hour hadn't yet begun, as Miller drove into the MCP HQ car park. Saunders' car was already there.

"Morning Keith!" said Miller, loudly as he walked into the department. He was surprised to see Rudovsky and Kenyon were already in, as was Saunders' girlfriend, DC Helen Grant. "Bloody hell. You can't *all* have pissed the bed?"

"Morning Sir!" said Rudovsky.

"Sir!" said Kenyon.

"Had a lie in today, Sir?" asked Grant.

Saunders just smiled.

"What's all this about?" asked Miller, smiling. He looked refreshed, relaxed and ready for whatever lay in store.

"We're just hoping for the best jobs... early bird catches the worms, Sir." Rudovsky raised her thumb and did a cheesy smile, which made Miller laugh.

"Come on Jo, tell me what you're thinking?"

"Okay Sir, I'm thinking me and Pete want to get over to Scarborough and pick Daniel Pollard apart."

"Pete, is this true?"

"Yes Sir, Jo text me at half-two this morning to let me know."

"What do you think you're going to find out?" asked Miller, concerned that Rudovsky might just be getting a little bit ahead of herself.

"Sir, with respect, I'll find everything out."

"Okay. Off you go. Scarborough is two and a half hour's drive. Pete, use your siren and see if you can do it in an hour and a half. Jo, I'll phone you in a bit for a chat. Don't go in with Daniel Pollard until you've spoken with me first. Understood?"

"Yes Sir!" said Rudovsky as she stepped forward and kissed Miller's cheek, standing on her tip-toes to reach.

"Get off me, you fucking knob."

"Love you too!" said Rudovsky as she headed for the door. Kenyon grabbed his car keys off the desk and followed quickly behind.

"Right, so, that's got her out of our hair for the day, anyway."

"Sir, Helen and I..."

"Want to go to Ashton and interview Jess?"

"Yes please. Just thinking, it might be a bit more productive if you weren't around."

"Yes, I totally agree. I was hoping that you'd fancy taking care of it. Is that why you're in so early, Helen?"

"Sort of, Sir. Keith was worried that you'd set off with him, and balls everything up because the chemistry is all to cock between you and Jess Pollard. So, he promised to take me to see Mumford and Sons, if I came in early and blocked you."

Miller laughed loudly at Grant's raw honesty.

"I didn't say that at all!" said Saunders, blushing slightly.

"Why the hell do you want to go and visit a Funeral Directors, anyway?" asked Miller.

"It's a band, Sir." Grant smiled, well aware that Miller was pulling her leg. The DCI turned to Saunders. "I bet you did say that, you two-faced lying bastard! Right, well, before you set off, I want a quick look at your game-plan."

Saunders grabbed his file. "Okay, I've got three key lines of enquiry that I wish to discuss..." The DI talked through the key points that he wanted to pursue during the interview with Pollard's daughter.

"Okay, looks good to me. Go on, off you go. I've got to sort out a breakfast press briefing, so I wouldn't have wanted to go anyway Keith, you back-stabbing piece-of-shit."

"Good. Alright, well, speak later."

Miller loved his team, he loved the brutal honesty amongst the officers and he didn't mind if the piss was being taken out of him from time to time. It made for a good team ethic if he was the butt of the joke just as much as the others. He did miss working as closely with Saunders these days, if he was honest. But he liked the new, emerging professional partnership between Grant and Saunders. Despite the fact that they lived together, it worked very well.

Miller opened the envelope which had been driven over from Llandudno the previous night. His hand was shaking slightly as he tried to insert the memory-stick into the USB port on the front of Saunders' PC. Within seconds of opening the file, he was watching the CCTV footage of Darren Jenkins and his 56 year-old school teacher relaxing in The Palladium.

The boy looked happy. That was the first thing that caught Miller's eye, and the realisation of how happy the missing kid was on Sunday afternoon, put him at ease. Darren was smiling, laughing, talking, then laughing again. It did just look like a father and son visit to the pub for tea, Miller could see why the bar manager had quickly arrived at that conclusion.

Miller was transfixed by the footage as Pollard struck up a conversation with Lee, the manager, and Darren went off to the toilets. The kid walked as though he was in no hurry, his body language didn't make it appear that he felt under any threat. He didn't seem paranoid or on edge, or eager to try and escape from Pollard. Miller was watching the boy as he had the perfect opportunity to escape from Pollard. But that just wasn't on Darren's agenda, in fact the way he was walking through the pub, towards the back door, suggested that the thought had never crossed his mind.

As he continued to watch the footage, Miller began to get a sinking feeling. He was beginning to think that perhaps this was, after all, a love thing. All the signs were there. It looked like Darren thought the world of Mr Pollard and this realisation troubled him, and sapped his positive energy as it dawned on the DCI that he really didn't have a clue what the hell was going on with this bizarre set-up.

Miller selected the clip that he wanted to present to

the press. It showed Pollard and Jenkins eating. They both had gigantic steaks in front of them and were talking away between mouthfuls, seemingly without a care in the world. The CCTV camera angle showed them both extremely clearly and would now provide the best photographic image of the two people that the police wanted to find as a matter of the utmost urgency.

"That'll do nicely!" said Miller as he tried to replenish his positive outlook from earlier. Despite the depressing thoughts that these images had inspired within him, he knew deep down that it was excellent content that would leave the British public in absolutely no doubt who they were being asked to keep an eye out for.

Once the edited footage had been sent to the press office and to central police comms for redistribution to every police force in the UK, Miller started working on his press statement. He was wary that he had to be careful how he explained the arrests of Daniel and Jess, but at the same time, he genuinely believed that Saunders' theory was spot on. They *did* know something, and Miller's insides flipped as he realised that he wouldn't have much longer to wait to find out exactly what it was that they knew.

Chapter Thirty

Ashton police station is the main police hub for the Tameside metropolitan area, of which Stalybridge, the home town of the Pollard family, makes up one of Tameside's eight towns.

Saunders and Grant arrived at the police station at 7.25 am, and were surprised to see press photographers and a couple of reporters standing outside. The media personnel had put two and two together and correctly guessed that Jess Pollard had been brought here. The sight of DI Keith Saunders and DC Helen Grant getting out of an unmarked CID car confirmed that their guess had been spot on.

"Detective Inspector, is it true that Jess is being held on suspicion of murder?"

"DI Saunders, have Darren's and Mr Pollard's bodies been found?"

"Can you confirm that Jess Pollard has been arrested because of her lack of emotion in last night's press conference?"

Saunders and Grant smiled politely as they fought their way through the press. It was a relief to get inside the police station's reception and close the door behind themselves.

"Good morning, I'm DI Saunders, this is DC Helen Grant, from the SCIU. We're here to interview Jessica Pollard." Saunders was looking forward to this. He had an unenviable record for cracking the vast majority of the department's most challenging cases, some through fluke, but most through brilliant detective work. As he and Grant were shown beyond the public area and into the main police station, he was absolutely determined to bring home the bacon on this one, as well.

Things had moved remarkably quickly thanks to Saunders' ringing ahead, and Jess Pollard was in Interview Room 2 with a duty solicitor, just twenty minutes after Saunders and Grant had arrived.

Jessica Pollard looked angry, upset and a little bit deflated, not to mention tired. It didn't look as though she'd managed to grab much sleep in her cell. She certainly didn't resemble the cock-sure, ball-breaker who Miller had indulged for over 90 minutes, just 14 hours or so earlier. Saunders and Grant smiled politely as they entered the interview room. Their warmth was not returned.

Once all the legal talk was completed and Jess was made aware of her rights, the interview got under way. DI Saunders began, whilst DC Grant made notes. She had been instructed to bide her time, but knew exactly when she was expected to step in.

"Okay, Jess, to get things started, do you know where your father is?"

"No." She was looking up at the ceiling, avoiding eye contact with anybody.

"Can you tell me where Darren Jenkins is?"

"No." The answer was followed by a huff.

"Can you tell me when you last spoke to your father, please?"

Jess thought for a minute. "It will have been last Tuesday."

"Was this face-to-face, or by phone, or by another medium?"

"Face-to-face. He came round to see mum but she was out. I made him a brew, we talked about a few problems I was having at work. And then he left."

"What time was this?"

"I don't know."

"Roughly?"

"Well, roughly between six and seven."

"And this was at the family address, where you live with your mother."

"Yes."

Jess wasn't looking remotely interested in any of this, and Saunders wasn't sure if it was down to arrogance, because she was 100% confident that she hadn't done anything wrong, or if it was an act, to pretend not to be worried and thus, convince the police that she was completely innocent of any wrong-doing. Saunders had seen "the act" a million times before, so it held no water with him.

"And when did you first become aware that your dad was missing?"

"Last Saturday. Mum was getting into a bit of a state. They'd had a row or something and she upset him. She'd not seen him for a couple of days and he'd been blanking her calls. She went round to apologise to him but there was no sign of him."

"Are you concerned about your father's welfare?"

"Not massively. Like I said to mum, he's just having a mini-breakdown or something."

"And would you say that abducting one of his pupils was part of that mini-breakdown?"

Jess looked at her solicitor who mouthed something to her. She repeated it. "No comment."

"We've been looking at your communications devices. It seems that you've made a number of calls to your brother over the course of the past few days. Can you tell us anything about that?"

Jess looked at Saunders with a cocky, sly grin. "Are you being serious? My dad is in the news for going missing with a pupil, and you are asking me why I've been talking to my brother? Is this a joke?" She added a fake laugh onto the end.

"No, I'm sure you recognise that this isn't a joke. I'm simply trying to work out why you have had so many conversations with your brother, when your phone records state that you rarely speak. Last month, for instance, you didn't phone him once, and you sent him two text messages. So, it doesn't strike me that you are particularly close."

"Hey! I just told you! My dad has run off with a kid from school! I'm quite entitled to speak to my brother about it. Aren't I?"

"Yes, yes of course you are. It's perfectly understandable. I'm just asking."

"Well, get some better questions then."

DC Grant saw her opportunity to ask a better question, whilst simultaneously stunning Jess Pollard with her first judder, following Saunders gentle warm-up.

"Jess, if what you are saying is correct,"

"It is correct." She said, huffing again.

"Can you explain why the high volume of calls and text messages between your brother and yourself commenced last Friday. A week ago today?"

"What? I..."

"You said that you were entitled to speak to your brother, since your dad was in the news for running off with a pupil. However, that story only came out on Wednesday lunchtime, six days after your father and Darren Jenkins disappeared, last Thursday."

Jess was trying to think fast. She'd let in an own goal there, and she knew it. Her face was heating up and her solicitor sensed the vibes.

"I don't know. No reason. Just talking."

"Jess, when we seized your phone last night, we discovered that all of the calls and text messages to your brother since last Friday have been deleted from the call history, and the text messages have all been deleted. In fact the last one was a text, from Daniel, saying 'yeah lol, and you're still fat and single.' That text was received over a month ago. Can you explain why you have deleted at least nine text messages to and from your brother, between last Friday, and last night?"

Boom. The second punch was harder than the first and seemed to have done more damage. Jess Pollard was dazed. Her solicitor recognised the signs, and pulled rank.

"Can I have a word with my client, in private please?" she asked.

"Of course." Said Saunders. "Interview suspended at," he looked at his watch. "Zero eight hundred hours."

Grant and Saunders left the interview room, closed the door and stood outside on the corridor. Grant held her hand up for a high-five but Saunders ducked it. She punched him in the arm.

"Oh, here we go," said Saunders, looking at the Sky News app on his phone. "The press conference is starting." He clicked "watch live," and Grant stood beside him, to see what Miller was revealing in this early morning press gathering.

*****

"Good morning," said Miller, as he sat down in front of the assembled press. "First of all, I'd like to thank you all, and the public, for an absolutely superb reaction to our appeal for information last night. As you'll all recall, I explained that we were centring our enquiries around the seaside town of Llandudno, in North Wales. Following a really excellent response, I am encouraged by the information which has been coming in to us. The first piece of evidence that we have which proves that Darren Jenkins and Philip Pollard are together, is this." Miller started playing the CCTV footage from the laptop, displaying it on the huge projector screen to his right.

"As you can see, Darren and Philip seem to be quite relaxed and in very good spirits. This is very encouraging, because not only is it the first sign that these two are together, as I said, but also, because it confirms that they are both safe and in good health. However, I must warn you all that this footage is now several days old. It was recorded at The Palladium pub, in Llandudno, on Sunday tea-time."

Miller let the clip play through for a few more seconds, before stopping it and replacing it with the photo of the motor-home, which had featured in the previous night's address.

"This motor-home, as I explained last time, has been hired from Tameside Camper Hire. The vehicle is a white, Eldiss Autoquest 6 berth motor-home, registration PN67 WYN. We still wish to locate this vehicle but we have no evidence that it ever left Llandudno as it has not passed an ANPR camera since Sunday, when it arrived in the resort. We know for certain that the vehicle is not in Llandudno, or in the wider area, as police helicopters have carried out a detailed overhead search. This leads us to the conclusion that the registration plates have been changed. We do know that the vehicle's tracking device was removed on Sunday, whilst in Llandudno, so we are working on the assumption that the vehicle's registration plates were changed at the same time."

This information was being welcomed by the press, it was all interesting stuff which could quickly be whipped up into sensational headlines.

"So, the message regarding the motor-home is unaltered. The photo of the vehicle is on the screen, and we want every member of the public keeping an eye out for it. We believe that it contains Philip Pollard and Darren Jenkins. However, we have no idea where it is now and enough time has elapsed since Sunday, for the vehicle to be literally anywhere on the British mainland. There are approximately two hundred and fifty thousand motor-homes registered with the DVLA in the UK, so we are completely aware of the challenges involved in spotting just one. Now that we have released the up to date CCTV of Darren and Philip, I am confident that there will be people out there in our communities who will have spotted this vehicle and its occupants. And if you are one of those people, we desperately want to hear from you."

Miller took a deep breath. "Okay, I'm sure all of you are aware of the arrests we made last night. I'd have preferred that these arrests hadn't been reported, but I'm fully aware that it is difficult to suppress these stories. Firstly, I need to make it clear that no charges have been brought against either of the two people we have taken into custody. Secondly, I would advise the press to tone the reporting down or you may well find yourselves in court, answering libel and defamation cases. Now, I know you all want to know why we have made the arrests but that information is confidential. All I will say is that we have reason to believe that the two people in our custody have information or access to information which is vital to this enquiry. They may or may not even know about this information, and there's also a chance they don't have any information at all. So, for a second time, I would urge you all to report on this case with caution."

Miller took a sip from his glass of water, as the press considered the gentle bollocking, and words of caution.

"Okay, once again, the key message coming out of my department this morning, is that we desperately need to find this motor-home." Miller pointed up at the screen. "We live on a tiny island and we're a nation on nosey-parkers. With that in mind, I am extremely confident that we will know where this vehicle is by end of play today. So, keep sharing the pictures online, keep reporting, and lets all pull together to find Darren Jenkins and Philip Pollard. No questions this morning please."

Chapter Thirty-One

Miller was pleased with how the press conference had gone, he thought he'd said enough to get the journalists and reporters to back off a bit as far as Pollard's son and daughter were concerned. He arrived back in the office, where the constables were busy answering incident room calls. Worthington and Chapman were sat at their desks, wondering where everybody else was.

"Morning," said Miller, in the general direction of everybody as he switched his phone back on.

"Morning Sir," said Worthington. The PCs waved as they continued logging the information which was coming in from the calls.

"Where is everyone?" asked Chapman. He looked pissed off, as usual.

"Oh, yes, sorry, Jo and Pete have gone over to Scarborough to interview Daniel Pollard. Keith and Helen are at Ashton nick, interviewing his sister."

"Oh, thanks for the invite!" said Chapman, feeling a little annoyed that he'd been left out.

"What?" asked Miller. He looked confused.

"You, you have your favourites, don't you?" Chapman was spoiling for a fight and Miller wasn't prepared for this sudden, unexpected confrontation.

"Wait, just a sec, what are you going on about, Bill?"

"Oh, nowt, its just, every time I come in here, the good jobs have been taken and we're left with the sweeping up!"

Miller didn't look impressed.

"What time did you come in, Bill?"

"Eight."

"And what time do you start?"

"Eight."

"Okay. Well, your colleagues, who also start at eight, were in before me, and I arrived at half-six."

Chapman looked a little wrong-footed.

"So, if you want the good jobs, get in earlier and get them, like the others do!"

Miller walked off towards his office, furious that Bill Chapman had the audacity to question him, when the issue was plainly and simply down to one thing. DC Bill Chapman was last in, first out, every day.

"Knob-head" said Miller under his breath as he closed his office door and checked the messages on his phone.

Saunders had text. "Jess Pollard's brief has asked for a break, Helen got her stuttering within a few minutes. I suspect we're getting a no comment interview when we get back in."

He checked the time of the text. 8.00am. Miller realised that he'd have just been starting his press conference at the time the text was sent, so was glad that he'd turned the phone off. He tried ringing Saunders, but it didn't connect. That meant he was back in the interview room with Jess Pollard.

*****

"Okay, interview suspended at zero eight-hundred hours, recommenced zero eight hours ten." Saunders nodded to Grant, who picked up where she'd left off.

"So, Jess, going back to the last question I asked you. Can you tell me why you have deleted all the text messages that you have received from your brother since last Friday?"

Jess Pollard looked stressed, and nervous. "No comment."

"Can you tell us why you deleted all of the text messages that you sent to him, between last Friday, and yesterday?"

"No comment." She couldn't look the police officers in the eye.

"Can you explain why you have deleted all of the call history logs of your phone calls with Daniel?"

"No comment."

"Presumably, you must have known that the calls and text messages would show up on your itemised bill?"

"No comment."

Saunders decided to step in. He didn't like the path this was going down.

"Jess, I know that you've taken advice from your solicitor. But I must warn you that providing a no comment response increases suspicion that you are somehow involved in your dad's disappearance and the abduction of Darren Jenkins. One thing to remember is that your solicitor won't be stood next to you in the dock, and your solicitor certainly won't be serving prison time with you. Please bear that in mind. I'm just thinking of the bigger picture here, these details will be taken into account when it gets to court." Saunders was trying to be nice, but Jess Pollard was ice-cold as she stared through him.

"My client is quite happy with the legal advice I have offered." Said the brief.

"Okay, just trying to help you out Jess. This only makes you look like you've got something to hide." Saunders nodded again at Grant, directing her to continue.

"Jess, where were you last Wednesday, between ten am and ten pm?"

"No comment."

"Did you see your dad on that day?"

"No comment."

"Did you come into contact with Darren Jenkins on that day?"

"No comment." Jess Pollard looked as though she was on autopilot, she was just answering as though she wasn't even listening, or hearing the questions which were being asked.

Saunders pointed to Grant's list of questions, specifically, the ones intended for a "no comment" scenario. These questions were designed to gauge reaction, more than anything else. Jess Pollard's physical reaction to them would tell the detectives more than any vocal response.

"Jess, obviously we are speaking to you because we are concerned about your father. Do you think that he is alive?"

"No comment." No emotional reaction either.

"Has your dad had any history of mental health challenges, specifically depression?"

"No comment." No reaction at all.

"What about self-harming?"

"No comment."

"Jess, because of the nature of your father's disappearance, we have to ask you if you've ever been aware of your father having a sexual interest in young boys?"

This one found Jess Pollard's button, and pressed it really hard.

"Oh for Christ's sake! That's disgusting! How fucking dare you!"

"Is that a no?"

"Yes! Of course it's a fucking no. God, you people. You haven't got a fucking clue!"

"No, well, that's a fair point. But we're trying to get a clue. That's the whole point of you being here Jess. We are of the suspicion that you know something about this matter and we just want to find out what it is."

"What, by trying to insinuate that my father is a fucking paedophile?"

"We're not insinuating anything. We're asking a perfectly understandable question under the circumstances."

"No comment. Unbelievable!"

"We believe that your father has taken Darren Jenkins away in order to groom him and have sex with him. Do you think that might be likely?"

"No comment." Jess was raging, the blood was pumping through her face, her pale complexion had turned red and tears were forming in her eyes.

"Your parents are separated, aren't they?"

"No comment."

"Do you think that might be a factor in your father behaving in the way that he has done?"

There was a pause. Jess Pollard was trying to control her breathing. Eventually, through gritted teeth, she said, "no comment."

*****

"Hello Sir."

"Alright Keith, what's happening?"

"We've taken a break. Jess Pollard is a real live-wire!

She's no commenting us but we've had a couple of reactions."

"Oh yeah?"

"Yes, so, Helen started getting under her skin, asking her if her dad was a paedo, stuff like that."

"Provocative!" Miller was smiling down the phone.

"Yes, quite. From what we both made of her reaction, she's not covering for that."

"But you think she is covering?"

"Oh yes, without a doubt. Something is definitely amiss. Helen got her in a spin early on, asking about the deleted phone calls and text messages from Daniel. Her brief had her no commenting after that."

"Anything else?"

"Yes, we got on about self-harming, whether her dad's dead, all that type of stuff. No emotional interaction, so its looking likely that she knows precisely what's going on."

"And that her dad's safe?"

"Yes, I think it's fair to make that assumption."

"Fucking hell. I knew there was something funny about her. So what's the plan now, then?"

"She's banged up again. I think we'll hang fire and see what Jo and Pete can find out off Daniel. And then take it from there."

"You've sent Jo the phone records, haven't you?"

"Yes Sir, she's had them since seven am. She's on it."

"Great. Okay, well, enjoy your nap."

"Cheers. Speak soon."

Miller hung up and rang Rudovsky.

"Alright Sir! I didn't know you were such a good kisser!"

"Shut up Jo. Where are you?"

"Scarborough. The home-town of Jimmy Savile."

"For God's sake Jo. There must be better things to associate Scarborough with?"

"Yes, Sir. Anyway, we're here, just chomping at the bit to get going with Daniel Pollard."

"Good, okay, well..."

Miller spent the next five minutes updating Rudovsky on the eventualities with Jess. He also filled her in on a few other details that had come to light. Rudovsky filled him in with a few details which North Yorkshire police had uncovered through the night too.

Things were looking good.

"Okay Sir, well, we'll go in now and rip this Daniel Pollard a new arse-hole. Speak soon."

Chapter Thirty-Two

"Hello Daniel," said DC Peter Kenyon, as the son of Philip Pollard entered the interview room.

He just nodded. He was a big lad, and he didn't look like the kind of bloke who would take any nonsense.

"Have you not got a solicitor?" asked Rudovsky.

"Don't need one." He'd retained his Manc accent, despite living over here for a decade. If anything, he had an exaggerated Mancunian accent, something the proudest ex-pat Manchester people did. Daniel sounded a bit like Liam Gallagher.

"Take a seat."

The custody officer who had brought Daniel Pollard in left the interview room.

DC Peter Kenyon read Daniel his rights, and explained the interview procedure, before starting the recording device.

"So, you have declined your right to have a solicitor present?" asked Kenyon, kicking things off.

"That's right."

"Okay, well, we've got a number of questions that we need to ask you in relation to your dad going missing."

Daniel Pollard shrugged.

"Are you worried about your dad?" asked Rudovsky, picking up on the dismissive body language.

"Have you ever met my dad?" asked Daniel.

"No. I've not."

"No, I can tell."

"What do you mean by that?"

"Well, let's just say, he's not the kind of bloke you need to worry about."

"But he has disappeared with one of his pupils." Said Rudovsky, playing the good cop.

"Well, yeah, I get that. But like I say, you don't need to worry about my dad."

"Thing is though," interjected Kenyon, "we are worried. It's not every day that a teacher just takes off with a pupil."

"Well I'm sure he had his reasons."

"What do you mean by that?"

"Nothing. I'm just saying, he'll know what he's doing. He's not gone mental or anything."

"You're talking as though you know something. Have you spoken to your dad about this?" Rudovsky was playing her nice cop role brilliantly. DC Peter Kenyon knew that it was only a matter of time before Daniel Pollard was introduced to the psychotic side of Rudovsky's personality.

"Nah, I've not spoken to my dad since... God, at least two weeks."

Rudovsky decided that she'd strike now, while Daniel was still toying with her.

"Was that on his normal phone number?"

"Yes, what... what do... what's that supposed to mean?"

"Your dad has two phones, doesn't he?"

Suddenly, Daniel sat up a little straighter. "No, I don't... as far as I'm aware, he only has one phone. Don't know anything about another phone. What do you mean?"

"Oh, it doesn't matter..."

"Well, yes, it does matter actually." Daniel seemed to want to assert some control in this conversation. It was noted mentally by Rudovsky.

"We'll ask the questions, Daniel, if that's okay." Kenyon was firm in his response, as the suspect locked stares with Rudovsky.

"Talking of phones. You've been talking a lot with your sister over the last few days. What can you tell us about that?"

"What do you want to know?"

"Everything. What have you been talking about?"

"This and that."

"About your dad being the number one news story in the country?"

"It came up." Daniel smiled widely.

"We've been looking at your phone."

The smile dropped slightly.

"There's no record of you phoning your sister on there."

Suddenly Daniel looked lost. That confidence and charisma had left the room.

"Thing is, we know, from your phone records, that you and Jess have been having a right old natter over the past few days. You've been pinging texts back and forth like there's no tomorrow as well."

"And your point is?"

"Well, my point is that there is no record of these calls and texts in your phone. It's almost as if you've deleted them all, for some reason."

"Nah, I've been having a bit of trouble with my phone." It was clear that Daniel was a fantastic liar. He didn't miss a beat with his reply.

But Rudovsky was just as sharp.

"All the other calls and texts are there. They've not disappeared from the call logs. The text messages are all there as well. The only ones missing are the ones to and from your sister."

"Don't know then. I'll take it down the shop when you let me out of here. Let them have a look at it." Daniel had a weird smirk on his face, which was intended to annoy Rudovsky. But it just empowered her. She loved dealing with narcissistic arse-holes, they were easy to mess with.

"Your sister must be having the same issues."

This comment got under Daniel's skin.

"What..."

"Jess. She must be having the same problem. All of her calls to and from you have been deleted from the call log as well. Same with the text messages. How weird is that?"

"Well, like I say, I'm no phone expert."

"Anyway, we'll come back to phones in a bit."

"What do you mean by that? Why do you..."

"Chill out. We'll come to that, I said. But first, I just want to ask you about this delivery note." Rudovsky pulled a folder out of her pile of paperwork and presented a photocopy of a delivery note. She placed it front of Daniel Pollard.

"For the tape, I am exhibiting a copy of evidence, item number 16B, taken from Daniel's workplace. It's a delivery note from East Yorkshire Commercials, dated Saturday the eighteenth of May, for two sets of front and rear number plates. Can you tell us anything about this delivery note Daniel?"

The suspect hadn't seen this coming. He was visibly rocked by the evidence before him, but he tried to appear cool.

"It's just a couple of sets of plates for a job. No big deal. Why?"

"Can you remember what the registration numbers were, that you ordered?"

"No. Course I can't. What a stupid question."

"Well I'm sure that your supplier will be able to tell us, when they open."

"I'm sure they can... but I'm not..."

Rudovsky opened her folder again.

"For the benefit of the tape, I am exhibiting a copy of evidence, number 21B. This is a screen shot of your internet browsing history last Friday afternoon Daniel. As you can see, you were browsing eBay, looking for Eldiss 6 berth motor-homes. Can you explain why you were doing that, Daniel?"

He looked shocked, and a little numb, but he carried on regardless, and came up with an answer.

"I've been looking for one. You know, for family holidays."

"So, just to confirm, you definitely weren't looking for similar vehicles in order to clone their registration plates?"

"No."

"You looked at a few models, but you didn't spend very long on the pages where the owners had obscured the reg plates. However, there are two vehicles that did have the registration plates displayed on the adverts. You spent several minutes on both of these pages. Were you reading up, checking that the vehicles were stationary at their point of sale?"

Daniel Pollard looked as if he was beginning to realise that he'd been sussed. But defiantly, he continued with his routine.

"This is getting a bit paranoid now."

"Is it really Daniel? Your dad hires a motor-home, goes on the run with a pupil from his school. And a few hours after he's set off in the motor-home, headed towards Scarborough, you're looking on eBay for the exact same model, and you order two sets of registration plates? Pull the other one Daniel, it's got bells on!" Rudovsky grinned. Daniel Pollard just stared at her.

"Is that all?" he asked.

"I bet you wish it was."

"Are you taking the fucking piss?"

"No Sir, I can assure you I'm not taking the piss. I'm building a bomb-proof, water-tight, brick shit-house of a file for the CPS."

"Well, I'm getting a bit fed up with…"

"Daniel, sorry to interrupt, but going back to your phone for a minute. We've had police officers investigating this all night. When the officers cross referenced your call logs with your actual phone calls, they noticed that the only calls you've tried to conceal are those to Jess, and those to another number. What can you tell us about this other number?"

"I don't know what you're talking about."

"Oh, I think you do. Think hard. Last Friday, while you were looking through eBay, you were on the phone to somebody, weren't you? For eight minutes and twelve seconds. You deleted it from your call logs. It's a bit weird, because that phone number you were connected to was only registered on the EE network an hour earlier."

"No idea. Can't remember."

"It was the third phone call that new number made. All three calls were to your number. The first call lasted almost twenty minutes. Come on Daniel, I'm sure you can remember, if you try really hard!"

Suddenly, it was as though Daniel realised that he had no more bullshit to offer. He had given up, his confident smile faded as he looked down at the table-top and said "Yes, okay. Fair enough. It was dad."

Mr Pollard sat bolt upright at his desk, holding the envelope in two hands and trying to muster the courage to open it. An anxious, giddy dread washed over him as he stared hard at the brown packet. He had nervously waited longer than six weeks for this moment to arrive, and now that it was finally here, he barely had the nerve to open the letter. The contents enclosed had the power to save his thirty-five year marriage or end it for good. It was a scary, yet strangely tantalising moment and Mr Pollard just couldn't bring himself to open it.

There was a quiet, half-hearted knock at the office door which audibly lacked confidence. It was the familiarly feeble sound which always heralded a teacher-to-pupil confrontation. Mr Pollard let out a loud groaning sound as he stood and strolled assertively across to the door, trying to guess which one of the usual suspects was standing behind it.

It was Darren Jenkins, or Daz Jenks, as he was better known around the school community. In the staff room he was known simply as "dickhead" to many of the teachers. This was the third time Jenkins had been sent to see Mr Pollard that week. And it was only Wednesday.

"Oh my God!" said the teacher grumpily as he opened his office door and saw Jenkins standing at his familiar spot, trying the complicated combo-look of innocence, victimisation and bafflement in one facial expression.

"What now?" said the smart, grey haired Head of Year 10.

"Mr Briggs sent me, Sir." Replied the pupil, manipulatively trying to make it sound as though it was no more than a simple errand he'd been sent on.

"Okay. Let the charade begin. What have you done now you little doughnut?" asked Mr Pollard, though he looked completely disinterested as he waved the teenager into the office.

"Don't know Sir. He just sent me out."

"For nothing?"

"Well, not really for nothing. For messing about."

"Doing what?"

"I don't know Sir."

Mr Pollard rolled his eyes at the ceiling and let out a long, exaggerated sigh. He paused for a painfully long, awkward amount of time before speaking again. The scenario was all too familiar to Mr Pollard, and he knew that this first part of the conversation was to be the most frustrating, just trying to ascertain exactly what Jenkins had done, that had warranted him to be sent to the most feared and respected teacher in the school.

"Do you know what Darren, I can't be arsed. Go and get Mr Briggs for me."

"Sir." Jenkins turned and casually walked back towards the class he had been excluded from. He jumped and skipped slightly as Mr Pollard's door slammed violently shut behind him. The frightening "boom" sound echoed all along the corridor as a sudden fear caught up with Jenkins. The pupil suddenly found that he was walking very quickly, his heart in his mouth from the terrifying shock of the slammed door.

Inside the office Mr Pollard sat down at his desk and stared at his computer monitor, willing himself to open Jenkins' disciplinary file. Mr Pollard was the school's longest serving and most feared teacher. His nickname amongst the pupils was "Well'ard" and it was a well-known rule that he wasn't to be crossed. But each year, a small handful of kids would ignore the advice and would foolishly gravitate towards him.

School legend had it that a pupil had once died because Mr Pollard had shouted so loudly at him. It was nonsense of course, but Mr Pollard kept the rumour alive by never actually denying that the incident had happened, when quizzed about it by curious kids. "It wasn't pretty." He'd mutter vacantly.

After a moment, the veteran teacher double-clicked Jenkins' progress file and looked dismayed as the red marks appeared on screen. He was on a final warning. One more red mark, and he was going to be expelled. There was a gentle tap at the office door and Mr Briggs appeared as the door slowly opened. Jenkins was stood behind the young teacher, looking slightly embarrassed. The cock-sure attitude was gone, Jenkins was beginning to realise that he couldn't argue and wriggle his way out of this one.

"Hiya Mark, come on in mate. Bring the school gimp in with you."

"Hello Mr Pollard. You wanted to see me?" Mark Briggs was a relatively new member of staff and was making great progress within the teaching staff.

"Well, Master Jenkins here said that you sent him out, and I just wanted to hear directly from you what exactly happened?" Mr Pollard gestured his colleague to sit down opposite him.

"Yes, well, he's in a silly frame of mind today, continually making a nuisance of himself. He kept shouting out in the class and was just being a pain. He had several warnings, but he's not up for any learning today. Sorry to send him to you Mr Pollard, but I had no alternative."

"No, no, don't apologise." Mr Pollard turned to Jenkins who was standing awkwardly beside Mr Briggs' chair. He was fidgeting with his hands behind his back and leaning to one side slightly.

"What were you shouting out?" Mr Pollard's voice was raised. He wasn't shouting, but he had just the right amount of volume to command the room as he stared psychotically at Jenkins. When angry, Mr Pollard had a piercing, frightening glare that cut straight through most people who faced him. But Jenkins was past caring about that, he had been through the ritual so many times that it was all becoming quite mundane. He just shrugged.

"What were you shouting?"

"Can't remember."

"Can you remember, Mr Briggs?"

"Yes. He was shouting "beans-on-toast." Said the junior staff member, in a manner so blasé and dismissive that it made Jenkins feel stupid. Mr Pollard raised an eyebrow and stared at Mr Briggs for a few seconds. Eventually, he looked over at Jenkins and began shaking his head.

"Beans-on-toast? Is that really the best you could come

up with?"

"Sir." Said Jenkins, acutely aware that in this setting, the hilarity of the sentence was lost on these old people who clearly didn't possess a sense of humour. The rest of the class thought it was hilarious.

"Can I get back to my year tens now Mr Pollard?" asked Mr Briggs, hoping to move things on.

"Yes, of course. Thank you for coming down here Mark, sorry to pull you out of your class. Now, just before you go, can you remind me what your priority is this year?"

"Well, I need to get decent exam results from my students, in order to get a full-time contract."

"So, you're not actually employed by the school yet?"

"No, I'm still a probationary teacher. If I can prove myself with my results this year, I'll get the job full time. If I fail, I'll have to leave in July."

"And just out of interest, how many years have you been working towards getting this job?"

"Six years."

"Did you know that Jenkins?"

"What, Sir?"

"That if Mr Briggs here doesn't do a fantastic job of teaching your class mates, he won't have a job in a few months time, despite investing every day of the last six years into it?"

"No Sir. Sorry, Sir." The young lad looked genuinely bothered by the statement.

"How is Mr Briggs supposed to teach and get good marks from his students when there's a tit shouting "beans-on-toast" out all the way through his lesson?"

"I don't know, Sir."

"Well, the point is, I can't do it Mr Pollard. It's physically impossible. Once the class are distracted, it can take five minutes to settle them and get them back to where they were, and that's why I sent him to you."

"And how are the rest of the class?"

"They are fine, they are trying really hard, and if we could just settle this one down, they'd be learning and gaining a lot more from the lessons."

Mr Pollard nodded sympathetically as he considered the difficulty that his junior colleague was facing.

"Okay! That's fine, no problem." The veteran teacher slammed both hands down on his desk and stood. The sudden movement and noise made Jenkins jump, forcing him to stand straight momentarily. "You get back to your class, Mark."

"Thanks Mr Pollard."

"Sorry Sir," said Jenkins as Mr Briggs stood from his chair.

"Thank you, Darren." Said Mr Briggs calmly, gently patting his hand against Jenkins shoulder before he left and closing the bright green door softly behind him.

"He is a lovely young bloke him, you know."

"I know Sir."

"Hard working, committed, enthusiastic, popular. He is first in every morning, last to leave at night. Brilliant bloke, he could become a head teacher one day with that work ethic. But not if his pupils don't score highly enough at the end of term. He'll be sacked. He'll be going home to his lovely fiancé and telling her he's got no job. God knows how he'll pay for the wedding. And all that, just down to the bad luck of getting you in his class. Poor bastard."

Jenkins didn't have anything to say. He looked down at his scuffed shoes and felt guilty about the seriousness of what Mr Pollard was saying.

"Funny though, beans-on-toast!" Mr Pollard fixed his glare on the teenager, daring him to laugh. Jenkins did not dare to laugh.

"Tomorrow morning, I'm getting you up in assembly. You'll come to the front of the school and stand beside me, and you will shout out 'beans-on-toast' to the rest of the school, all the way through. Is that okay?"

"Why Sir?" Jenkins began to look concerned, panicky almost. The colour drained from his face.

"Trust me on this, you'll love it. The whole school will be looking at you, the kids, the staff, all looking directly at you, all thinking you're a legend."

"Sir, they'll all think I'm a dick."

"Nah, don't be so ridiculous. They'll all think you're absolutely amazing! Trust me on this. Tomorrow morning, nine o' clock sharp, I want you stood next to me in that assembly. Each time I go silent, that's your cue to shout out 'beans-on-toast' at the very top of your voice. It'll be a riot!" Mr Pollard laughed and rubbed his hands together. "This is going to be brilliant!"

"I can't, Sir."

"Well you will, Jenkins." Mr Pollard raised his voice as he hammered home his authority. "This isn't a debate. I'm not asking for a favour."

"Sir, please. I'll never hear the end of it. It's stupid."

Mr Pollard turned around slowly in his chair and faced the window overlooking the lush, green hills which extended right across to the valley towards Mossley, and Saddleworth Moors in the distance. He stared out across the view that he loved so much for what seemed like an age. Finally, he spoke again. When he did speak, he had his back to Jenkins and continued to glare out across the picture-perfect landscape.

"I'm just trying to work out why you don't want to do it. I'm offering you an attention-seekers dream-come-true here. The eyes of the entire school will be fixed on you tomorrow morning. But you don't want it. You like to shout out during class, despite being asked loads of times to stop. But here is the chance to do it to a much wider audience, with full permission, and you don't want to do it." Mr Pollard span back around slowly in his chair and faced the troubled pupil. "That's a massive contradiction isn't it?"

"Sir. I just don't think that it's a good idea."

The teacher stared at his shabby looking pupil for a moment, Jenkins black hair looked greasy and his acne problem was getting worse. He had a few stray black hairs on his top lip which looked more like chaotic ball point pen marks underlying sore looking zits, than the grown up, moustache-look that Jenkins was obviously going for.

"Well, you know me Jenkins, I'm a fair man. I'm going to offer you a deal. You can either turn up and shout beans on toast all the way through my assembly, or you can write me a two-thousand word explanation of the reason why you don't want to do it. It's your call."

Jenkins didn't look at all phased by the mammoth project that Well'ard was offering him. It was his passport to freedom.

"Thanks Sir."

"If there is any repetition, I'll rip it up and you'll be shouting 'beans-on-toast' for half an hour."

"Yes Sir."

"If it's not on my desk by 8.45 tomorrow, you're doing the assembly. If you don't turn up tomorrow, you'll be suspended for a week, and as you're on your final warning, you'll be excluded for good, you'll be gone. No more school, no chance of sitting your GCSEs. No future. Clear?"

"Sir. Thanks."

"Right, now go and stand outside my office until bell."

"Sir."

Jenkins turned slowly and walked out of the office. Mr Pollard began typing notes onto the computer as the door closed.

The brown envelope from Tameside Metropolitan Council still sat ominously on his desk, unopened. Mr Pollard continued to type, once again fighting a nagging desire to just open it and read the potentially life changing news that might be contained. He didn't quite feel ready to unseal his fate just yet.

*****

"So, come on, out-with-it, what did Well'ard say, Daz?" asked Jenkins' best friend Michael Donnelly, as the two made their way out of the school gates surrounded by a six-hundred-strong scrum of excitable kids eager to get home to their computers and televisions.

"Nowt really. Didn't seem that arsed. He thought it was pretty funny I reckon." Said Darren, though he didn't sound too convincing. He followed his remark up by saying "beans-on-toast" in a squeaky voice which received a big laugh off Michael.

"Eggy bread!" replied Michael, to the amusement of

Darren.

"Hoi Daz, you spaz! What did Well'ard give you?" shouted Paul Coates, the much feared fifth year who was "cock of the school."

"Nowt!" said Darren, smiling over his shoulder as the well-built sixteen-year-old caught up him, and Michael.

"You are such a twat mate. Honestly, I bet Well'ard wishes you were dead." Paul Coates' small entourage laughed mockingly as Darren tried to shrug the remark off politely. "In fact, we all wish you were dead, you absolute shit-splash." Paul Coates leant towards Darren and forced out a big sweaty burp, blowing it right into Darren's face. It smelt of fizzy Vimto and cheese-and-onion crisps. The hot stench made Darren retch, which delighted Coates and his gang of grinning, boisterous followers.

"What a twat!" said one.

"Ha ha ha, you sad bastard." Jeered another as the small group shouldered rowdily past the pair and headed towards their bus. Darren stood there feeling embarrassed and vulnerable, his eyes watery from the retching.

"God, I hate them bastards," offered Michael. "Come on, forget them."

For the rest of the walk home, Darren seemed quiet and thoughtful, it was Michael who did most of the talking. Michael shared the same sense of humour as Darren, and the two had been friends since primary school. Michael had always skilfully stayed out of trouble though, where Darren just seemed to be in constant detentions and isolation periods. Michael instinctively knew when to wind it in and settle down in class, but Darren just never seemed to know when to stop joking about. It often caused a bit of tension between the friends, mainly because Darren felt that Michael was equally as bad as him, but never got caught.

"You coming out tonight?" asked Michael as the pair sauntered slowly along the back-to-back, red-bricked terraced streets towards their homes.

"Nah, can't, still grounded. And I've got something to do for Well'ard anyway."

"What?"

"Two-thousand word essay about why I said beans-on-toast!" Darren didn't seem as gutted as Michael had expected.

"Honestly? Shit, that sounds harsh." Michael had never heard of such a tough punishment.

"It's got to be on his desk before school or he's getting me expelled."

"Fucking hell, that's a bit much isn't it?" Michael stopped outside his house and leant back against the front door.

"I know yeah. So that's my night taken care of. Seeya tomoz." The two friends fist-bumped, and Darren continued along the street.

Once he arrived on his own street, Darren was dismayed to see his dad's shitty old car parked up outside the terraced house. He let himself in the front door and closed it quietly behind him. After putting his bag in the cupboard, he crept quietly up the stairs to his room.

"Darren! Is that you?" shouted his father up the stairs. Darren rolled his eyes at the ceiling.

"Yes, hi dad, how come you're home?"

"Got an early dart. Why are you creeping upstairs? Are you in the shit again?"

"No!" said Darren, a little too urgently, which inadvertently revealed his guilt as he shouted downstairs from the landing.

"You better not be. Can't be arsed with any more of your bullshit pal. Now come down here and make me a brew." Darren reluctantly went back down the steps he'd ascended and breezed into the living room. Mike was lay on the settee watching a TV quiz show.

"You're in the shit again aren't you? I can tell. What have you done now, you little dick?"

"Nowt dad, honest." Darren didn't sound very convincing.

"Well summat's up – why else would you go creeping off up the stairs like that? Do you want a smack?"

"No. I didn't even know you were in dad. I've got coursework to do, wanted to just get on with it, get it out the way."

"I'm calling bullshit on that! My car's outside. Should have gone to Specsavers if you didn't see it. Anyway, just make me a brew will you, I can't be arsed listening to any of your shite. And do us a couple of rounds of toast, as well."

"Sure."

Darren did as he was asked, going through quietly into the kitchen as Mike shouted out answers to the television quiz. By the time the kettle had boiled, his father had loudly answered three out of three incorrectly. The teenager had a difficult job trying not to laugh, and could feel a dizzy excitement building up within him. Mike answered each question with such confidence that the awkward silence or tut that followed each of his incorrect shouts was irresistibly amusing and rewarding to Darren. He listened carefully to the fourth question, hoping his dad would get it right to avoid any awkward eye contact when he took the brew through. Darren dropped a tea bag in his dad's cup as the host asked a bonus question.

"Okay, for double points, who had a hit in 1978 with the LS Lowry inspired song, Matchstalk Men and Matchstalk Cats and Dogs?"

"Houghton Weavers!" shouted Mike urgently.

"Brian and Michael!" said the television contestant who had buzzed in first.

"Brian and Michael is... correct! For 9 points! Well done."

"Fucking bollocks this!" said Mike, dismissively. Darren couldn't help but laugh as he stirred the brew, trying hard to do it as quietly as possible. He disguised the laugh as a cough.

"Where in the world am I? For six points, in front of me I see a perfectly symmetrical building, but where in the world am I?" asked the corny TV presenter.

"Taj Mahal!" shouted Mike.

"Paris, at the Eiffel Tower." Buzzed the contestant.

"Oh, bad luck. I'm not in Paris. For three points I can offer it to you Maureen."

"Taj Mahal!" Shouted Darren's dad, louder this time, in a desperate bid to help Maureen secure the points.

"Tower Bridge, in London?" suggested Maureen, with a look of worried uncertainty.

"No, I'm afraid you're both wrong. Where in the world I am is India, at the Taj Mahal."

"Get in!" shouted Mike at the television. "Should have listened to me Maureen, you gormless old boot!" Mike laughed loudly and held his hand out for a high-five as Darren walked in.

Darren placed the brew down on the floor beside the settee where his father was sprawled out. The teenager clapped the high-five.

"Here you go dad, toast is just coming now."

"Thanks. Did you hear that then? Smashed it there for six points!"

"Yes, nice one dad" said Darren, with a smirk on his face as he walked back into the kitchen to spread some marge on the toast, doing well not to blurt out his observation of the earlier questions.

After returning and handing the plate of toast to his dad, Darren headed upstairs to start work on the two-thousand word essay for Well'ard. As he sat down on his bed with his A4 lined pad, it occurred to him that he wasn't feeling remotely anxious or stressed about the task. If anything, he was quite looking forward to getting stuck in.

*****

Mr Pollard arrived home shortly after 6pm, still clutching the unopened envelope. He knew that it was getting silly now, he'd had it in his possession for more than eight hours. Before the break-up, his wife Sandra made fun of his strange habit of not checking his lottery ticket. He reasoned that as long as he had the unchecked ticket on his person, the dream was still alive. Only after he'd checked the lottery numbers against the ticket would the fantasy end. He liked to prolong the anticipation.

But this was slightly different, the letter he had waited for contained a simple yes or no. A stop or go. The very thought of opening it and reading the contents made his belly flip over.

He placed it down on the kitchen work top.

He went for a shower and came back through to the kitchen. After stabbing the film lid of his lasagne ready-meal several times and loading it into the microwave, he poured himself a large glass of red wine and started unloading the stacks of coursework, which he planned to mark through the evening. As he stared at the microwave, watching the plastic container revolve around on the turntable, Mr Pollard's mind wandered back to the situation with Darren Jenkins. He wondered if he had dealt with the boy reasonably. The threat of making him stand up in assembly and completely humiliate himself was probably going a bit too far, and the thought made him feel guilty. But he'd been known to do much worse. Perhaps he was going soft in his old age, he considered.

In the past, before his marriage fell apart, Mr Pollard would talk about his day, and go over the finer details with Sandra, analysing any situation that he was unsure about. In his heart of hearts, he knew that it was this self-indulgent behaviour that had proved a significant factor in the break-up of his marriage of thirty-six years.

These moments made Mr Pollard feel lonely. It wasn't often, but when something at work was bugging him, he really missed having Sandra's opinion to help put things into perspective. Most of the time, he actually enjoyed the new experience of living alone, in a strange way. The independence, the solitude and the quiet were new experiences that he didn't mind at all. This fact made him feel quite guilty, but after a life full of noise and activity, and his needs always being the last on the list, the new life that he was adapting to was presenting some surprising outcomes.

The microwave pinged. Mr Pollard opened the door and began dishing out the lava hot meal onto his plate. He swore under his breath as he burnt the tip of his thumb on the film lid. With regards to Jenkins, he'd just have to wait and see if the lad would turn up with the essay in the morning.

*****

Darren finished his explanation at around about ten o' clock, went into the bathroom for a pee and to fill his glass with water from the sink. He returned to his neat little bedroom, and got into bed on the top bunk. Although it was more of a letter than an essay, the young lad had got so much out of his system, he felt completely relaxed for the first time in his entire life.

Darren had always found it hard to sleep, bedtime was a difficult time for him, it always had been, for as long as he could remember. Pointless, endless thoughts would run around his mind for hours. Thoughts like; "If you were walking on ice in the Arctic and it broke and you fell in the icy waters below, would you be able to get out, and if you did, how would you get dry, and if you did get dry, would you freeze to death because you didn't have dry clothes? And if you did have dry clothes, how come they hadn't fallen through the ice anyway? You wouldn't have had time to pull your back-pack off and throw it clear. Do Penguins have knees."

Tonight though, the thoughts that Darren had shared in his essay had completely cleared his mind. He put his head on his Manchester United pillowcase and fell into a deep, calm sleep.

*****

The following morning, Darren found himself walking very quickly to school, occasionally breaking into a jog. He had whizzed through his paper-round, arrived home, changed into his uniform and had left the house before 8 o' clock. He was in school for quarter past eight, he'd never seen the school so deserted and quiet, not even after a detention. The desire to give his essay to Mr Pollard was overwhelming him, he literally could not wait to hand it over and share his words. It quickly transpired that he was being a little bit too enthusiastic though. When Darren arrived at school, there was no sign of Mr Pollard. He wasn't in his office and he hadn't arrived at the staff room yet either.

Darren went up to the school office. After hearing the details of why he was on school premises so early, Mrs Horsfield, the kind-faced school secretary explained that Mr Pollard didn't usually arrive until eight thirty. Darren was crushed, he really wanted the essay to be read, right now. He walked back through the school and stood at his usual spot, outside Well'ards office, and decided to give his essay a quick read through to pass the time.

Dear Mr Pollard,

As you requested earlier today, I am going to write down a two-thousand word explanation about my misbehaviour, and mainly about why I don't want to say beans-on-toast in assembly. Sir, I know what you mean when you say that you can't understand why I come out with stuff in class when I'm not supposed to, but now you say that I can do it in assembly, I don't want to do it. I am glad to have this chance to try and get my side across about it and I hope you think that it makes some sense anyway. Here goes.

Today, everyone was laughing at me shouting out in Mr Briggs class and yesterday I was in your office for the same thing in Mrs Dawson's class and the day before for shouting out in Mr McGuire's lesson. Sir, every time you ask me why I do this stuff I just say I don't know. You always go mad at me and you say that I must know. But the truth is, I do know, or at least I think I know why. I want to try and explain it to you, as it is the worst thing in my life. I have hardly no friends because of it, the teachers all hate me because of it, my dad thinks I'm special needs and you Sir, who has always been really good to me, you are also getting sick of me now.

When I think about what you said to me today, you are right, it doesn't make sense that I don't want the whole school's attention on me. The truth is Sir, I would happily live the rest of my life without anyone ever looking at me again. I hate this part of me that shouts out stupid things like beans-on-toast or Sunday-roast, or summer-on-the-coast, or whatever stupid crap it is.

I hate that when the room goes quiet, I have this urge inside me to fill the quiet. I feel uncomfortable when it goes quiet, nervous I suppose, so I just do stuff so everyone laughs, or

I get sent out. When it goes quiet, it's like I feel that it's my job to do something. I don't care about the quiet when I'm on my own or stood out in the corridor but when I'm in a big group, I can't help it. It just happens. My dad does it as well. My aunty Julie does everyone's head in because she doesn't stop talking, not ever, and my dad says it's because she can't handle silence. Whatever it is that makes her like that, I think I've got it Sir! But I just want you to know that even though I know I do it, I do try to stop myself all the time, it's just by the time I realise I'm doing it, it's too late. I really do try but I can't do it. Most of the time, when I shout out, or say something cocky or cheeky or make fun out of someone, it's like I don't even know I'm doing it. It's only afterwards when I'm sent out or in your office that I'm trying to work out what I've done or why I've done it. Because I'm so confused about everything that's just gone on, I normally deny it anyway, which just gets me in even more trouble.

Sir, my nickname is Daz the spaz because of my behaviour. It's not funny to everyone else, I know they laugh, but its laughing at what a fool I am, how far I'm taking it. I know they're not laughing because the joke is funny. If I could stop acting like this, I would do, I know that for a fact. On Monday in Mr McGuire's class, I'd only just come out from your office and within five minutes of being in the class I was swearing under my breath and squeaking my chair on the floor. I was like, what am I doing? I was thinking about what you'd said and that I had already been in your office twice. I had to try really hard to stop doing it. It takes proper hard effort to stop myself, and I can keep it up for a few minutes before I find myself doing something wrong again like throwing a pen at someone. Then I get told off and start arguing back at the teacher, pretending that I haven't done anything. It's like I'm not in control of myself.

Seriously Sir, even though it's embarrassing, I'm finding it dead easy to talk about it by writing this, but there's something definitely wrong with me, I swear to God, I'm not just trying to get on people's nerves, I can't help it.

When I try really hard to keep still and quiet, my mind just goes blank, and I just sort of drift off. I'm trying to listen to the teacher and write down all the stuff but I just sort of go into a dream world, like when the telly has all that snow thing on it when the aerial comes out and my eyes start watering and I'm yawning like mad, all the words the teachers are saying just sound like they're under-water or something. It looks like I'm crying because my eyes water so much when I'm concentrating on sitting quiet and doing the work.

This will seem weird, well, it is weird, but it's not just at school I have this. It happens when I go to the pictures, I'll be looking forward to going to see the film for days but when I'm in the cinema, and the film's on, I start going to the toilet or kicking the chair in front of me. Afterwards, I get home and I think about how I've missed half of the film. It's exactly the same as when I'm at school, except there's no teachers telling me off. It's weird, Sir.

The thing is, I've been really worried about this for years but I have never felt like I can tell anyone. Hopefully, you won't think I'm being cheeky Sir, but I can't do school. It's not just school though, its life. When I'm with a group of people I have this urge to do stuff that always ends up with me getting in bother. I was with a load of lads a few weeks ago and we were all just walking down towards the train station and for some reason that I still don't understand, I just walked over someone's car. Everyone else was walking on the pavement and I just jumped up and walked over it, then everyone laughed and was pointing at me, so I walked over the next one. I swear I don't remember thinking oh I'll jump on these cars and everyone will laugh at me and like me. When I stopped, one of the lads who was there called me a retard and punched me in the face, and everyone laughed again.

There is no thought in this stuff at all, it's not planned out you see. I hope this is making sense to you Sir, but I doubt it is really. The next thing that happened was the police came round to my house and said I was on CCTV and I got took down to the station, got a caution and obviously my dad went ape about it. I've lost my telly and playstation, got grounded, got a police caution on my record and everyone thinks I'm a freak. So, all I'm saying is, I don't sit here trying to think of ways that I can really drop myself in it. It just happens. My dad is like 'why do you jump up on a car?' and I say I don't know and that angers him even more because he thinks I'm just being cocky or something, then he batters me as well.

It's the same at school, at the youth club and everywhere. Half of the time someone is after me because of the way I carry on. I'm always being cocky and giving abuse to people. I'm always watching around corners and checking who is around whenever I go out. There are five people after me at the moment, so it's just as well I'm grounded really. I have to watch my back going to and from school, but luckily it's pretty safe at school. I wish more than anything that I didn't have to live like this. I hate it. My life is nothing but hassle.

The only time that I'm not doing all this stuff is when I'm on my own. I can go out all day on my own, travelling about on the buses and trains, going for walks and looking round places and I go all day without the slightest problem. If I'm sat on the bus and a load of other kids get on I just sit there looking out the window, I don't try and get noticed or anything. I don't even make eye contact, even if they're trying to talk to me and ask me where I'm from. It's weird because if they were kids from my school I'd be rubbing my bare bum on the windows or something. Everyone would be laughing and saying I'm a retard but I'd just laugh about it. But when I get home I sit by myself and start thinking why did I do that, what's the point!!

Sir in this essay you wanted me to explain why I don't want to get up in assembly. Well, it would just be another thing for people to give me a hard time about, to talk about what a weirdo I am. You are right though, what is the difference? As I try my best to understand whatever it is that is wrong with me, I still can't say why it is okay for me to say beans-on-toast all the way through class though. When I know why, I think I'll probably know enough about it to make it stop.

Even though I do try really hard, I can't stop. So now Sir, I am saying to you that I want to leave school and just forget about my exams. I know I'm holding everyone back, I know I'm wasting your time, all the teachers and just causing a lot of stress for my parents. I feel really bad about what you said about Mr Briggs. It's not my goal to get him sacked, like you say he is a nice teacher and I really like him. But even though you said that, that I might be the reason for him getting sacked, I still won't be able to do anything about my behaviour. That sounds really cocky Sir, but it's not. It just sums up the truth.

I know for a fact that I won't be able to stop myself from doing some absolutely stupid stuff in that class, all the time knowing that I might be making a teacher who I really like lose his job. I bet you think I'm being cocky writing all this stuff down, speaking my mind but it's not cocky sir, this is just me being honest and truthful. If I could just sort myself out I would. But I know, after all the years of trying for all the reasons I've said, I can't do it.

The point of this essay was why don't I want to stand in assembly shouting beans-on-toast? Well the answer is because I don't ever want to come back to school again, I don't want to be known as a dickhead and I don't want the constant trouble that I'm in, just for being me. This is just who I am, I'm no good at school, I can't do it, I can't learn anything. I need to be the centre of attention but even when I am, I don't really like it anyway. That's what it all boils down to Sir. Some kids are good at football, some are good at maths and science. I'm just good at disrupting the class and making a tit of myself. Well it would save us all a lot of time and trouble if we just went our separate ways to be honest.

I've still got about a hundred and fifty words to do sir, so what I would just like to say is that even though you are always being really awful to me, I do like you. You're the best teacher at Astley High and I have the most respect for you. I hope you can see what I'm saying here in this essay, and as I have already said, I truthfully hope that you can maybe see this from my side and let me leave.

Thank you for giving me this opportunity to express myself. It's been really helpful for me, and I hope it's not been too boring for you.

Darren Jenkins

Darren was really happy with his letter. He noticed a few repetitions in it, but overall, after sleeping on it, and reading through it again, he was pleased with the document. He looked impatiently along the corridor, willing Well'ard to hurry up so he too could read it. Darren had never felt so excited about anything in his entire life. But as he stared along the familiar school corridor, his excitement was turning into frustration that the teacher wasn't appearing. He decided to start reading through again.

He'd only got through the first few paragraphs when he heard Well'ard's heavy shoes approaching on the shiny tiled floor.

"Bloody hell! Have you wet the bed Jenkins?!" boomed Mr Pollard as he got nearer, his unmistakable smile lit up the corridor.

"No Sir. I've done your essay, Sir." Jenkins was holding it out at arms-length, looking extremely pleased with himself. Mr Pollard rolled his eyes at the ceiling.

"Let me get in the office first, you little twerp! Here, grab this bag."

Mr Pollard unloaded his heavy bag of coursework onto the pupil and fumbled around for his keys. Eventually, he unlocked the office door and entered. The door made its familiar, loud squeak. Jenkins followed excitedly and placed the books down on a desk.

"Sir, if there are bits of it that you think are cocky, it's not sir – I'm not trying to..."

"Shut up a minute Jenkins. I'm not ready for you at this hour. Just leave it there on my desk and I'll have a look at it later."

Jenkins looked absolutely crushed. "Sir, are you not reading it now?"

"No. Don't be daft, I've only just walked in. I've got loads of things I need to do before I can look at that. Just leave it there." Mr Pollard bent down, reaching under his desk and turned his PC on. He looked at Jenkins. The boy was devastated.

"But sir," he pleaded.

Well'ard laughed mockingly. "For heaven's sake Darren – will you just put it on my desk and piss off out of it!"

After a brief pause, Jenkins placed the letter on the

desk, and walked slowly out of the office. He had tears streaming down his face. Mr Pollard was oblivious as he unpacked the coursework and arranged the pile neatly. A few seconds after the door closed behind Jenkins, Mr Pollard heard the forbidden sound of running along the corridor, then a loud bang as a door slammed against a wall, followed by the unmistakable sound of shattering glass, reverberating along the echoey corridor.

"What the bloody..." said Mr Pollard as he rushed over to his office door to see what was going on. There was nobody around, but the corridor floor was covered in broken-glass.

*****

Before he knew what was happening, Darren was walking along the canal, headed out of town. Quite what he was doing here, or where he was headed was unclear. Nothing really made much sense to him. He just felt that he needed to get away and spend some time alone.

Darren hadn't meant to break the door at school. Like so many things that plagued his young, but eventful life, it had just happened. He had just thrown it open a bit too hard as he ran away from Well'ard. But he knew that nobody would believe that. This would just go down as another "incident" and yet another black mark against him. He was on his last, last chance. He would probably get excluded now.

"Fuck 'em." He shouted, as he kicked a stone which danced along the canal towpath, before finally plopping into the cut.

As the thoughts of the trouble he faced ran around his mind, Darren felt an overwhelming burden of bad luck. It never made sense to him why things would just escalate so quickly, why there was always a black cloud of trouble hanging over him.

Darren had no firm idea of where he was going, or what he was doing. The thought of going back home and facing his dad, and Well'ard, and all the dickhead kids who made his life a constant misery filled him with loathing. He'd really felt that his letter to Well'ard was going to be the start of a new chapter.

Never before had Darren felt so happy, or relaxed, and even feeling positive about the future. He always felt that he was stuck on a never-ending hamster-wheel of problems, bollockings and restarts. That letter had made him feel like the cycle was finally over. And, Well'ard couldn't even be arsed to read it, something that was so personal, and that had taken him nearly six hours to write.

As Darren saw it, he was just the unluckiest kid in Britain. He dwelled on his situation as he walked along the side of the derelict mills and factories. Most of the broken windows along here were his, but he wasn't interested in throwing any stones today. He wasn't wallowing in self-pity or feeling sorry for himself. He was just recounting how badly his luck seemed to run.

As he approached the town centre, Darren was unsure of the next move. He didn't particularly want to walk around Stalybridge town centre because he knew it wouldn't be long until a police officer or truancy officer pulled him up and asked him why he wasn't at school. He knew that the security guard at Tesco phoned school if he saw anybody in Astley High uniform, so he'd have to stay away from there. Knowing his own luck, Darren imagined that a police officer and a truancy officer would come walking along this canal towards him at any moment.

He stayed on the canal, under the bridge, just leaning over the barrier and staring into the water. After a short while, the fuzziness of everything that had happened began to pass. Darren started to regret the decision to run out of school. But it was done now, and he couldn't face the thought of going back into school. He decided that he would just have to stay-put for now, and hope that no more trouble would be headed his way for the time being. His thoughts began to turn to his dad. He was bound to know about him bunking off by now. Although he was beginning to feel calmer and more settled, the problem hadn't gone away. Darren resigned himself to the fact that he would just have to deal with that when he got back home, probably with a good kicking as well.

As Darren sat and contemplated the situation, and worked on explanations to try and give himself the easiest way out of this latest mess, he realised that the only answer was to run away. Just fuck off and get away from everything. Within seconds of this thought popping into his mind, Darren Jenkins felt an electrical buzz running through his body. His hands and feet were tingling and his tummy was doing somersaults as his heart-rate quickened. Darren started walking at quite a pace, back in the direction he'd come from.

*****

After the school assembly, once it had become clear that Jenkins was nowhere within the school community, Mr Pollard went to see the Headmistress to explain the situation, and ask what steps should be taken next. The child's welfare is entrusted to the school once a pupil enters the building. Now that Jenkins had effectively absconded, there were certain procedures that needed to be adhered to. As this had not happened for a couple of years, Mr Pollard was uncertain what the latest procedure was, or what the next course of action should be.

"STOP RUNNING! ARE YOU A MAD PERSON?"

Mr Pollard shouted at the top of his voice to a year nine who had obviously forgotten himself in an attempt to get where he was going a little bit quicker. Pollard instantly switched into Well'ard mode and stopped the boy from continuing by stretching his arm out, blocking his way.

"Sorry, Sir." Said the petrified kid, looking as though he was about to burst into tears.

"If you run, that means everybody else can run. And that means we will all be trampled on, our limbs crushed to dust. Is that what you want?"

"No, Sir." The little lad looked sad, and scared.

"If we allowed everybody to run we could all be poisoned to death by the fast-flowing fumes of Lynx Africa. Do you have a death-wish?"

"No, Sir."

"Good. Now go on, be on your way. If I see you running again I will personally throw you in the pig-swill bins out back!"

"Sir!"

Mr Pollard continued on his way, following behind the boy as he walked ridiculously quickly.

Eventually, Mr Pollard reached the Head's office. The Headmistress, Mrs Houghton was twenty years younger than Mr Pollard and had been at the school for less than a quarter of the time. There was a certain amount of animosity between the two – but both managed to get along professionally and kept their personal views to one side. Mr Pollard thought that Mrs Houghton was a good role model for the pupils and above all else, that was his number one interest. But he didn't particularly like her, in his view, she was more of a politician than a teacher. In short, Mr Pollard thought that Mrs Houghton was full of shit.

"So, he's done a runner?" asked the Head.

"I'm pretty certain of it, I've done the rounds and he's not in any of the usual hot spots. A couple of his form group saw him running out of the school gates as they were heading in to school."

"What time was this?" asked Mrs Houghton.

"I'd just arrived at school, about half eight. He wanted me to read an essay that I'd set him. I told him that I'd look at it in a bit, but he just went off on one." Mr Pollard placed the folded-up writing paper on his superior's desk.

"Have you managed to read it yet?"

The loaded question irritated the teacher. "No, I've been looking for him!" Pollard raised his voice slightly, unintentionally.

The Headmistress looked disinterested. She picked up the paper and began reading. The gesture undermined Mr Pollard slightly, who was sitting redundantly across the desk. Mrs Houghton sighed a few times as she read and Pollard tried to guess what each sigh implied, whether it was a noise of frustration at the boy, or a noise or irritation directed at Mr Pollard's handling of the situation. Several minutes passed before Mrs Houghton looked up from the essay and made eye contact with the head of year.

"Well, I can see why he's upset. He's poured his heart and soul into this."

"Yes, but the world does not revolve around Darren Jenkins. I told him I'd read it, but I'd not even taken my jacket off. What does it say?"

"In a nutshell, he's saying that he's tried, but he can't behave and that he wants to leave. It's all very positive stuff, surprisingly mature – I'll give him that."

"So, what do we do?"

"Have you phoned his father?"

"Yes, no answer."

"What is your timetable this morning?"

"I've got year 9 for maths in second period."

"Okay, well I would suggest that you go to his home and see if he's there. Have a quick drive near the usual hangouts as well. Try and get him to come back and we can all have a good chat about the future. Frankly, I'm at a lost cause with the boy and I want him out."

"We can't just kick him out. Those days are gone. We have a duty to manage his behaviour, the units are all full. There's nowhere for him."

"I know that. But I can't throw any more resources at a kid who is set on messing about. He'll fail his GCSEs anyway and he'll drag half of his class down with him. Most concerningly, his failure grades will pull the school's over-all results down. We can't have it, the stakes are too high."

Mrs Houghton was using this situation as a way of asserting her own authority over Mr Pollard. The comment seemed to do the trick and Pollard stayed silent.

"Anyway, we have far more pressing matters with Jenkins at this point-in-time. Do you want to go now, try and track him down. If you find him, bring him straight to me."

Mr Pollard had a strained and difficult rapport with his superior. He really wasn't keen on her, but none-the-less, he genuinely wanted to be liked by her. Her guard was always up around him. He had always assumed that she was cautious of him and it troubled him. Mr Pollard had enjoyed a good working relationship with all of the school's staff, but Mrs Houghton was very aloof. She had her inner-circle of brown-nosing staff and they tended to be young, ambitious and unlikely to question any of her decisions.

It was almost skilful how she had wrong-footed him. She had just engaged him in a conversation about Darren Jenkin's future with the school, and then just as he'd attempted to make a case for Darren, she'd pulled the rug out and effectively suggested he had better things to be thinking about. It was this kind of daily awkwardness which drove the wedge between them.

Mr Pollard had twice avoided going to the Christmas staff meal out of a genuine concern of being belittled or embarrassed by his boss.

And, if he was being brutally honest, it was also because he'd been anxious that after a few glasses of Merlot he might tell her exactly what he thought of her.

"Yes, of course. On my way." He grabbed Jenkins' letter off the head's desk, before leaving.

*****

It was almost ten-thirty by the time Mr Pollard had pulled his car up outside Jenkin's address. He looked at his watch and worked out that he had fifty minutes before he was due back in school to take his class. He wondered if that would be enough time to talk to Jenkins, calm him down, and get him back into school. He got out and closed the car door and looked up at the property. It looked reasonably well kept, there were no obviously outward signs of a dysfunctional household.

Mr Pollard knocked at the door. A minute passed before a face appeared at the window, grinned and then disappeared again. A few seconds later the door opened slightly. The grinning face was wedged between the door and the frame.

"Hello. Mr Jenkins?" said the visitor.

"Yeah?"

"I'm Mr Pollard, from Astley High."

"Yeah, I know you are. Fuck me! You've not changed one bit!" Mike Jenkins had a look of cocky sarcasm across his face. Mr Pollard just looked puzzled.

"Don't remember me, do you? Shit, I can't believe

that!"

"I'm sorry…"

"Michael Jenkins. Used to teach me, God, twenty-odd years ago now!"

It only took half a second. "Bloody hell, yes, I remember now." Mr Pollard suddenly had flashbacks of this man as a boy, a hell-raising, gobshite, pain in the arsehole of clusterfuck proportions. "So, you're Darren's dad? I hadn't realised…"

"Yeah, course I'm his dad. What's he done now?"

"Can I come in?"

"Nah mate. In the middle of summat."

"Oh…"

"So, what's he done now, the little prick?" Mike took a cigarette packet out of his jeans pocket, took one out and lit it as he leant against the doorframe.

"Well, he's come to school this morning and then he ran off, we are trying to locate him and get him back into the school environment. I just wondered if he'd come back home?"

"No, course he hasn't. He knows I'll kick fuck out of him if he does. Why's he ran off?"

"Well that's the peculiar thing, we're not sure and that's why we want to find out where he is and get to the bottom of what's wrong."

The boy's father blew smoke out his mouth and stared aggressively at Mr Pollard.

"Are you sure," Mike pointed a finger at his old teacher's chest, "that it's not because you're being a twat with him? Because you were a mean old twat with me, I hated your fucking guts when I was his age." Mike suddenly had a wild look in his eyes, and Mr Pollard suddenly felt vulnerable, for the very first time in his adult life.

"You were a right nasty old bastard with me!" continued Mike. "Always on my fucking case, giving me shit. You're a fucking bully pal. And that's why he's run off."

"Well, no. Er…"

"Don't answer me back dickhead. I'm not a little fucking kid anymore. I'll break your nose sunny Jim." Mike was squaring up to his old school master. The adrenaline had started to build in Mr Pollard, he was determined to stand his ground, he could not allow Jenkins Senior to intimidate him.

"Right, well, I think I'd better be going..."

"You're not going anywhere 'til you tell me why my lad's run off."

"Really Mr Jenkins, I must leave now." Mr Pollard turned and began returning to his car.

"Yeah, that's it, shit-head, off you go. And if you see Darren, tell him I'm going to break his fucking legs when I get hold of him. Ta ta, knob-head."

Mr Pollard stopped dead. He wasn't having this. Despite his better judgement, he turned back around and walked straight up to Jenkins Snr. He stood, with his face inches away from his aggressor's.

"You know what, you were the most horrible kid I ever taught, out of ten-thousand. Of course I remember you, I could never forget."

Jenkins looked down at the floor. His arse had gone.

Mr Pollard turned again and the door was slammed shut behind him. He hurriedly got into his car, started the engine and pulled out of his parking space and began rattling and vibrating as his car drove down the cobbled street. Tears filled his eyes as he drove, it was the combination of anger, shock, adrenaline and sadness, all in one heavy, sudden dose.

Mr Pollard pulled the car up again once he'd got around the corner at the bottom of the street. The tears began to fall freely and the teacher found himself sobbing like a baby. His mind was filled with thoughts and questions. How could he not have realised that Darren Jenkins was the product of the most impossible kid he'd ever taught? How had he got caught up in alpha-male bullshit with a grown man at his age? Where was Darren? Why hadn't he just read the lad's letter? All these questions were rushing around his head. After a few moments, the tears began to subside and the confusion cleared.

"God, I hated that little bastard!" He began to laugh, as it occurred to him that he would only cry some more if he didn't. A big bubble of snot burst from the teachers nose and he laughed again, wiping away the tears on his sleeve. A few minutes passed, he had calmed down, took stock of the events and regained some sense of reality. Compared to his father, Jenkins junior was an angel. He decided to read his pupil's letter and grabbed it out of his inside pocket where he'd stuffed it after leaving Mrs Houghton's office half-an-hour earlier.

Pretty soon, Mr Pollard was in tears again, as a fuller picture of the boy's life became depressingly clear. Jenkins' letter had made a real connection with him.

But all that had to wait for now, Mr Pollard realised with a start that he needed to update Mrs Houghton. He had a maths class to teach in five minutes. He grabbed a packet of hankies out of the glove-box, wiped his face and blew his nose and tried to regain his composure before phoning the school and asking to speak to Mrs Houghton.

As he waited for the call to connect, it occurred to Mr Pollard that it had been a good thing that he'd not read the letter until now. Coming face to face with Darren's father had made the content read so much more profoundly. The young lad's wise words had hit home and had certainly given the experienced teacher some food for thought. He was nervous as he waited for the head to answer the phone, although he suspected that she was just exercising her authority by leaving Mr Pollard waiting. "Come on!" he said, under his breath as the stupid music-loop played out. Finally, the call connected.

"Mrs Houghton!" she said.

"Hello, it's Phil Pollard."

"Oh, yes. How did you get on?" Mrs Houghton didn't sound particularly interested.

"No sign. I went to his house, he wasn't there. His dad is aware of the situation, although he was making some rather troubling comments. I've had a drive around the area he lives, and the town centre. He's not hanging about town, that's for sure."

"Oh, right." Mrs Houghton didn't sound particularly happy, making Mr Pollard feel, as she always did, somewhat inadequate.

"Thing is, I'm supposed to be teaching in a few minutes. I was wondering if you could organise some cover? I want to keep searching for Darren. I'm quite concerned."

"Well, we don't really…"

"Seriously Mrs Houghton, I'm informing you that I have concerns about Darren's well-being. Can you arrange cover for my class, please?" Mr Pollard was uncharacteristically assertive. Mrs Houghton side-stepped his question.

"What was the father's response?" she asked.

"I'll come to that, but can you organise the cover? Class starts in two minutes."

"Yes. Hold on." Mrs Houghton sounded pretty pissed off with Mr Pollard as she placed him on hold again, reintroducing him to that annoying music. A couple of minutes passed before she recommenced the conversation.

"Okay, Mr Hampson's taking it."

"Thanks."

"So, you were going to tell me what happened with the father?"

"Well, that was a very strange experience. I used to teach Darren's father. I didn't realise at first, but Michael Jenkins was the worst behaved kid we've ever had at this school, certainly in my time."

Mrs Houghton sounded intrigued. "Ah, like father like son, eh?" she said it in quite a relaxed and friendly way, which sounded unusual. "So, what was his response?" she asked, her formal tone brushing away any friendliness that could have been found a few seconds earlier.

"He said that I was a mean old bastard with him when he was a pupil here, so he assumes that I'm being mean on Darren as well."

"And do you think he has a point?" she asked the question in a very matter-of-fact way.

"No. As I say, Jenkins' dad was a different kettle of fish, he was the biggest nightmare we've ever had. He was evil. He was completely different from Darren. I maintain my view that Darren is a nice kid, there's lots to like about him. But his father was genuinely impossible. Not just at school, but in the town as well, he was a one boy crime-wave. He was a bully, a thief, a compulsive liar. Truthfully, he was out of control. In the end, when he was starting the fifth year he started creeping around one of our teacher's houses. Miss Carter she was called."

"What, really?" Mrs Houghton suddenly sounded interested in what Mr Pollard was saying.

"Oh yes. He'd become quite infatuated with her, started hiding in her back yard, spying on her when she was at home. Eventually, he somehow started getting into the house. One night as she was getting changed, she saw him hiding down the side of her bed, lying down on the floor. God knows how she managed to stay calm, but she did and pretended she hadn't seen him. She went downstairs and phoned the police, whispering that there was an intruder upstairs. They grabbed him, and he was sent off to a young offender's unit."

"Good God!" Mrs Houghton was clearly disturbed by what she was hearing.

"Oh, like I say, he was a real piece-of-work. Still is as well, by the looks of things."

"That's turned my blood cold."

"Yes, it was a very difficult time for Miss Carter. Really shook her up, took her a while to fully recover."

"Okay, well I think I've heard enough. If he is aware that Darren has run off from school, the responsibility for the boy's well-being is now back with Mr Jenkins."

The school bell rang out for its familiar five seconds, interrupting the call. Both teachers waited for it to stop before continuing with the conversation.

"Is that it, then?" asked Mr Pollard.

"Until he comes back into school, he's not our problem."

"Can I please request some more time to look for him? I've got a bad feeling about all this, especially after what happened with Johnny."

"Well, we can't really justify..."

"No, no, totally agree. Okay perfect, thanks very much. I'll soon find him and bring him back. Thanks again."

Mr Pollard hung up. He knew that Mrs Houghton had been about to refuse him the extra time that he was requesting. But she could jump in the sea, as far as Mr Pollard was concerned. He didn't care about her, or her ridiculous power-trips. His priority was finding Darren Jenkins and having a good chat with the lad and somehow trying to work out a way to get him one last chance.

And then he just appeared, from around the corner, looking thoroughly miserable and carrying a loaf of bread by his side.

Darren walked straight past the vehicle. He was lost in his own world and hadn't noticed his teacher sat there in the car. Mr Pollard considered beeping the horn at him but thought better of it. Now that he finally had sight of the lad, it would be a bad decision to scare him off. Mr Pollard looked in his rear-view mirror as Darren slowed his pace as he reached the corner of his street. He peeped around the edge of the end-house and quickly pulled his head back. He looked as though he was swearing to himself. Mr Pollard assumed that Darren had seen his dad's car parked outside the house and realised that his plans of watching TV and eating his loaf of bread were in ruins.

Mr Pollard decided to get out of the car. Darren was standing at the corner, leaning against the wall, possibly waiting for his dad to go out, assumed the teacher. He walked up slowly and quietly towards the lad. Darren hadn't sensed his presence, he was, as he so often tended to be, lost in his own thoughts.

"I read your letter." He said, softly to the back of the teenager.

Darren's shoulders stiffened. Then dropped again. He didn't turn around, he just stayed, leant against the wall, with his back to the teacher.

"It made me feel very proud of you. I can't ever remember reading such an honest letter. Its very well written as well, and very mature. It displays a wisdom way beyond your young years, Darren." Mr Pollard was talking quietly, and softly.

Darren turned to face him. He had tears in his eyes.

"Really Sir?" he asked, half-smiling, half-emotionally confused.

"Yes, seriously Darren. It was really, really good. The hand-writing was a bit shitty though."

Darren laughed suddenly, and it forced a big snotter

out of his nose, which he wiped away quickly with his sleeve.

"We need to talk."

Darren looked down at the floor. "We're always talking, it's all we ever do, Sir."

"I know, I know, I get that. But this letter changes everything."

Darren looked up at his teacher again and another tear appeared.

Mr Pollard was fibbing, it wasn't so much the letter that changed everything. It was the knowledge of this poor lad's domestic circumstances that had changed everything. Certainly in Mr Pollard's mind, anyway.

"Come on, get in the car and we'll go and get a McDonalds or something. Whatever you want. Don't forget your loaf."

Part Three

Chapter Thirty-Three

Miller's phone rang. It was Rudovsky.

"Hi Jo."

"Sir, do you love me?"

"What, yes, course I do."

"How much?"

"A lot."

"More than that, please."

"Okay, I love you like an incontinent old Aunty."

"More."

"Okay, I love you like a moody sister."

"No, come on Sir, for fuck's sake..."

"Alright Jo, I love you as much as I love rum n' raisin ice-cream at the seaside on a hot summer's day, and England just won the World Cup."

"Good, that's better, and well, you're going to love me even more than that, now that I've got you Philip Pollard's new mobile phone number."

"You what?"

"Seriously."

There was a silence that lasted way too long. Eventually Miller spoke again. "Well, dip me in dog-shit."

Rudovsky explained the outcome of her interview with Daniel Pollard. Miller was listening with a huge smile on his face. This was a remarkable result and even though Rudovsky seemed keen to take the credit, it had all stemmed from the work of the North Yorks force and before that, Saunders' suspicions of Daniel's sister, Jess.

"This is amazing Jo. What do we know about the phone?"

"I've been onto EE, the network provider. They're running a report now. If it's switched on, they'll be able to identify the nearest mast that it's connected to. If the phone's GPS is switched on, we'll have a location of his exact spot. Just waiting for a call back, so if I hang up on you..."

"Yeah, no worries Jo. Brilliant work mate."

"Well, you know…"

"So, Daniel isn't concerned about Darren's welfare?"

"Nah Sir, not in the slightest. He's more worried about how much trouble he's in!"

"Good. Well, let's prepare for him to be transported over here, get all the paperwork signed off and what have you while you're waiting for EE to get back to you. Is he alright to travel with you and Pete?"

"Yeah, can't see why not. He's not violent and he doesn't smell. I've a sneaking suspicion that he thinks he's Johnny Marr, though."

"Brill. Okay, well get back to me as soon as you've got the details of the phone."

"No problem Sir."

Miller hung up, dialled his number two and recounted the conversation to Saunders.

"Fucking hell!" said the DI.

"You've got that right Keith! Looks like we'll have a location just as soon as the phone operator has got back to Jo."

"That is really cool, Sir. Can I get Jess back in, and let her know?"

"Yes, I think you should. But be careful, we can't charge her just for deleting a few phone records out of her device. So give her the news that Daniel has coughed and try and insinuate that he's dobbed her in as well. Nothing too heavy, her brief will be onto you, just enough to bring out a bit of self-preservation. Judging by the level of phone interaction between them before all this started, I don't think they are particularly close. She might reveal something in a bid to save her arse. I'd like to see her charged, if we can."

"No problem Sir. I'll buzz you back in a bit. Oh, and if you speak to her, tell Jo she'd better fuck off if she's after my job."

Miller laughed loudly. "You mean, tell her you send your congratulations?"

"Yes. Great result that. Speak soon."

*****

"Hello again, Jess." Saunders was smirking, whilst Grant stared down at her paperwork. Jess Pollard's solicitor was glaring at Saunders, but he couldn't care less.

Jess said "Hello." But the greeting lacked warmth and contained a hint of sarcasm.

"Well, have I got news for you?" said Saunders, once the interview was officially reconvened.

Jess Pollard just stared dispassionately ahead.

Saunders continued. "Your brother, the one who's phone calls and text messages you've deleted, has also deleted his phone logs!"

Jess shrugged and stared at the wall behind Saunders' head.

"But it wasn't just your number he was deleting. He's deleted your dad's new number, too."

Still no reaction.

"But the cool thing is, he's had the sense to confess to what he knows, once he realised that the cat was out of the bag."

"Really?" said Jess Pollard, attracting a severe look from her solicitor.

"Yes, really. He's in a lot of trouble you see, assisting an offender, perverting the course of justice, aiding and abetting. So, he's seen the light, and told us everything he knows."

Jess just stared ahead, she had the apathetic expression of a teenager being nagged for not tidying up.

"Everything, Jess, including the content of your communications over the past week. So, you might want to keep that in mind."

"Right, fuck's sake!"

"Now, I must advise you..." The duty solicitor suddenly looked stressed, but Saunders interrupted.

"Your brief is trying to get you to wipe your arse with a broken bottle here, just saying."

Jess shot her solicitor a dirty look. And started talking, it looked as though the scare-mongering tactic was about to pay off.

"This has got nothing to do with me, okay? I didn't ask

to be dragged into it. I told Daniel to leave me out of it. But he kept phoning, telling me what dad was involved with."

"And would you like to tell us what he said that your dad was involved with?"

Jess took a deep breath and started rubbing her eyes. Her solicitor nudged her firmly. She looked at the solicitor, and read the expression. She averted her gaze to Saunders.

"No comment."

*****

"Go on, Jo."

"Hi, okay, just had EE on. The phone has not been picked up on their network since yesterday, at seven minutes past two, fourteen oh seven hours, Sir."

"Switched off?"

"Yes possibly, switched off and battery out, or..."

"Or?"

"The phone is in an area with zero coverage."

"Well that's interesting, there aren't many places that aren't covered these days. Have you got the last known location?"

"Yes, we've got it, Sir. The signal was picked up near Forfar, Scotland."

"Forfar?"

"Sir, it's about fifteen miles north of Dundee."

"Yes, I know where it is Jo. The football team were famous for having the most ridiculous football result ever. What was it, Forfar four, East Fife five!"

Rudovsky didn't appreciate the joke. She was too concerned with the case that she was working on. She completely blanked Miller's sporting anecdote.

"Sir, the phone pinged a mast in Dundee, then another in Forfar, and it lost contact near Northmuir, heading in the direction of Glen Clova."

"Heading north?"

"Yes, Sir."

"What's north of Dundee, Jo?"

"Not sure, the Highlands?"

"Aberdeen."

There was a silence, followed by a heavy sigh. Rudovsky had sussed it. "He's taking Darren home, to his mum."

"Yep. That's my new favourite theory mate! When was this, yesterday afternoon?"

"That's right, Sir."

"Okay, this is sterling work. I'm guessing that they will be in, or around the city of Aberdeen, probably planning to speak to mum."

"EE are going to alert us the moment that number registers back on their network."

"So presumably, in that case, they've not hit Aberdeen yet. Maybe they're still out of network range. Tell you what, Jo, give EE another call and see if they can generate a map of the areas that they don't supply coverage to. It might help."

"No worries, Sir. What are you planning?"

"I don't know, mate. But I think I'd better go and speak to the big cheese."

*****

Miller had taken a map of the Aberdeen area with him to DCS Dixon's office. He wanted to demonstrate the vast expanses of rural landscape in this part of the world.

"As you can see, Sir, this part of Scotland is wild, it's what, ninety-per-cent rural?"

Dixon nodded. The point was easy to understand. Trying to find a specific motorhome here, over many hundreds of square miles of wilderness and rural, one-track roads was going to be a mammoth task, especially when it was the middle of May, and the region was likely to be overwhelmed with holiday-makers in white motor-homes.

"Let's take a deep breath, Andy."

Miller didn't like the sound of this. It was the prerequisite of Dixon throwing a spanner in the works.

"What?"

"If Pollard was in Forfar yesterday morning, then in

reality, he could be anywhere now."

"But, Sir…"

Dixon held his hand up in front of Miller's face, silencing him immediately.

"Let me finish Andy, please." He said.

Miller nodded.

"Now, let's look at this objectively, with a cool head, and we'll arrive at a better conclusion. Agreed?"

Miller nodded. Dixon was right. Miller had learnt this lesson many times. A well planned, fully considered approach always won over an all-guns-blazing, knee-jerk reaction. It was the difference between Neil Young's profound lyrics in his song "Old Man" versus the utter mystery of Donald Trump's late-night "Covfefe…" Tweet.

"Make a brew, Andy. I'll have a coffee, no milk, one sugar."

Miller stood and silently walked out of Dixon's top-floor office and headed for the "hospitality" room a little further along the shiny corridor. He entered the room where the posh filter coffee was already made and waiting to be poured beside fruit bowls and mountains of individually wrapped biscuits and health-food cereal bars. All this was for the bosses and the visiting dignitaries. It certainly wasn't meant for ordinary coppers from the lower-floors.

Miller poured two cups of coffee and put several of the cereal bars in his pocket. There weren't many perks in this job but nicking free snacks off the top-floor was definitely one.

"Here we go," said Miller as he shuffled back into Dixon's office and placed the cups on the desk.

"Very good." Said Dixon, as though it was 1952. "Pass me the map that I've just printed, please." The Detective Chief Superintendent pointed at the printer which Miller was standing next to. The print-out was a map of the UK on A3 paper.

"Just pop it down a minute, let the ink dry. It's a bugger to wash off once you get it on your hands."

Miller looked at his finger-tips. They were green and blue. He smiled at Dixon sarcastically, but the DCS wasn't looking at his DCI. He was reading something on his computer screen.

Eventually, he looked up and gestured for the map.

"Thanks. Okay. Friday last, Pollard went from Manchester to Scarborough, then on Sunday, he was in Llandudno, travelling via York, Skipton and Chester."

Dixon drew two lines onto the map in thick, black marker. The first mark was a straight line, as neither Dixon, nor Miller knew the precise route that Pollard had taken on the first day. The second line was a little more precise. Once he'd finished, he showed Miller the randomness of the first three days of the motorhome's activity. The map suddenly had a large S shape which went from the welsh coast in the west, to the north Yorkshire coast in the east.

"We don't know the route he took on Friday, but we do know that he came back this way." Dixon traced the huge S shape with his finger. "As far as we know, there is no rhyme nor reason for this peculiar route from Scarborough to Llandudno."

"Does there have to be one, Sir?" asked Miller. He didn't look as though he was understanding the point.

Dixon took the tip off his marker and scored a thick, black line along the land between Llandudno and Forfar, half-way up Scotland, creating a large "tick" shape. In this context, Miller began to see how strange the route was. It looked stupid.

"Now, the point I'm trying to make is a simple one, Andy. Pollard doesn't know where he's going, so why the hell would you?"

"Sir, to be fair, we know why he went to Scarborough."

"Yes, I accept that, to pick up the number plates from his son. But the thing I can't understand is this..." Dixon drew another line from Scarborough to Forfar. It was a very neat journey, staying close to the east coast all the way up.

"Do you see?"

"No. What?"

"If his intention was to go to Forfar, then he's gone a pretty strange way. Via Llandudno!" Dixon laughed at his own joke.

Miller stared at the map. It was totally insane. Miller nodded slowly, he knew that his boss had a point.

"Based on this completely random and erratic activity, I

think it would be unwise to assume that Pollard is anywhere near Forfar right now. He's had enough time since yesterday afternoon to be in Brighton, or Cornwall by now." Dixon pointed to the two examples he'd given, on the south-coast of England, locations as far away from Forfar as he could find.

"But the lad's mum lives in Aberdeen, Sir. There's a strong argument for them going up there."

Dixon nodded. "I agree, in theory. But that would contradict this." Dixon retraced the S shape between the east and west coasts. "Not only that, but if Pollard is trying to evade the law, it would be quite foolish to travel anywhere near the boy's mother's address."

Miller blew out an exasperated breath. Dixon was right. It was the first rule of detective work, never try to guess what a crazy person is going to do next.

"Andy my advice is simple. Forget Forfar, or Scotland, or anywhere for the time being. He could be anywhere on this map. As soon as you get your next piece of evidence which points to a location, lets do this exercise again, and see if any kind of pattern is emerging. But for now, we sit tight."

"I agree, Sir, in principle. But we know the new registration plates now. Rudovsky's running an ANPR report off as we speak."

"Good. If she comes up with anything, we'll look at this map again."

"Sir."

"Come on Andy, it's a marathon, not a sprint. You're close to grabbing him. Now is not the time to let rash emotions get in the way of skilfully crafted thoughts."

Miller knew that Dixon was right. It was just a disappointment, feeling that he had Pollard in the net and then realising that he had nothing of the sort.

"Think about that stunt with the tracker device, Andy. For all we know, Pollard might have stuck this phone under a wheel-arch on a truck. There's not enough evidence here to justify travelling up to the Scottish highlands."

"Okay, Sir. I agree."

"We might be talking about this again in five minutes so

put your bottom lip back up near your face, Andy."

Miller stood and left Dixon's office, annoyed that his boss was so calm and collected, and rational. He knew that he needed to work on this skill-set.

As he made his way down the stairs, away from the relative luxury of the top-floor, he felt his phone vibrating in his pocket. He took it out and saw that it was Rudovsky calling.

"Jo." He said.

"Sir, I've been onto the firm that made the new registration plates for Daniel Pollard. Both sets correspond with the two vehicles he was checking out on eBay last Friday afternoon."

"Go on,"

"One of the fake plates has pinged an ANPR camera this morning."

"Where?"

"M6, near Carlisle, south-bound."

This was unbelievable. Miller stopped dead outside the SCIU department's doors. Dixon had been spot-on.

"So, he's heading south now?"

"Yep. Totally. I've looked at the ANPR photo, it's the same vehicle, same markings on the back."

"Could you see the occupants?"

"One male driving, Sir. Looks like Pollard, but its not a HD image. Physical profile looks right, though."

"No sign of Darren?"

"Negative, Sir."

"What time was this Jo?"

"Just after nine."

Miller checked his watch. It was quarter past twelve.

"Shit. He could be anywhere now."

"Anywhere, Sir?" Rudovsky sounded confused.

"Yes. He's just driving around randomly. Could be headed back up the other side of the motorway for all we know."

"Yes, I've got all the ANPR logs since Sunday. He has been all over the place in this motor-home. We've had him in the Peak District, then over to Hull, then he's gone up to

Inverness…"

"Fucking hell."

"Then down to Glasgow, then back over towards Aberdeen yesterday. It looks like he's having a real tour of the north of Britain."

"Jo, I need these reports as soon as you can fire them over."

"Already sent them, they're in your e-mails, Sir."

"Brilliant. Any news on that phone?"

"It's not been switched on since yesterday. I've checked the areas that aren't covered, and there are no black-spots on EE's network in this part of Scotland. So, the conclusion that EE have come to is that its switched off and the battery has been removed, otherwise it would have pinged a mast."

"Right. Okay. This seems to get weirder by the minute, but the nets closing in now we have that new registration plate."

"Yes, and the minute Pollard turns his phone on, we'll have his precise location."

"In theory…"

"What do you mean by that, Sir?"

"Oh, Dixon's got me paranoid. He's put it in my head that the phone might be stuck under a truck, to send us off the smell."

"He's talking shit. How could a phone with no battery attached to it send anyone off a smell. He's talking bollocks."

"Would you say that to his face?"

"No."

"Didn't think so."

"But trust me. He's chatting shit Sir. That phone will either be switched on again, or it won't."

"Oh, that's a compelling thought Jo!"

"Well what I mean is, he'll turn it on when he needs to, or, he's chucked it away. If he's put the radio on in that motor-home, he'll know about Daniel and Jess being arrested. So he might have chucked the phone."

"Yes, the thought crossed my mind too. Anyway, get your arse back over here with Pete and your prisoner. I want a chat with him."

"We're just going through the transfer paperwork. The custody sergeant's being a bit of a jobsworth about it all."

"Okay, tell him to phone me if he doesn't pull his finger out. I'll threaten him with a phone call off the Chief Constable."

"No worries. Alright, keep your phone on, EE have got me on speed-dial."

"Cool. On your way over here, give Darren's mum a call, see if she knows what the hell is going on."

"It's on my to-do-list."

"What else is on it?"

"Well, one of the things was to have fish and chips on the front."

"Sack that. But if we get a positive result on this job, I'll take all of the team to Llandudno for a chippy tea, and a few pints. I owe a big favour to the manager of Wetherspoons. We'll have a laugh."

"Deal."

"Brill. See you in a couple of hours."

Part Four

"Come on, Darren, just get in the car."

"I don't want to go back to school, Sir. What's the point? Just to sit through a lecture and then get expelled."

"I know. I agree with you. I just said, I'll take you to McDonalds."

"KFC?"

"If you like. I want to talk to you about your essay." Well'ard held open the passenger door, and Darren walked solemnly towards him. He got in.

"Good lad," said Mr Pollard as he closed the door. Darren just sat there with his school-bag between his feet. He was clutching his loaf of bread on his lap.

"Were you planning on feeding the ducks?" said the teacher as he got in the passenger seat and clipped his seat-belt. Darren ignored the comment, and just stared out of the window.

"Stick your belt on, mate."

Darren reached over his shoulder and grabbed the buckle, clipping it into the slot without a word.

Mr Pollard turned the key and started driving the car slowly away. He recognised that encouraging this frosty silence was the best idea. He knew that Darren would snap out of this bad mood soon enough, but not if he was being nagged.

"Where's the nearest one?" he asked, gently. He knew, of course, but he thought that he'd divert Darren's thoughts for a minute or so.

"Ashton, I think."

"Ashton? What in the town-centre?"

"No, it's... do you know where the cinema is?"

"I don't, I hardly go into Ashton. Last time I went to the pictures in Ashton it was the Metro. Loved that place."

"It's hard to tell you because I just get the tram there. But its like down from IKEA."

"Oh, got you! I know now, Ashton Moss. They've got a Frankie and Benny's and a Five Guys there as well, haven't they?"

"Yeah, and McDonalds."

"No problem. I know where I'm going now. Leave this to me!"

Mr Pollard continued driving, heading through Dukinfield, past the Morrisons supermarket.

"I remember when this was a great big cotton mill, here." He said as he waited at the traffic lights. Darren didn't seem too excited by the observation. Mr Pollard decided to continue talking anyway. He'd seen that Darren was beginning to mellow, so decided to carry on with the distraction tactic.

"It was gigantic, had about a thousand employees. All these houses you can see were built by the mill owner, and the staff worked there 6 days a week, then paid half of their wage back to the mill for their rent. The Victorian mill owners were an unscrupulous bunch!"

Darren didn't say anything. He just sat there quietly.

"There's a photo of the mill, just inside the doors in Morrisons." Mr Pollard sounded as though he was really interested in what he was saying.

"Sir, are you in the team for the boring Olympics?"

Mr Pollard looked at Darren and laughed loudly.

"You cheeky little sod! I'm not boring!"

"No Sir, definitely not. Everything you just said was fascinating. Truly." Darren pretended to yawn and made Mr Pollard laugh again.

"Well, okay, maybe I am a bit boring. But I'm not Olympic medallist standard."

"Oh, you are. Trust me. Gold medal, Sir. No question."

Mr Pollard laughed again. Darren's dead-pan delivery was even funnier than the brutal insult. Once he'd stopped laughing at Darren's outrageously cheeky comments, Mr Pollard decided to stay quiet and leave the history lesson out. But Darren seemed happy enough with the reaction he'd received. He kept sniggering at himself.

"You think you're funny, don't you?"

"Well, you laughed!"

"True. I'll give you that, you're a good comedian."

"Thank you. I try my best."

"Do you know something, a weird thing I was reading

the other day?"

"Oh my God, this isn't about a mill is it?"

"No. It was about comedians, it was saying that all the best comedians were always in trouble at school for joking around. I was just thinking about it, how they've become millionaires and hugely successful celebrities. I bet their teachers must be gutted when they see them on telly now. Or if they get the DVD for Christmas. I bet it really hurts!"

Darren seemed interested in this. "Like who?"

"Oh, loads."

"Peter Kay?"

"No, not sure about him. He went to Uni, so I doubt it. But have you heard of Russell Brand?"

"Yeah. Course I have."

"He was always in trouble at school. What about Kevin Bridges, do you know him?"

"Aw yeah, the Scottish guy, he's proper funny."

"He was expelled from school."

"Really?"

"Yes."

"Have you heard of Frank Skinner?"

"No, I don't think so…"

"You know that song that comes out whenever England are playing, Three Lions?"

"Yeah, course."

"That's Frank Skinner, and his mate David Baddiel. They were the biggest TV stars in the 90s."

"Wasn't born then, Sir!"

"No, no, I bet you weren't."

"No, Sir, I actually wasn't. I was born in the year 2002."

"God. A year after nine eleven. That makes me feel old."

"You are old."

"Alright, bloody hell. Anyway, the point is, Frank Skinner is a comedian, and another one who was expelled from school. There's so many of them. It was a really interesting article."

"Sir, if you're trying to tell me that I've been expelled, in a nice way, I'm not bothered. Like I put in the essay, I just want to leave anyway. I can't stand the thought of another year of this bullshit!"

"Well, listen, if it did come to that, you'd be joining a pretty cool bunch of stars. People like Adele. She was expelled, the most successful British female singers of all time! So was Lily Allen."

"Honestly? Darren looked shocked.

"Ever heard of Eric Clapton? You might be a bit young to know who he is. He was expelled."

"Yeah, I know him Sir."

"There's loads of mega-stars who were expelled from school. Stephen Fry was. Amy Winehouse. Cheryl Cole. Lewis Hamilton. Who's the cleverest bloke you've ever heard of?"

"Albert Einstein?"

"Correct. Expelled."

"Shut up!"

"Seriously. Albert Einstein was expelled from loads of schools."

"You're making this up!"

"Who's the richest bloke you can think of?"

"Richard Branson."

"Expelled."

"Shut up. You're blagging my head Sir!"

"Honestly. You know that Ed Sheeran?"

"Course."

"He couldn't stand school, just like you. He walked out at fifteen."

"Right, wait a minute Sir. You've spent the last four years warning me that I need to behave better or I'll get expelled and my life will be over and today you're telling me that basically everyone who is doing well in life was expelled!"

Mr Pollard didn't reply, he was concentrating on his driving as he negotiated a round-about on the outskirts of Ashton. Once he had got around and into the correct lane, he apologised for his sudden loss of conversation.

"Sorry, I hate that roundabout. I always get in the wrong lane. Anyway, sorry, what you were saying... oh, about leaving school, like Ed Sheeran did?"

"Yes, I'm done, Sir."

"Thing is though, Darren, you've got to go, until you finish year eleven. They're the rules of the law."

"I know, I know, but if school want me out anyway, it just... it makes sense doesn't it? Like what you were saying about Mr Briggs yesterday. Doesn't make sense to keep me there, doing everyone's head in, making Mr Briggs lose his job. Here it is, here on the left."

Mr Pollard started indicating as the KFC sign suddenly dominated the view.

"Ah, brilliant. I'm starving."

"Same!"

"Have you had your breakfast?"

"Nah."

"What are you having?" asked Mr Pollard as he pulled into the car park.

"I'll just have some chips, and popcorn chicken please Sir."

Mr Pollard locked the car and caught up with Darren who was already by the entrance of the fast-food restaurant. The smell of fried chicken filled the air.

"Ah, smell that! That's the best smell, Sir!"

"Yeah, my mouth's watering." Darren held the door open for his teacher. "Cheers. So, what do you want, popcorn chicken and a portion of fries?"

"Yes please, Sir."

"Is that it?"

"Yes, thank you."

"Alright, grab a seat, I'll be back in a minute. What drink do you want?"

"I'm alright, thanks."

Darren went to find a seat whilst Mr Pollard went to the counter. He felt sad for the boy, just asking for popcorn chicken and chips. Both items were off the budget menu. And he'd obviously felt cheeky asking for a drink. The polite gesture touched Mr Pollard.

Several minutes later Mr Pollard walked across to the

table with a tray stacked up with food.

"Flippin' heck Sir! Are you hungry?"

"Ha, don't be cheeky. It's not all for me, you moron." The teacher started passing food across the little table to Darren.

"There you go, chicken zinger tower burger, fries, corn on the cob, and a hot wing! Side of beans, side of gravy. Oh, and your popcorn chicken. Here you go."

"Sir, you shouldn't... thanks, but..." Darren looked embarrassed by his teacher's generosity.

"It's a special deal or something that they're doing today. Order popcorn chicken and you get a free zinger tower box meal. I think that's what the guy said, anyway." Mr Pollard had a mischievous look on his face but avoided eye contact as he grabbed his own food from the tray. "Oh, and a free Coke as well. You might as well have it, I don't drink that rubbish."

"Thanks Sir."

"Hey, don't thank me. Thank the Colonel."

"Come on Sir, I'm not a total nugget. Thanks a lot, it's nice of you."

Mr Pollard made eye contact with Darren and smiled. "I bet you won't remember this, but I've owed you lunch for about four years now." Mr Pollard opened the tub of gravy and gestured Darren to help himself.

"No. What do you mean?" Darren looked puzzled by the statement.

"You were in year seven, and I had you for maths, it was period before dinner and I'd let it slip that I'd forgotten my lunch. You stayed behind after class and offered me half of your sandwich. Do you remember?"

Darren laughed. "God, yeah, I do now."

"Do you remember what I said to you?"

"No. Not really, Sir."

"I said that it was very kind of you and I said that out of thirty-two kids in the class, you were the only one who stayed back to offer me some lunch."

Darren bit into his huge chicken burger and smiled as he chewed.

"Can you not remember? I told you that you've got a very kind heart, and that you should never lose that quality. And as I've watched you growing up, I've seen you acting like a right pain the backside. But you've still got a heart of gold."

Darren looked a bit embarrassed. He wasn't comfortable with receiving praise. It didn't happen very often.

"So, thanks for sharing your sandwich with me that day. It was horrible, though."

Darren laughed and a bit of his bun flew out of his mouth, which made him laugh again.

"I hate cheese! I was gutted when I bit into it! I thought 'oh no, what have I accepted for my lunch!'"

Darren was laughing loudly and Mr Pollard joined in. Eventually, they calmed down and got on with their meals.

"Anyway, I owe you an apology, about this morning..."

"No, Sir, forget it. Doesn't matter now."

"Yes, it does matter. I was NGAB."

Darren looked completely thrown.

"Bang out of order, I should have seen how much it meant to you. I could have just sat down and read it. But I was being an arsehole."

"It's fine."

"It's not fine. It's far from fine mate. You're facing loads of trouble now, for breaking that door and running off from school. We're probably talking about expulsion, and it will be my fault. It's totally out of order, and I'm really sorry."

"Shit happens, Sir."

Mr Pollard bit into his burger and nodded. He spent a few moments chewing, and he looked lost in thought.

"Yes, that's true. Shit does happen. I'm going through my own difficulties at the moment. I think that's why I was being such a toe-rag this morning."

Darren looked a little embarrassed. He wasn't sure how to respond to his teacher talking about real life stuff. It wasn't normal to have a window into a teacher's world.

"Thing is, we've got a lot in common. You're not the only one who wants to leave Astley High. Obviously, don't say nowt to any of your mates. That Michael Donnelly you go around with has got a right mouth on him!"

Darren laughed. It was true, but it just sounded weird hearing Well'ard saying it.

"But yeah, I tried to leave, at the end of this year. But the education authority wouldn't let me. So, I'm stuck there, and if I have to stay, you can bloody well stay with me!"

A silence filled the space between the two people. It felt uncomfortable for them both. Darren thought of a question to ask, just to plug the awkward silence.

"Why do you want to leave?" he asked.

"Well, that's a good question! You should ask my wife that. She's the one who wants me to leave. Oh, it doesn't matter."

"No, go on, Sir."

Mr Pollard ate some of his fries as he considered the question. Darren had opened up to him, so he decided to reward that openness, and share a little from his own private life.

"Well, our kids have grown up now. And, well, she says I care more about my job than I do about her. It's funny really, because she's always been proud of how hard I worked. Anyway, we've separated. But she said she'll have me back if I take early retirement. I went round there last night to open the letter from the education. I gave it to her and she read it out. It said that I'd been unsuccessful in my application for redundancy. So, she slung me out!"

"No way. Bad times."

"Yes, you're right there. And, I suppose I was still angry about it this morning and took it all out on you. I'm really sorry, Darren."

"Like I say Sir. Doesn't matter. I'll become a comedian!"

"You probably will mate. You probably will. But now I'm worried about your dad."

"My dad?" Darren suddenly looked stressed.

"Yes. I'm afraid I had to go round to your house..."

"He's a knob-head, Sir."

Mr Pollard laughed loudly at the young lad's cutting remark, it had come from nowhere.

"Seriously, he is. He doesn't give a toss about me. He hates me. That's why I'm…"

Suddenly Mr Pollard was the one who looked stressed.

"That's why you're what?"

Darren shrugged.

"Talk to me, Darren. What were you about to say?"

The difficult silence descended again. Eventually, Darren thought of his options and decided that there was no point holding back. He just came out with it.

"I'm running away."

Mr Pollard put the last piece of his tower burger into his mouth and started chewing. He used the time to process the information and to think of something constructive to say. It took him a while to think of the words, but once he did, he came straight to the point.

"Do you know what, under the circumstances, I can totally understand you arriving at this decision."

That wasn't the statement that Darren had expected to hear from Well'ard, his face made it obvious.

"However, it is possibly the worst idea you could have had."

This dismissive remark put Darren on the defensive.

"Why, what choice have I got? Go home and get battered off my dad, then get kicked out of school, and get battered again? Then be stuck in the house with that bastard every day? Seriously, Sir. You don't know what it's like." Darren looked angry, and sad. All of the light-hearted fun from the past few minutes was long forgotten as Darren faced the bleak reality of his situation.

"Listen, mate, I'm not disagreeing with you." Mr Pollard desperately wanted to share his views about Darren's dad and talk about his experiences, both historical, and more recently, an hour or so ago. But he had to be professional. He needed to neutralise Darren's mood first. There would be no point talking to him whilst he was feeling like this.

Mr Pollard thought he had a great diversion. "Have you ever heard of the eighteenth-century saying "softly softly catchee monkey."

Darren shook his head sombrely.

"In modern language, I imagine that it translates as 'chillax blud, get out of my grill, and everything will be sick, you get me?"

Darren tried to laugh, but it was borne from politeness rather than genuine humour. Mr Pollard read the signs and continued.

"The thing is, half of the problems that you have come from making quick decisions. As you get older, you'll realise that you need to slow that impulsiveness down. You'll get that eventually. But I need you to trust me on this, just running off and hoping for the best might seem like a good idea now. But after a couple of days of sleeping in doorways, and old blokes offering you a bit of money for sex, you'll realise that you've made a mistake."

"I'll tell them to fuck off, Sir!"

"Yes, I'm sure you will Darren. I have no doubt about that. I'm just saying, you don't need to find out. We can work out a better plan than just setting off and hoping things will work out."

Darren looked at Mr Pollard and maintained eye contact. "Sir, I appreciate what you're saying. But I've got to go. I just don't know why you're being so nice. I've been nothing but a pain in your arse since I started at Astley High."

"Listen, you've not…"

"Sir, I know I have been a pain. But I've never meant to. None of it, I don't walk to school in the morning thinking 'oh I know, I'll try and annoy the teachers today and end up in Well'a… in Mr Pollard's office. I just can't help it. I can't behave, I can't sit still, I can't learn anything. I just want to get off Sir, I've had enough of everything."

Mr Pollard stayed quiet. He had listened and now he was considering the words that his pupil had shared. He remained silent for a minute, looking out of the window and watched as one of the big yellow trams went past, heading towards the town-centre.

Finally, Mr Pollard spoke. "Tell you what, let's talk this over properly, later. If you don't want to go home, or come back to school, then I can let you chill at my flat for a few hours. Then, when I've finished school, I'll come home and we can talk this thing through properly. It will give me a few hours to think things over and look into what options we have."

Darren didn't look too impressed. It was obvious to Mr Pollard that he just wanted to get going with his loaf of bread and start this exciting adventure.

"Come on Darren, please, do this for me. What time is it now?" The teacher checked his watch. It was 11.30. "Right, by the time I drop you off at mine, then get myself back to school, we'll be talking about three hours, and I'll be back, and I'll have a few ideas. And if you really want to do it, just get away from everything, at least I'll know that I've tried my best to talk to you about things first."

"There's no point, though..."

"Well lets just wait and see. I might be able to sort you out with a place to stay through Social Services, or through the council. At least let me try, let me see what options are open."

In the back of Mr Pollard's mind were two unsatisfactory outcomes to this. First was the prospect of Darren going home, and taking a beating off his dad, if not something far worse. As far as the teacher could read the situation, Darren's other option was to head off to a life on the streets. For all the shit that Darren had given Mr Pollard through the years, he liked the kid, always had, and if he was honest, he liked Darren Jenkins even more now that he knew what kind of a nasty bastard he lived with.

"Like you said in your essay, Darren. No matter what you try to do, it all seems to go wrong. There's no reason to believe that this trend is going to alter now when you head off into the night with nothing. So, will you come and sit at mine for a few hours? And I promise you, I'll have some good news for you when I get back."

Darren smiled warily. He didn't like feeling as though he was taking advantage, and he hated feeling as though he owed a favour. As far as he was concerned, Mr Pollard had every right to just laugh at him and the latest stupid position he found himself in. After all, this wasn't Well'ard's fault. It was his, and his alone.

"Come on mate, don't turn down a good offer. I've got Netflix on my telly."

Darren smiled. Seemingly, Netflix had swung the deal. "Right, nice one Sir. Cheers."

"Good lad. Right, come on, finish your Coke and let's make a move."

Darren drained the cup, making a loud slurping sound as he sucked up the last of the pop.

A few minutes later they were heading back towards Stalybridge.

"Can you remember some of those people I mentioned earlier? The ones who got expelled?"

"Yes." Said Darren.

"Go on then, what were they called?"

"Well, there was Amy Winehouse, Lily Allen. That guy who sings Three Lions, Ed Sheeran, Richard Branson. Oh aye, Eric Clapton. Einstein!"

"Not bad. Can you remember any of the others?"

"Kevin Bridges!" said Darren. He seemed pleased with himself.

"Good. And if you managed to learn that piece of useless information today, then that proves your theory wrong that you can't learn anything. Doesn't it?"

"Sir."

"You see, its not that you can't learn. You just learn differently from everybody else in the class. Just try and remember that."

"Yes, Sir."

"What can you tell me about this supermarket we're going to go past in a few minutes?"

"It used to be a mill."

"How many staff worked there?

"A thousand."

"See! You can learn. Oh Lord above us! Thank you for this gift! It's a miracle!" Mr Pollard raised his hands to heaven, leaving the steering wheel unattended.

Darren laughed. Mr Pollard had completely lost the plot, and it was genuinely funny. He'd never seen Well'ard acting stupid like this, and it really tickled him.

"You're worse than me for acting the goat, Sir!"

As Mr Pollard's car approached Stalybridge, the mood inside calmed down a little, as the seriousness of this bizarre situation caught up on the teacher.

"Okay, let's get something clear. I'm going to tell Mrs Houghton that I haven't been able to find you. It will buy us a bit of time to sort this mess out. But you must stay at my flat, don't go out or anything, it's vitally important. There's some stuff to make a brew, and there's stuff to make a butty."

"I'm totally stuffed, Sir! Won't want anything more to eat until tomoz."

"Yes, I must admit I could do with a nap after all that KFC! Just promise me that you'll stay inside?"

"Scout's honour, Sir."

"And don't be putting it about on Facebook that you're chilling at Well'ard's on your phone."

"I haven't got one."

"Well, if you just stay at mine for a few hours, and keep your nose clean, I might sort you out with my old i-phone, I got upgraded to the latest one a few months ago. I'm only going to throw the old one. Seems a waste as it works fine."

"No way. Thanks Sir."

"If you do as I say!"

"I will."

"Good lad."

Mr Pollard arrived at his flat and stepped out of the car quickly. Darren was right behind him and followed as his teacher walked speedily around the back of a row of houses, through a gate, and up a metal staircase. Mr Pollard opened the door and waved Darren inside.

"Right," said Mr Pollard as he closed the door behind himself. "Kitchen, front-room, my bedroom's through there and the bathroom is through that door. The TV remote is on the bookcase. See you in a few hours."

*****

Mr Pollard arrived home at 4pm. Although he had told Darren that he was going back to school, he'd had second thoughts and had stayed in his car at the end of the street, keeping an eye out for Darren running off again. He'd been concerned that Darren would give in to his impulsive nature and go off to start his running away adventure. Mr Pollard had felt that it was a big risk, especially as Darren's mood had been so volatile earlier. He wanted to be on hand and try and stop him if he did try and make a run for it. Work could sod off, as far as the teacher was concerned.

The teacher had spent the time in his car productively, ringing around the council, the Citizen's Advice Bureau, the local homeless charities and social services. Although his calls had been fruitless, he was in a great mood, mainly because the youngster had kept his word, and stayed put in the flat.

"Alright Darren?"

"Sir!"

"Not been rooting have you?"

"No Sir."

"Really? You can't beat a good root in somebody else's house! I'd have been in all the drawers at your age." Mr Pollard laughed as he filled the kettle with water.

"Do you want a brew?"

"Yeah, go on then. Cheers."

"What do you have?"

"Tea two, ta."

Mr Pollard made the drinks and went through into the front room and placed them down on the coffee table. Darren took the remote control off the table and muted the programme he'd been watching. He was sat upright, his hands clasped on his lap, looking quite tense. Mr Pollard smiled, imagining how he would have been sprawled out all over the settee just minutes earlier. He had very good manners, for all of his academic faults.

"So..." said Mr Pollard, "we've got a situation here. I've phoned Social Services, don't worry I haven't named you, or identified you in any way. But I asked them what options there are for a fifteen-year-old lad who is facing permanent exclusion from school and the potential for a beating off his dad. Do you know what they said?" Mr Pollard looked serious. He had very kind, gentle eyes when he was being nice, and very scary, intimidating eyes when he was being horrible. Today, he was being nice.

"Don't know Sir. Did they say it's my own fault?"

"No, not quite. They said that due to your age, they have no powers of intervention until a crime has been reported. What that basically means is that they won't be able to do anything until after your dad has beaten you up."

Darren didn't look particularly shocked or surprised. "Nah, I didn't think they'd do out. They don't care about teenagers. It's all about the little kids. That's the way it should be, anyway."

"I asked them what the situation would be if your dad did beat you up. They said that they would take advice from the police and do their own assessments. Whilst all this was going on, they'd secure you accommodation in a kid's home, or in temporary foster-care."

Darren didn't say anything.

"What do you think about that?"

"Not a lot."

"You don't think that's an option?"

"What, get battered off my dad so I can get put in a home full of knob-heads? I'm good, thanks." Darren smiled, he wasn't being ungrateful, he really appreciated Mr Pollard going to all this trouble on his behalf. But it was apparent that he thought that this was a shit idea.

"Obviously, I wouldn't send you down there to get beaten up. But he has done it before, hasn't he?"

Darren stiffened up and looked down at his lap. It was obvious from his sudden change in body language that he was uncomfortable with this conversation. Mr Pollard recognised the signs. Abused kids were remarkably loyal to their abusers, and it was this fact which allowed, often encouraged, further abuse.

It was time to change the tune.

"Anyway, that's what I found out... not much!" Mr Pollard leaned forward and grabbed his brew off the coffee-table. He thought he saw a tear forming in Darren's eye, but didn't stare, he didn't want to invade the lad's privacy. He took a sip of his brew and cursed the temperature as it burnt his lip.

"I'm sure you told me that you were going up to live with your mum when you left school?"

Darren wiped his eyes casually with his sleeve.

"That's what's happening, Sir. But that's a year away."

"What if I can arrange a new school for you, up there? I'm sure I could. I could explain your situation, everything that's gone on, with your Johnny, and your mum leaving and everything."

"I can't Sir. Dad's threatened mum with all sorts if I go and live with her. He's saying its all about my education, but mum says its just about control. He said that if I move up there, he'll come and burn the house down while we're all in bed. He's said all sorts, like he'll kill himself, and he'll kill my grandad." Darren was filling up again. Mr Pollard really felt for the lad. He shouldn't be carrying this shit around with him at this age. He should be enjoying the best days of his life. Instead, he was living an utterly miserable existence with a nasty, sadistic bully, and being used as a pawn in Michael Jenkins twisted game of emotional chess.

"Right, mate. Listen to me. I can't stand the thought of you going out there and trying to make the best of this situation by running away from home..."

"But Sir,"

"Hold on a minute mate, let me finish. I can't just let you walk out there knowing, because I'm a boring old fart, what dangers you will face on the streets. And I can't let you go back to your dad's knowing he's going to take his unhappiness out on you again. So, we've got a real dilemma here."

"Thing is though, Sir. When I run away, dad's always alright with me for a week or two afterwards."

"Well what you're saying there is that you'll run away, but come back in a few days?"

Darren shrugged. It was obvious that his plan was quite relaxed. He didn't have a clue what he was planning.

"I'm just... I don't know. I get excited when I think about just setting off."

"What, as though you're going on holiday?" Mr Pollard smiled affectionately.

"I don't know Sir. Never been on holiday. Not a proper holiday. Apart from going to stay with Granny and Grandad." Darren took his brew off the table and took a sip, nodding appreciatively. "Good brew that, Sir."

Mr Pollard laughed. "Cheers. Right, I've got some stuff to sort out, a few more enquiries to make. I'll go through to my bedroom and let you watch your programme in peace."

Chapter Thirty-Four

Donna Moran, the owner of Tameside Camper Hire couldn't believe her eyes, as she looked out of her office window. She gasped at the extraordinary sight before her. Her missing motor-home, the subject of a national police hunt, was pulling up on the forecourt outside.

Her heart was suddenly thumping hard in her chest. She knew the vehicle, she knew every sticker, every curve, every detail on it. This was the pride of her fleet, and despite it having different number-plates, she knew that it was hers. It was home, and it looked as though it was in immaculate condition.

This had not been the outcome she'd been expecting. In fact, the thought of seeing this vehicle in one piece again had not crossed her mind since Wednesday night, when she'd phoned the detectives who were searching for the missing teacher.

Donna grabbed her mobile phone off her desk, and scrolled through her call log, looking for DI Saunders' number. A fear had gripped her. Her finger was shaking noticeably as she pressed Saunders' phone number and then the "call" icon. It took a second to connect.

"Hi Donna. Everything alright?" said Saunders.

"He's here. Just parking up now."

There was a silence that lasted a few seconds longer than it should have. Clearly, the detective she'd been dealing with on this had been taken by surprise, too.

"Pollard?"

"Yes. I've got to go."

Donna hung up and stood up to look through the side-window of her little office. Pollard was getting out of the motor-home.

*****

"Hi Keith."

"Sir, Pollard's just turned up at the camper hire place."

"What?"

"That's what I said as well. He's just arrived."

"Mate, is this a joke?"

"No. I'm still in Ashton, I'm on my way there now with Helen, it's only up the road. Can you organise the response?" It was clear from Saunders' voice that he was in the middle of a major adrenaline rush.

"Yes, yes, on it. Cheers."

Miller hung up and tried to take stock of the enormity of that phone call. There were so many questions suddenly revolving in his head. Was Darren with Pollard? That was the first, and loudest of the questions.

He dialled Dixon. "Sir, It's Miller. Pollard has just turned up at the Tameside Camper Hire shop, it's on Huddersfield Road, Carrbrook. Please get onto control and tell them to send the nearest officers, I'm on my way now." Miller hung up and ran out of the office, shouting Chapman and Worthington to follow.

"Get over to Tameside Camper Hire, business premises, on the hurry up!" He shouted as ran.

*****

Rudovsky was sitting in the back of the CID car with Daniel Pollard, as Kenyon drove back from the Yorkshire coast. They were on the top of the Pennines, high above Greater Manchester. She was bored, as she looked out of the car window at the weird old farm-house that the motorway split into two to swerve around.

"Stubborn fucker!" she muttered as a smile crossed her lips at the thought of the old farmer who'd refused to sell his land to the developers. He'd won his argument but was trapped in-between two of the busiest motorway carriageways in Great Britain. Rudovsky loved this story, because she knew that she'd probably have stayed put, too, and eventually died from smugness and tinnitus from the trucks passing by non-stop in the front and back garden.

Rudovsky wanted to relay the story to her prisoner, but she thought better of it as he was in a right mood. Daniel Pollard seemed furious, he couldn't believe all this fuss.

Rudovsky's phone began vibrating in her pocket.

"Hello, DC Jo Rudovsky speaking."

"Oh, hi Jo, it's Dawn. Darren's mum?"

"Yes, hi, what's... is everything okay?"

"Yes, fine, I'm just ringing to let you know that he's here. He's just walked through the door."

Rudovsky was stunned. That had come from nowhere.

"I... you, are you talking about Darren?"

"Yes, he's here, he's fine."

"In Aberdeen?"

"Yes, that's right. Okay, just thought I'd let you know."

"Wait, where's Pollard?"

"I don't know. I've not really found out what's going on, I must go. I'll phone you back in a few minutes."

Rudovsky moved the phone from her ear and stared at it. "What the fuck..." she muttered, as she pressed the screen and dialled Miller.

*****

"Hi, look, sorry about everything that's been going on." Philip Pollard was walking, quite casually, towards Donna. She was standing on the step, outside her office. She couldn't speak, she was rooted to the spot, holding onto the metal hand-rail. He was acting normal, and she just couldn't figure out how she was supposed to react. This was Britain's most-wanted man, casually walking towards her with a cheerful smile on his face.

"I imagine you've called the police. But before they arrive, I'd just like to settle up with you. I owe you some money for a new tracker, and you'll need to change the number-plates back. The original ones are in the cupboard under the sink." He was still smiling, and he looked as calm, and as trustworthy as he had done when he'd turned up a week earlier and paid cash to hire the motor-home and left a £1500 deposit with his bank card.

Donna didn't say anything, she was speechless.

"I bet this is a shock. But listen, you've no need to worry. Your motor-home is in excellent condition. We've looked after it well for you."

"What's... where's the kid?" Donna managed to speak, though her voice sounded strange and wobbly, through the fear.

"Oh, he's at his mum's, up in Aberdeen. He's fine, don't worry. It's not like they were saying in the papers." Mr Pollard had a really kind, gentle expression on his face.

The faint sound of police sirens could be heard in the distance.

"So, do you want to settle up? In fact, do you know what, just keep the deposit. That will more than cover the cost of a new tracker, and to pop those plates back on. Think of what's left as compensation for stressing you out."

Mr Pollard stepped forward and handed the key to Donna, before turning and heading over towards the wall by the entrance to the forecourt. He sat down on the wall and waited as the police sirens got louder.

Donna went into her office and locked the door.

Chapter Thirty-Five

Philip Pollard's arrest had been straight-forward enough. As the first police officers arrived in a panda car, he stood up from his seated position on the wall and extended his hands for the cuffs. He was searched and placed in the back of the police car, where he waited unceremoniously for a couple of minutes, before a police van arrived at the scene.

The disgraced teacher was led quietly from the car, to the van, and officers were just closing the internal cage door as Saunders and Grant arrived.

The DI parked dramatically in the middle of the busy road and leapt out of the driver's seat. The police constables were just about to lock the back doors of the van when he arrived.

"Is it him?"

"Yes, Sir." Said the police officer.

"Let me see."

The back doors of the police van were opened, and Saunders leant his head in.

"Where's Darren?" was all he asked of the prisoner.

"He's with his mum."

"Definitely?" asked Saunders, looking a little thrown by that straight-forward response.

"Yes. He just text me, five minutes before I pulled in here. The officer who arrested me has got my phone. It's the only number on it."

"Right. And is he okay?"

"Darren? Yes, of course."

Saunders hadn't been prepared for Philip Pollard's calm and helpful manner. It surprised him, and he wasn't sure how to react, just as Donna had struggled to find the correct manner ten minutes earlier.

"Right. Cheers." Saunders turned to the police constable who was standing beside him. "Alright, take him in."

The back doors were slammed shut once again and the police van drove away, it's siren blaring as it headed up Huddersfield Road, headed for Ashton police station three miles away. Saunders noticed that the police presence had grown quite considerably and neighbours were starting to gather across the road, trying to find out what was happening.

"There's been a crash."

"No, it was an armed robbery at the caravan place."

An attractive young mum walked across the road and headed for the nearest police officer. "Hi, I'm Claire, I live up there. This is my son, Alfie." The young lad smiled warmly at the police officer. "Has someone been stabbed?" she asked.

"No, it's the missing teacher, he just brought the motor-home back!" It was as though the copper couldn't believe it either. Claire and Alfie headed back across the road to share the news with the local community.

Shortly after the nosey-neighbour had left, Miller arrived. He was disappointed to learn that Pollard had been taken away already. He listened to Saunders assessment of the situation, before going across to see Donna in her office. She described Pollard's weird manner, him talking as though he'd just got back from a lovely week in Skegness, not a week on the run, being hunted by every police force in the UK.

It was a weird one, no question. But Miller was happy that it had come to this conclusion. After all, less than 48 hours ago he had been combing the cliffs of North Wales in the chopper, looking for bodies. It was looking like a good result.

*****

Miller and Saunders were sitting in interview room 3 at Ashton police station, just an hour after Pollard had turned up at Tameside Camper Hire.

Philip Pollard looked relaxed but there was something else about his demeanour that Miller couldn't quite put his finger on.

"Okay, Philip Pollard you have been arrested on suspicion of child abduction, you do not have to say anything, but it may harm your defence if you do not mention when questioned something which you later rely on in court. Anything you do say may be given in evidence. I should warn you at this stage that we are investigating this case thoroughly, and we expect that we will be pressing multiple charges, once the investigation has been concluded."

"Yes, I understand." Said the teacher, nodding confidently, as though this was a business meeting.

"You've refused the offer of a solicitor. Do you understand that you are advised to take legal advice, before you proceed with this interview?"

"Yes, I understand. But it's fine. I don't need anybody."

"Okay. Well, DI Saunders, my colleague here will now ask you some questions relating to the abduction of Darren Jenkins."

"Yes, that's fine."

"Can you confirm that you abducted Darren Jenkins on the morning of Thursday 16th May?"

"No comment."

Saunders and Miller looked at one another. That wasn't in the script. They both turned their heads back towards Pollard who was sitting straight across the desk from them.

"Can you confirm that Darren Jenkins has been with you for the past eight days?"

"No comment."

This was a bizarre turn-up. Neither Miller nor Saunders had anticipated a no-comment interview from a man that had effectively just handed himself in. It was weird.

Miller decided to have a man-to-man with Pollard. "Philip, I'm not sure that you understand the format here. We're interviewing you to give you the opportunity to put your side of the story across, which will be beneficial to your case when this comes to court. Not *if* it goes to court, we're talking about *when*. So, I would urge you to desist from the no comment answers, as it will harm your defence. Replying with 'no comment' is usually the tactic of an interviewee who doesn't think we have enough evidence against them to make a charge. Your case is quite the opposite, we've got so much evidence we'll have to decide which highlights to use in the court case." Miller was being gentle, and quite sincere. This was a shit idea that Pollard was pursuing, there were no two ways about it. He wanted the teacher to know that he was making a mistake.

"No comment."

"Well, I've said my piece Philip. Is it your intention to say no comment throughout this interview?"

"No comment."

"Okay, well, thanks. I think we'll leave this here for now. We'll probably interview you again in the morning before we charge you. Interview suspended at eighteen hundred hours."

Miller pressed stop on the recording device, and Pollard leaned forward. "Please don't think I'm trying to be awkward. But I prefer to say my piece in court." Pollard looked sincere, and quite apologetic.

"It's your right to do that Philip. But court could be six, eight, ten months away. You won't get bail. You'll be remanded in custody until your trial."

"No, I quite understand that. Which prison do you think I'll be sent to?"

"Aw God knows. Probably Forest Bank, if you're lucky. But the prisons are all over-crowded at the minute, so it could be anywhere."

"Sure, I understand. I know a young lad in Forest Bank actually. So at least I'll have a friend!" Pollard smiled widely, and Miller couldn't help but reciprocate.

"I know. He asked me to go down there and see him. Kieron, you mean?"

"Yes!" Pollard treated this as though it was the greatest coincidence that had ever occurred.

"Yeah, he wanted to convince me that you're a good man, and that there's no way you'd do anything to harm Darren."

"That was good of him."

"Yes, he was extremely worried about our suspicions that you were having some kind of a sexual relationship with Darren."

Mr Pollard smiled and nodded. "Well, that's nice to know. He's very much like Darren. And he was right of course. This was never about sex."

"I believe you. Which makes it all the more annoying

that you are no commenting."

"Don't worry. It will all become clear in the end."

"Anyway, we'll pick this up in the morning."

"Sure. Okay, well, thanks."

Chapter Thirty-Six

Police Scotland had been alerted to Darren's appearance at his mother's house by the Manchester force. In a missing person's case, the file cannot be closed until a police officer has personally met with the person and can confirm that the person is safe and well. As this was such an extraordinary case, the procedure was far more complex than usual today.

Two female police officers were despatched from Aberdeen's Queen Street police station, with the instruction of identifying Darren Jenkins, and checking the reports from his mother, that he was indeed, safe and well.

Dawn Jenkins opened the front door of her parent's home and nodded the two officers into the property. As she closed the door behind them, she noticed a few neighbours standing by their gates across the road, having a good nosey. Police cars always got tongues wagging and it was no secret that it was Dawn's son who'd been in the news for the past few days.

"Ah, so you must be Darren?" asked the first constable, a young probationer, not a great deal older than Darren herself.

"Yes, hello," he said, sitting on the settee next to his grandfather.

"Can I have your autograph, please?"

The joke settled the tension, and the police officers asked a few basic questions of Darren, such as where he had been all week, who with, and how he had arrived at his mother's home.

Darren answered the questions, he seemed very calm, happy, possibly excited. The two officers made their notes and left. The whole encounter had taken less than five minutes. As they left, they advised that CID officers would need to come and interview Darren, and that it will probably be sooner rather than later. Dawn Jenkins agreed that the family would stay in the house and wait.

A couple of hours later, two plain-clothes police arrived, and Dawn led them through to the dining room.

"Hello Darren!" said the older looking detective, seemingly full of beans. "My name is DS Stephen Henry, and this is my colleague DC Michael Baird."

Darren nodded towards the two detectives and smiled.

"So, quite a week eh?" It was the younger detective who was speaking.

Darren smiled again and nodded.

"We need to ask you a few questions about everything that's gone on, if that's okay?"

"Yeah, course. Here do you mean, or in the police station?"

"I think we'll be fine here, for now."

"Has he handed himself in now?" asked Darren.

"Yes, yes, a few hours ago. Mr Pollard is in police custody down in Manchester. The detectives down there are going to speak to him in the morning. But before they can do that, we need to find out a few facts from yourself."

"Yeah, its not a problem. Happy to help." Darren grabbed the salt and pepper pots from the table-top and began fiddling with them.

"We have to ask you some very personal questions as well, so it might be a bit embarrassing with your old ma sat here!" It was the younger officer, DC Baird who had made the gentle joke, smiling warmly at Dawn. But Darren's response was quick.

"Well, if you're going to ask me if Phil touched me, or raped me, or even tried to do anything sexual, the answer is no. He's not like that."

"Phil? Is that what you call him?" asked Darren's mum.

"Yeah. Well, it started getting a bit weird calling him Mr Pollard and Sir. So he said, just call me Phil."

This detail caught the detective's imaginations, and Darren sensed the suspicion, so added a bit more detail.

"It felt a bit strange at first. But he'd say something like 'do you want a brew?' and I'd say 'yes please Mr Pollard.' After a while, he just said 'look, we've both left school now. You might as well call me Phil.'

"Well, you're correct Darren, that was one of our questions. Usually, in a case like this, the person who has abducted a young person has done it for some kind of sexual motive."

"Yes, I get that. But it wasn't about that."

"So, in your own words, would you like to tell us what it was all about, then?" DS Henry asked the question.

"In my own words?" asked Darren, with a cheeky glint in his eye. His sarcasm was lost on the older detective.

"Aye."

"Okay well basically, I told Phil that I was running away from home, and he wouldn't let me. He said I'll end up in a doorway, being beaten up by drunks, getting a drink problem or getting into drugs. He said that all the homeless in Manchester are addicted to spice. But I told him that there's no way I'm going home. So, he said he'd look into finding me somewhere to go. Anyway, he couldn't find anything, he'd rung the Social, Citizen's Advice, Shelter, loads of places. Basically they told him that there are tens of thousands of teenagers looking for alternative accommodation, because of family problems."

"And are family problems at the heart of the matter?"

"Yes. Very much so," said Dawn. "Darren's father has made numerous threats of violence against us, he said he'll burn this house down. He's said he'll kill himself if I take Darren away from him. He's a very messed-up person."

The two detectives nodded sombrely. It was a familiar tale, one they'd heard hundreds of times before.

"Phil said that he'll let me run away if I came up with a proper plan. But he said there's no way he's just letting me disappear into thin air."

The two detectives traded glances. This was all beginning to take on a different angle. They'd come here to ascertain whether sexual penetration had occurred, and if not, what lesser sexual activities had taken place.

"What do you think was in all of this for Mr Pollard?" asked DC Baird.

Darren shrugged, and let out a loud sigh.

"He's just a really nice man," said Dawn, filling the uncomfortable silence.

"You know him?"

"Oh yes, I know him quite well. I was in to see him at

least once a fortnight because of Darren's behaviour. Wasn't I?"

Darren nodded.

"Seriously, he's a lovely man." Added Dawn, nodding as though she was reminding herself.

There was another silence, as the detectives thought about the next question. They really hadn't been prepared for this outcome.

"Basically, I came up with a plan, which was to hitch-hike up here to my mum's. I was going to knock on the door and just say, 'I don't care if he kills himself. I want to be here.' Phil thought that was a good idea, but he said that it was too risky to hitch-hike, and said he'd bring me up. But he said that he wanted to teach me a lesson that I'll never forget."

Part Five

"Right, I've got a few errands to run. I'll be about an hour, an hour and half. Don't go out of the house, and don't contact any of your mates on Facebook. If the word gets out that we are together, we won't get very far. I'll be arrested on suspicion of being a kiddy fiddler."

"Yes Sir."

"And run yourself a bath. You look like a bloody chimney-sweep!"

Two hours later, Mr Pollard arrived back at the flat. He was in a great mood, and his hands were full of bags from JD Sports.

"Hello? Darren? Come in here and have a look at this," he said, placing the bags down on the kitchen table. Darren wandered through from the living room, still wearing his school uniform from the previous day.

"What's…"

"I've got you some new stuff! You can't go and see your mum in that tatty old uniform. Look at your shoes, they're falling to bits." Mr Pollard was smiling, as Darren walked over to the pile of bags.

"For me?" he said, his eyes were filling with tears.

"Yes. Have a look, I hope I got the right stuff."

Darren looked slightly dazed, almost embarrassed. It was clear that he didn't know the etiquette when faced with a load of JD Sports bags which were full of goodies for him.

"Come on, you flipping drongo, don't just stand there with your gob open."

"But…"

Mr Pollard recognised that there was an issue. He quickly sussed out that the young lad was uncomfortable accepting charity, he'd demonstrated it the previous day at KFC. "Come on Darren, you can't wear that school uniform. It's just some new stuff. You can pay me back for it when you've got a job."

The comment did the trick. Darren said "thank you," and stepped forward towards the bags. This was the kind of moment he had dreamt of. This was an unbelievable dream-come-true moment, there was very little that Darren wanted in terms of material goods, apart from the latest clothes. He began feeling each bag and worked out what each one contained. He grabbed the bag which contained the shoe-box first. He opened it very carefully, pulling at the drawstring, and easing the box out of the carrier bag gently.

"No way!" he said, as he read the label on the red Nike box. "Air Max 90's!" Darren opened the box, and the tears were flowing down his face as he grabbed one of the navy-blue trainers and held it out to look at it. He couldn't believe it. He'd always wanted a pair of these. He sniffed the shoe, inhaling the fresh Nike smell that he had only ever experienced in the sports shop, looking at the trainers, wishing and hoping for a pair of his own some day.

"Sir, are you sure? They're a hundred quid these!" His voice was quivering with the excitement and the emotion.

"No, actually, I've changed my mind!" Mr Pollard was touched by how thrilled the lad was. "No, I'm kidding. Of course I'm sure. Come on, have a look at the other stuff." The teacher was smiling widely as Darren placed the trainer back in its box, ever-so carefully. He took another bag from the table-top. It contained a big item, as the carrier was swollen. Once again, Darren opened it very carefully, and recognised what it was immediately. It was a North Face coat, another item that he had dreamed of owning. The tears were streaming down his face now, and he looked extremely innocent and vulnerable, a far cry from the cocky, boisterous kid that Mr Pollard knew from the school.

Darren tried the coat on, his hands shaking as he tried to do up the zip.

Next, he opened the bag with the tracksuit, then a bag with some t-shirts, and underwear and socks. He opened the last bag very slowly, savouring the moment, as though he never wanted this amazing experience to end. Once all the items were piled up on the table, Darren turned to Mr Pollard, and looked him squarely in the eye. "Thank you so much, Sir. I will pay you back. Honest."

Mr Pollard felt a stinging sensation in his own eyes, he was shocked by how much this meant to the youngster. He decided to quickly move the conversation on.

"Right, well, I think you should go and get changed, let's have a proper look at your new clobber. Go in the bathroom and get changed. We need to be out of here in five minutes flat."

A couple of minutes later, Darren Jenkins stepped out of the tiny bathroom, walking around as though he was a foot taller as he paraded his new outfit. Mr Pollard was in his bedroom, throwing socks and underwear into a suitcase. He glanced across and saw Darren as he walked towards the bedroom door.

"Wow, look at you! You look exactly the same as every other teenage scrote in Tameside now!"

"Aw, Sir, these are sick! Honestly. I've wanted these clothes for years!"

"They suit you." Mr Pollard was smiling. He'd missed these moments as his own kids had got older, and the magic of giving them new stuff was lost. "Do you like them, then?"

"Aw, God. I can't even..."

"Well the worst thing is that you're not going to be able to walk through town in them, showing them off. We need to leave right now." Mr Pollard threw some more of his clothes into the suitcase, and zipped it shut.

"Right, listen to me. I've got another surprise for you. I need you to go and stand in the phone box at the end of the street and wait for me to pick you up. I'll beep you when I'm there."

"What's the surprise?" asked Darren, looking at the reflection of his new clothes in the mirror.

"You'll see when I beep you. Right, go on, I'll be about ten minutes."

Ten minutes later, true to his word, Mr Pollard sounded the horn of the motor-home. Darren looked confused at first, but stepped out of the phone box and walked over to the vehicle. As he opened the door, he saw Mr Pollard sitting in the driver's seat. He had a massive smile on his face.

"Welcome aboard!" he said, as Darren jumped into the

cab. "Stick your seatbelt on mate."

Darren did as he was told, as Mr Pollard began driving the vehicle up Mottram Road, and out of Stalybridge.

"Now before we get into any arguments, that big double-bed at the back of the van is mine!" said Mr Pollard, with a playfully serious look on his face. "The settee behind you turns into a bed. That's yours!"

Darren was stunned by the vehicle. Everything in it was posh and new. He was straining his neck, looking over his shoulder to stare at the kitchen, the dining area, the settee that was going to be his bed.

"Next to your seat is a button, just at the side. Press it." Said Mr Pollard, as they continued up the hill, towards the house that he had spent the past twenty-odd years living in.

Darren pressed the button, and his seat started rotating slowly, turning away from the road ahead, to face the interior of the motor-home. Darren shouted "whoaa!" and laughed loudly.

"Now you know what it's like to be a judge on The Voice!" said Mr Pollard, laughing at his cheesy joke, as Darren's chair continued to rotate.

"It's got central heating, a bathroom, full kitchen, thirty-two inch plasma with freeview, DAB radio and a bedroom at the back. This is what they call the dogs bollocks of mobile homes!"

"What, so this is what we're going to my mums in?" Darren was grinning from ear-to-ear.

"Yes, but remember yesterday, when you told me that you've never had a holiday? Well, I've hired this for a week. So we can go straight up to Aberdeen now, and we'll be there for eight o'clock tonight..."

"Yeah?"

"Or we can take our time and make a holiday of going up."

"Holiday, Sir!" said Darren, as he pressed the button on the seat and began revolving around again, back towards the front of the cab.

"You don't have to. If you want to go straight there, it's absolutely fine."

"No, honestly Sir. I want to have a holiday. It'll be sick!"

Mr Pollard went quiet, as the vehicle passed his marital home. A huge sadness welled up inside him, a numbing cocktail of regret, loss and a tinge of bitterness. This building, those bricks and mortar had meant everything to him at one time. And now, he was driving away from it, saddened that the marriage he had hoped to save was now finished. The words and the anger that Sandra had spat at him two nights earlier when he'd let her open the letter had hurt him deeply. He'd not even wanted to apply for early retirement, he had been excited a few years earlier to hear that he'd be able to work an extra two years, up to the age of sixty-seven when the retirement age had been extended. It had been Sandra who had made him apply for redundancy. Her vile insults were still ringing in his ears. Mr Pollard felt tears well up, and they stung him.

"Well, if you're coming with me, I'm putting you in charge," said Mr Pollard.

"What?"

"I'm going to leave the planning of the holiday up to you. I'm just your driver. But, there's one condition…"

"Welcome to the BBC News Channel, I'm Simon Shields and our top story this hour. Philip Pollard, the disgraced school-teacher of Grey Street, Stalybridge has this morning appeared before Tameside Magistrates Court in Manchester, charged with the abduction of 15 year-old Darren Jenkins. The case has been committed to Preston Crown Court. The 56 year-old school teacher has been remanded in custody pending a date for his trial. In court, Mr Pollard only spoke to confirm his name and address. He was dressed in police-issue grey track-suit and looked quite relaxed and happy as he was led away. We have this exclusive footage of Philip Pollard being led into the prison van at the rear of the court building in Ashton-Under-Lyne just moments ago and once again, in this footage, he does not look upset or ashamed. In fact, the best word to describe his demeanour is relaxed."

The screen switched from Simon Shield's head and shoulder shot and showed Philip Pollard walking towards the white G4S van wearing handcuffs. He was talking to a prison officer and the footage suggested that the two men were sharing a joke.

"The search for Philip Pollard came to a dramatic conclusion yesterday as we have been reporting over-night. Today, the attention has switched from the search for the teacher, and onto the welfare of the pupil who had been caught up in all of this for the past nine days. Our reporter Vici Scott is in Aberdeen where 15 year-old Darren Jenkins turned up quite unexpectedly yesterday afternoon. Vici, what's the latest where you are?"

The image on the screen switched again, this time to a young and happy-looking reporter who was standing on a very ordinary road in the middle of a housing estate. She was surrounded by many other reporters and journalists, all of whom were being held back by a police cordon-line which was being manned by two solemn looking police officers.

"Yes, good morning Simon. I'm here on Ash-Hill Drive in

Aberdeen, and as you can see, there is a massive media presence here today as reporters from all over the UK wait to hear more details from the youth who had been abducted for eight days at the hands of his school teacher, Philip Pollard."

"Yes, there is certainly a great deal of activity there Vici. Any news on Darren?"

"Not as much as we would like to be honest. The only news that we have received so far is that Darren is okay, and that he is staying here in Aberdeen with his mother and grandparents for the foreseeable time."

"Have you had any information about the events of the past eight days Vici?"

"No we haven't Simon, and police here are remaining extremely tight-lipped about the situation. We are being told that the family wish for the press to respect their privacy at this difficult time, but with so many questions about this case, it is proving very difficult to find out exactly what has been happening, and of course, that important question of how Darren is coping."

"The Magistrates court case has concluded Vici, as I'm sure you will have heard. Philip Pollard has been remanded in custody until the case reaches Crown court. There has been no new information released from the court, or from police officers in Manchester. So although it is good news regarding the safe return of Darren Jenkins, there are still plenty of question marks hanging over this case."

"That's right Simon. And I suppose that myself and my colleagues here, close to the family home, are hoping for a few words with the family, or with Darren. But as the time goes on and with absolutely no response from the police officers or the boy's family, that is looking more and more unlikely."

"Okay Vici, we'll leave it there for now. On to other news now, and..."

Chapter Thirty-Eight
6 months later

Preston Crown Court had seen some major criminal cases in recent years. Many high-profile trials had taken place at this famous red-brick building.

The hugely expensive trial of Dale Cregan, the drug-dealer who killed two young, female police officers in an unprovoked attack in Hattersley had taken place here. His trial had been one of the biggest security operations the UK security services had ever undertaken, as dozens of police vehicles escorted his prison van to and from Strangeways prison each day, and armed police officers trained their guns on the building from nearby roof-tops.

Preston Crown Court was also memorable for shocking the nation to its core with the trial of Dr Harold Shipman, the family GP who was sentenced to 15 life sentences for the murder of 15 of his patients, although the true figure was later revealed to be at least 215 people, and possibly as many as 260.

The court had also held the trial of the killers of Sophie Lancaster, in a case which broke the nation's heart. The promising, beautiful young woman had been attacked and beaten by a gang of youths in a Lancashire park, simply because of the clothes and make-up she had been wearing.

And today, Preston Crown Court was facing another high-profile case, as the trial of Philip Pollard was due to get underway, 6 months after the teacher's disappearance with one of his pupils had dominated the news here, and across the world.

It was a windy, dark and grey October morning in the north of England, but the weather hadn't deterred the press, they were all there outside the famous, circular shaped building in full force. All of the major broadcasters were there, PA, Sky, BBC, ITV, CNN, with their expensive outside-broadcast vans. And they were joined by broadcasters and journalists from much smaller, but equally as relevant media establishments from Mr Pollard's community, such as Tameside Radio, the Manchester Evening News, the Tameside Reporter and many of the Greater

Manchester news and broadcast companies that had made the thirty-mile trip north.

The public gallery was full, and many disappointed members of the Stalybridge community were left standing outside the building, having failed to gain access to the court. As the morning went on, the tension and expectation from the press, and the public, continued to build. This had been a very strange news event during the summer. And although it had all seemed to have been resolved without anybody being hurt, physically at least, there were literally thousands of questions that the public wanted answers to.

At the very top of the pile was a very simple question. What was it all about? Why would a celebrated, well-respected teacher destroy his career, and his personal life, as well as his distinguished reputation? Many, many other questions were also waiting to be answered. Was this a love story? Did Mr Pollard do anything to Darren Jenkins? The public were desperate to hear all of the dark and grisly secrets from this strange case which had fixated them for a few days earlier in the year.

Finally, the wait was now over, and the answers to these, and many other questions would hopefully be revealed through the course of the forthcoming week.

The court case was opened at 9.30am by Judge Gilbert Francis QC. For the next hour, he explained the role of the court, how the trial would run, and then defined the job of the jury, for the benefit of the jurors.

Following a brief explanation of the case, Pollard was called. He stood in the bullet-proof, glass-encased dock, flanked by two prison-officers and faced the judge and jury. He was asked to tell the court his name, age, address and his pleas in relation to the two charges, of child grooming, and abduction, of a fifteen-year-old child.

"How do you plead to the first charge?"

"Not guilty." Said Pollard, his head bowed.

"How do you plead to the second charge?"

"Not guilty, your honour."

Suddenly, the calm, detached mood of the court-room

changed, as an angry voice shouted out from the public gallery.

"How can you say not guilty? You fucking nonce!"

From his position in the dock, Mr Pollard couldn't see who'd shouted it, but he recognised the voice. It was Michael Jenkins. That voice had taunted the school-teacher for years, it was just a little deeper, and a lot more bitter now.

The Judge stared at Jenkins Snr, and turned to the court usher. "Is that the boy's father?" he asked quietly. It was inaudible to most of the people in the packed court-room. The usher nodded discreetly and mouthed something. The judge turned back to face Michael Jenkins.

"That will be the first, and final interruption to this court. As you are the boy's father, I will allow you to stay on the understanding that any further interruptions will result in you being dismissed from this court for the remainder of this trial. Is that completely understood?"

Jenkins nodded apologetically. His hammy outburst had sounded so rehearsed and disingenuous, it was obvious that it had been on his to-do list for several weeks, probably since Pollard's pleas had been received at the pre-trial hearing. He looked pleased with himself, as the trial got under way.

The prosecutor gave a long, and extremely damning assessment of the accused, making endless innuendos and assertions that Mr Pollard was a sexual predator, who had taken the boy, Darren Jenkins away for no other reason than to have sex with him. When the prosecution lawyer had finally finished outlining his case, Mr Pollard spoke. He was defending himself, and this was his opportunity to put his outline of the case forward.

"Sir, with the greatest of respect, I have listened carefully to the evidence against me, and whilst it has been very uncomfortable to hear my name linked to the sordid suggestions and innuendos made about myself, I accept that it has been necessary, and the proper thing to do."

"Thank you, Mr Pollard."

"However, as this trial continues, I'm sure that there will be further attempts to make this trial about my conduct, and naturally, to explore my motivations. But I would just like to make it clear that this was, and has always been about the welfare of Darren Jenkins. As a teacher, with extra responsibilities as a head-of-year, I have always taken my responsibilities extremely seriously. On the morning of May the sixteenth, I was faced with an extremely difficult situation."

Mr Pollard went on for the next five minutes, speaking clearly and succinctly about the events which led to him finding Darren Jenkins, close to his home address.

"I had literally just hung up my phone on the headteacher, who was in the process of instructing me to return to school, when Darren appeared from around the corner, near to his home address."

"Why, may I ask, did you defy the instruction of your superior?"

"Because I was extremely concerned about the welfare of the pupil in question."

"And had you passed that information on to the headteacher?"

"Yes. And I was told, I can't remember the exact phrase she used, but it was something along the lines of 'if you have told his father that he has absconded from our care, then it's no longer our problem.' The insinuation was that I had done my job and that I should return to school."

"Yes, I quite understand that, Mr Pollard. But I, and I'm sure the members of the jury will also join in me in wondering what your motivation was to, as you put it, 'hang up' the telephone and continue to look for Darren?"

"I felt that I should respect the duty-of-care that I had towards him, and I was profoundly concerned about his welfare and his state-of-mind."

"Yes, and that's all well and good Mr Pollard, but if your line-manager had instructed you to return to the school, then surely you were duty-bound to follow orders and do just that?"

"Well, in the calmness of this court-room, I would be inclined to agree with you. But the circumstances of that day were not calm, and as far as I was concerned, my priority was to find Darren and to ensure that he was okay."

"I'm sure most rational thinking people can agree in

principal with that. But is it not possible that this is nothing more than a cover-story? A smoke-screen? I think it's quite plausible that you can quite easily hide your real motivations behind the heavy cloak of this safe-guarding excuse?"

"I am simply answering your questions in an attempt to provide an honest account of what happened. If you insist on pursuing this red-herring and insinuate that I had sexual desires for Darren, then I'm afraid you are only going to confuse the matter and make it a lot more complicated than it actually was." Mr Pollard wasn't trying to be smart, but his reply certainly came across that way.

"Whether you think that my line of questioning is confusing the issue, or not, I shall persist with my questioning, thank you."

"But you're barking up the wrong tree."

"I think it would be wise to leave that decision to the jury Mr Pollard, don't you?"

"Yes, I do. But you are deliberately trying to lead them up a dead end. I'm just conscious of wasting everybody's time." Mr Pollard smiled politely towards the jury. There was an awkward sound, hard to distinguish if it had been a cough or a stifled laugh from one of the twelve jurors.

"So, back to the issue. You refused to return to school. Can you explain why you would do that?"

"I've already said. I was concerned about the welfare of one of my students. He had left the school in a very disturbed state and I was aware of the problems that he was facing."

"And would you care to enlighten us as to what these problems were?"

"Yes, Darren was on a final warning. I had just upset him, albeit unintentionally. He was very angry and ran away from my office. He accidentally smashed a door in the school corridor as he ran. He would have been under no illusion that this action was going to result in his exclusion. I wanted to find him, apologise for my own actions which had upset him, and try to work out a solution to the problem with him."

"You say that you upset him. What did you do?"

Mr Pollard explained the situation with the essay and

how he had flatly refused to read it, which resulted in Darren storming off and breaking the door.

"So, let us be absolutely clear with regards to the timeline of that fateful morning. The incident with the broken door occurred at what time?"

"I had just arrived at school, so it will have been approximately eight-thirty."

"And at what time did you leave the school premises, and go to look for Darren?"

"That will have been roughly ten o'clock."

"Ten o'clock. Some ninety minutes after Darren had run away?"

"That's right."

"I'm not trying to be insolent, Mr Pollard, and please forgive me if that is the way I sound. But isn't ninety minutes a long time to elapse? Did you not think that leaving an angry, upset pupil, whom you were so concerned about, for a whole ninety minutes was a little excessive?"

"No, not particularly. Ninety minutes is a very long time in a teenager's life. To you or I, perhaps it would seem an excessive amount of time. But in the case of an upset teenager, in my experience, ninety-minutes can see a number of different moods. From sadness, to happiness, via despair and hysteria. Ninety minutes is an extremely long time to sustain an emotional episode. Half an hour, in my experience, is a long time to maintain an emotional episode. Usually, a teenager would have calmed down and been distracted by something else. By the time that I had left the school to go and look for Darren, both myself and the headteacher had reached the conclusion that he wasn't coming back."

"So you had wasted that vital ninety-minutes on the wrongful assumption that Darren would return to school?"

"Yes. That's usually how these things happen. In normal circumstances a teenager storms off somewhere, calms down, thinks about a new bike or a new games console or whatever it is that occupies their mind, then they come and apologise, and the event would be forgotten about."

"You see, I'm inclined to think that..."

"Sorry, do you mind if I interrupt you?"

"No, go ahead."

"Thank you. I'm not being funny, but this jury, they're just ordinary people, picked at random from society, aren't they?"

"Yes, I can confirm that being the method of selection for jury service."

"So, if all these people are just normal, everyday folk, do you mind if I ask why you talk like that?"

"Like what, may I ask?"

"As though you're in a Dickens novel."

"That's absurd. We are standing in the Queen's Crown Court."

"Yes, I know that. But I'm just concerned that people are nodding off over there and I want them to know what happened."

"And know what happened Mr Pollard, they shall."

"All I'm saying is, instead of asking me all these questions, using all these old-fashioned words and phrases, and making me stop and start after two minutes, why don't I just tell you what happened, and then if there's anything you're unsure about, you can quiz me about it after? That's how they do it on TV."

There was another muffled cough from the jury. Followed by another. The prosecution lawyer looked a little bit embarrassed, following this patronising dressing-down. In a bid to save face, he walked across to where the twelve jury members were sitting. The prosecutor had the undivided attention of the men and women who ranged all ethnicities, ages and employment backgrounds.

"Ladies and gentlemen of the jury. You all heard what Philip Pollard just suggested. I must point out at this juncture, that this is a most unorthodox request. The legal system in this country is, I admit, very traditional. And I am very proud to say, our legal system has an excellent record for bringing justice and fairness, it is a system which is recognised and admired the world over." He spoke to each and every member of the jury as he addressed them, holding eye contact with each person for several seconds.

"However, if you are all in agreement with Mr Pollard's wish, I am quite prepared to let him explain the events in the manner which he describes."

The nodding and gentle gestures of approval from the jury was unanimous.

"Okay, Mr Pollard, I think that the jury are united in their agreement."

"Thank you. Right, well, let's start at the beginning. I've been Darren's head-of-year for the past four years. I first got to know him about a month or so after he started at the school. He'd been kicked out of his lesson for being disruptive. Now, being disruptive in class is obviously a major issue for teachers because it makes life hard for the teaching staff as well as the kids who are trying to learn. The problem with disruptive kids is that they don't fit into the education design we have. Trying to get disruptive kids to learn in a class of thirty other kids is the same as trying to get square pegs into round holes. The current methodology of 'sit down, shut up and learn this' simply doesn't work for these kids."

For the first time since the trial had begun, the jury looked engaged and interested in what was being said. The glum, sterile atmosphere seemed to have subsided a little, and one or two of the jurors were smiling.

"Now before I go any further, I'd just like to explain a bit about my experience as a teacher. I've been doing this job all of my life, from leaving University. After a while, you begin to realise that practically every class that you teach has the same dynamic mix of characters. Every single class that comes along is the same as the last and they keep coming along, every single year. It's no different today than it was in 1982 when I started my career in teaching. Kids are all the same, and that is the thing that teaching has taught me. I would like to demonstrate what I mean by that." Mr Pollard was looking at all twelve members of the jury as he addressed them. "Now, as I describe this class to you all, I want you to please cast your mind back, and think about your own school, and your own class-mates."

The jury members nodded their understanding of what

Mr Pollard was saying.

"I think you'll all agree that your class had a swot!"

There was an embarrassed laugh amongst the Jury members. It was clear from their faces that they could picture their own class swot.

"You all know who I mean!" said Pollard, smiling as he addressed the smiling faces. "Teacher's Pet. The one who has their hand up to answer every question. First in with their homework, which was always perfect, last to leave the classroom after the bell had gone. The person in the class that you wished you'd sat next to when it was a test."

There was another gentle laugh. Pollard laughed silently at all of the grinning faces. They knew exactly who he was talking about.

"Every class has a swot. I've not taught a class that hasn't had one. What about, casting your mind back to when you were at school, what about the class sports-star? Did you have one?"

The jury were nodding and smiling.

"Yes, the kid who was the star footballer or netballer, or the fastest runner who was going to win gold in the Olympic games in a few years time. Then there was the geek! Did you all have a geek? A kid in your class who was so immensely brainy about a specific topic, whether it was politics or history or steam trains? Every class has one. They also have a lazy-bones in there as well."

Another polite laugh escaped the jury, only it was louder than the last, but not loud enough for this court-room to be classed as a comedy club.

"I see the lazy-bones in every class I teach. The lazy-bones has never done their home-work, their shoe-laces are never tied, they arrive at the lesson a minute after everybody else, looking like they had just fallen out of a tree. And they never do any work. Their hand-writing is atrocious!" Pollard delivered his remark in a very animated way and the laugh that it received was noticeably louder.

"But, the lazy kid never does any harm, it's only themselves they let down. Not like the class bully. Did you have one? Oh yes, of course you did. I bet you can visualise him or her right now and you can recall the fear they used to put into you. The nasty comments, the vicious remarks. And the class bully always has two mates, who aren't nice, but they're not quite as bad as the bully."

There were some nods and grumbles of acknowledgement.

"I can guarantee that you all had a fat kid, a skinny kid, a tall kid and a short kid in your class. A great singer? A future actor? A poor kid, who's shoes were falling apart? Did you have a specky-four-eyes? Was there a ginger?"

Once again, the jovial mood within the jury was noted by the sounds of restricted laughter. Mr Pollard may have been in prison for the past six months but he still knew exactly how to engage an audience, the first skill of teaching.

"Then there was the popular kid, the nice one that everybody liked, and everybody wanted to be like. You all wanted to have the same clothes and the same house and the same parents as the most popular kid in the class. They had the best holidays, the best Christmas presents, their parents had the best car. Oh, you're nodding, but it still goes on. You may have left school several years ago but I could be describing a class of today's year eights to you. That's second years in old language. The kids you had in your class, they're all here, every year, they keep coming back, year after year, without fail. I bet you all had a shy kid, the one who never spoke to you, the one you invited to your birthday, but they never came. So, after a few years, you stopped inviting them. There would have been a cocky kid with a chip on his or her shoulder who couldn't answer a simple question without offering up a sarcastic comment. I know, you're all nodding. I also believe that your class will have had a good-looking kid, who members of the opposite sex always fancied. And your class will have had the ugly kid, or the smelly kid nobody wanted to sit near."

It was clear to everybody in the court-room that Mr Pollard was spot on in his analysis. Suddenly, his voice changed, the upbeat, enthusiastic tempo suddenly gave-way to a more serious, laboured delivery.

"Finally, your class will have had a Darren Jenkins. A nice enough kid, didn't mean any harm, but was permanently annoying. Shouting out, saying stupid stuff, drawing male genitalia on the blackboard and getting caught red-handed as the teacher walked in. The Darren Jenkins in your class will have fallen off his chair at least once a lesson, he or she would have spent the lesson making silly faces at others, throwing scraps of paper across the classroom or tapping their pen against the desk. Eventually, in almost every lesson, the Darren Jenkins that you knew, would be sent out and made to stand in the corridor, where they'd then start staring through the glass in the door, trying to make the class laugh. Then, the teacher would open the door and send the Darren Jenkins from your class to the headmaster's office."

Mr Pollard stopped for a moment and the sudden silence in the court was unsettling. He took a sip of water from a transparent plastic cup.

"Just like a fast runner and a swot, and a shy kid, every class I've ever seen has a disruptive kid. Darren is a disruptive kid, he's a total pain in the back-side to teach. But as a person, he's kind-hearted, he's funny, he's very bright, he's a great artist. He's considerate, his manners are impeccable. I think he will go on to have a great future doing something that will benefit others, perhaps nursing, or teaching, or helping homeless people. But, for now, he's disruptive and schools aren't geared up to deal with that. School's can cope with shy kids, lazy kids, cocky kids. But as I said earlier, schools can't get square pegs in round holes. The only answer in a lot of these cases is exclusion. Just get rid of the problem, move the problem on to another school. Currently, in this country, we are excluding thirty-five kids every day. That helps the schools hit their GCSE result targets, sure. But the difficulty with that policy is that a lot of the time, that kid's life is ruined before its begun. We are failing these kids, many of them will never recover and will face a life of unemployment, homelessness, addiction issues, poor self-esteem and a life-long supply of return-tickets to prison. Basically, these children go on to lead a miserable existence in most cases. And it's only because their brains are working too fast for the classroom environment. It's a scandal."

Pollard looked at the jury and then across at the judge. "Exclusion. Kicked out of school, kicked out of the system at fifteen years old. That's what we were going to do to Darren, the day he disappeared. And I'm ashamed to say that there was a real sense of relief amongst some staff members when he broke that door on that morning in May. That's not a reflection on those members of staff. It's a reflection on the obsession with grades, results, targets, and the school's performance indicators. It's no different from the council moving homeless people on. It doesn't solve the homelessness issue; it solves nothing."

The jury were listening carefully to Mr Pollard's words.

"It was that day when I found Darren walking the streets, carrying a loaf of bread and planning to run away from home, that I realised that I had let him and hundreds of other kids just like him down. Hundreds of them. Darren had written me the letter I described a little earlier. It had taken him six hours and a lot of courage, and I'd refused to read it because I was in a bad mood, maybe a bit hung-over or whatever my issue was that morning. That was why he ran off, throwing back that door and smashing it. But as I sat in my car near to his house that morning, I read his letter, and do you know, I wish that I had read it thirty years earlier. Because if I had, I may have treated all those hundreds of kids like Darren differently. In his letter, he described the loneliness, the isolation, the desperation he felt. Just for being himself. Just for being born with the mind that he has." Mr Pollard took another sip of his water as his captive audience sat silently, waiting to learn more.

"The reality of that morning was very depressing. I had just spoken to Darren's father, who told me that he is sick of his child, and when he next sees Darren, he's going to break both of his legs."

There was a gasp from the jury and the public gallery. Surprisingly, there was no sound from Michael Jenkins. The boy's father just looked down at his shoes and the gesture was noted by all of the jurors, who had been made aware of his presence earlier, with his cringy outburst.

"As far as I could see, this lad was in a great deal of

danger. He wanted to run away from home, which as we all know is a bad idea. But I couldn't try and convince him to go home because his father had just told me that he would inflict violence on him. So, I was stuck. I couldn't take him back to school because the head had already told me that Darren was being excluded. I knew that I wasn't going to be able to alter that decision. And so, I decided to contact social services myself and see what options were available. I soon discovered that there were no options, not unless I waited for both of his legs to be broken. Now let's be honest here, I'm usually a very resourceful man who can get things done. But not this time. I was stuck. I had a fifteen-year-old kid here with no school to go to, a threat of serious danger at home, and a desire to run away and make his own path in life with seventeen pounds and fifty pence in his pocket. I wasn't prepared to let that happen. So yes, what I did was unprofessional, it was out-of-character, it could be argued that it was foolish. But I did it for Darren's benefit, and I have absolutely no regrets. Given the same scenario today, I think that I would most likely do the same thing."

Mr Pollard looked hard at the jury.

"That week, Darren had his first ever holiday. I taught him, all week, everything from map-reading to cooking, to improving his hand-writing and a lot more besides. I can honestly say that I was devastated when it was time to return the motor-home because I had enjoyed such a good time with him."

Mr Pollard stopped talking and drained the last of the water from his transparent cup.

"Okay, thank you Mr Pollard. I think that sums up the side of the story that you wish to portray."

"No, not quite. Those are the details of what happened. The facts are extremely clear. I took Darren to a place of safety…"

"It took you a week to drive from Manchester to Aberdeen, a journey which, according to the satellite navigation system I have in my car, would ordinarily take five hours and fifty-five minutes from Stalybridge."

"As I have already said, I took him on holiday."

The Prosecutor laughed theatrically. The jurors looked on with an expression of mystification on their faces, they didn't appear to get the joke.

"This story gets more bizarre with each passing comment. You state that the reason that you abducted Darren Jenkins was to remove him from danger and to take him to a place of safety. On the face of it Mr Pollard, that is a very commendable thing to do, albeit foolhardy and irresponsible not to inform anybody of your good intentions and ultimately launching a missing-persons investigation which has cost the state an estimated six-million-pounds, not to mention the anguish and upset that this preposterous 'holiday' bestowed upon the boy's parents and grandparents."

"I couldn't inform any..."

"Mr Pollard, I wish to explore the details of your holiday, if I may."

"Of course. But I think that you should probably ask these questions of Darren."

"And why do you say that?"

"Well, the holiday was Darren's. I was merely his driver and his guardian."

There was the sound of unrest in the court-room, whispers, coughs, uncomfortable shuffling of feet. The prosecutor looked confused.

"I'm sorry, but what is that remark supposed to mean?"

"Well, it's simple enough. I hired the motor-home and advised Darren that I had it for a week. I asked Darren if he wanted to go straight up to his mother's house and if so, I said that I was going to have a touring holiday on the way home. I was having difficulties with my marriage-breakdown and there were mounting problems at school. I really needed to get away for a bit and do some thinking. Naturally, I hadn't mentioned this, but that was my intention. Darren said that he would like to stay with me and have a holiday. The lad had never been on holiday before, except for visits to his grandparent's house in Scotland. Can I have some more water please, its dry in here."

The Court Usher took a fresh cup of water up to the dock.

"Thank you. So, I gave Darren an ultimatum. I told him that he was welcome to spend the week with me but that he would be in charge of everything. I pulled the motor-home up in Mottram and I put a thousand pounds on the coffee table. I told him that this was our budget for the week. It will have to include food, diesel for the van, days out, camp-site fees. I also gave him a map of the UK and told him to plan a route, starting at Scarborough, where we were spending the first night as I had some business to attend to. The rest of the journey was down to Darren. So, I really think that it would be best to ask him about it."

At this point, the judge interrupted.

"I think that is enough information for this morning's proceedings. At this point I suggest a short adjournment, and we will hear the victim's evidence after lunch. Court rise."

Chapter Thirty-Nine

Darren Jenkins was standing in the witness stand, taking his oath as Mr Pollard faced him from the dock. Darren looked taller, and older, and he appeared much smarter than the former teacher had previously seen him, as he stood in a new suit with a grey tie. Puberty and adolescence had matured the young boy dramatically in the six months since the teacher had last seen him. He still had his cocky smile and his unwavering self-confidence though, which pleased the man standing accused of his abduction and of grooming him.

"Darren Jenkins, as you will all be aware, is the former pupil of Philip Pollard, and the young man that this whole case revolves around." Said the prosecutor to the jury.

"Darren, I would like to ask you some questions about the circumstances which led to you being abducted by your teacher."

"Yes Sir, but I just have to say, it's wrong to say abducted. I asked him if I could stay with him."

"Yes, well firstly, I would like to advise you that it is grossly bad-mannered to make interruptions. May I ask that you refrain from interrupting me in that manner, please?"

"Yes Sir, but I'm just saying, its bang out of order slagging Mr Pollard off. He didn't abduct me."

"Darren, in the eyes of the law I'm afraid that Mr Pollard did indeed abduct you. He took you away from your legal guardian without consent, or without even informing your guardian that you were safe and well. In this court, that crime is classified as abduction."

"I'd run away from home. So, it's me that you should be telling off. Not him." Darren pointed at Mr Pollard, who looked different himself. He had an awfully grey, pale complexion from his time in prison. He was thin, and he looked as though he was ten years older than he had been when Darren had said farewell to him in Scotland, six months earlier.

"I would prefer that the jury decides on that matter, Darren. Now tell me, if you can, why Mr Pollard took you away in the motor-home."

Darren explained the story, from the start beginning with the broken door. He spoke confidently about his thoughts and feelings on that disappointing morning. He talked about wondering what to do as he wandered along the canal, then having the idea to run away, before telling the court about his visit to the paper shop to get his wages early.

He continued, explaining the moment he saw Mr Pollard at the bottom of his street, and about the KFC lunch, smiling as he described Mr Pollard's lie about getting a Tower meal free with the popcorn chicken. Darren's story continued to being dropped off at the flat, to staying the night, and then the treats that his teacher had bought for him from JD Sports.

The prosecutor interrupted Darren, during a natural pause.

"So, bearing in mind the fact that this was a teacher that you had previously had a very fraught relationship with, did you not think that it was peculiar that he was showering you with expensive gifts all of a sudden?"

Darren seemed to be thinking hard about the question. After several seconds, he spoke. "What does fraught mean?"

There was a gentle laugh from several jurors. They weren't laughing at the fact that Darren didn't know the word in question, more his comical delivery in response.

"Let me re-phrase. You and Mr Pollard had a long history of conflict. Therefore, it might have seemed strange that he was suddenly giving you all of these expensive items. Was that how it seemed?"

"No, I told him that it was too much. He said that I can pay him back for it all when I've got a job and that. And I've been saving. I've got sixty quid for you so far, Sir." Said Darren in the direction of the dock. Mr Pollard smiled and nodded.

"And how much do you imagine the items cost?"

"I've already worked it out. I know exactly how much I owe him."

"Do you think that there was the possibility that Mr Pollard bought you those clothes for a reason?"

"Yes, he did buy them for a reason. He said I needed to look smart for my mum." Darren looked over to his mother who was sitting in the public gallery, several rows away from Darren's father. She smiled at her son encouragingly.

It was clear on the face of the prosecutor, that dealing with confident teenagers with fast tongues was not his usual forte.

"Darren, are you familiar with the term grooming?"

"Yes Sir."

"Can you please describe to myself and the members of the jury your understanding of what that term means?"

Darren looked at the jury. "Well, it's when a man... well, doesn't have to be a man, could be anybody of adult age, when they tidy their beards up."

Laughter erupted throughout the court-room, it looked like the judge smirked for a second. The jury, the public gallery and most notably, Mr Pollard laughed at the cheeky gag, which had been timed brilliantly.

The prosecutor didn't look amused. "I think you are fully aware of what I meant. I was referring to sexual grooming."

"Is that when you have a bit of a tidy-up downstairs?"

There was another laugh and Darren seemed to be enjoying himself winding the prosecutor up. It was just like being at school.

"No, no, I know exactly what you mean Sir. Sexual grooming is when you buy presents and stuff, trying to get a little kid to start having sex with you. But like I said, that's not happened, so its getting a bit boring now."

"Has Mr Pollard ever broached the subject of sex with you?"

"What does broached mean?"

"Has he ever tried to start a conversation about sexual activity?"

"No, not that I can think of... no, actually, wait. Yes, he did once..."

Suddenly, the light-hearted atmosphere gave way, and a heavy silence fell on the court-room.

"Go on," said the prosecutor.

"It was only once, but it was when we were at the KFC in Ashton, the morning I ran away."

The jury member's eyes all switched from Darren and focused on the man standing in the dock on the other side of the court. He didn't look remotely concerned.

"Mr Pollard told me that young lads like me, living on the streets, will be asked for sex off strange old blokes, in return for food and money and stuff. It was when he was trying to convince me that running away was a bad idea. That's the only time he has ever mentioned anything to do with sex or anything like that to me."

"When you slept in Mr Pollard's home on the evening on Thursday the 16th of May, can you please tell the court where you slept?"

"On the settee."

"And what about in the motor-home?"

"On the pull-out bed. Mr Pollard had the bedroom at the back."

"Did Mr Pollard, at any time, suggest that you should share a bed?"

"No. Why would he? Why do you keep trying to make out that he's a weirdo?"

"Mr Pollard has got a reputation for being quite an angry personality. Whilst you were with him, did you witness this side to his character?"

Darren thought about the question. He looked confidently at the prosecutor as he made his reply. "Yes, I'm not going to lie, there was one occasion when we were in the motor-home. He totally lost it."

"And would you like to describe what happened?"

"Yes Sir. We were driving along on the motorway with the radio on. The DJ kept singing over the songs in a really annoying way. After a while, Mr Pollard started screaming and shouting at the radio. He was banging his hand on the dashboard shouting 'this man is a bloody imbecile!' and turned the radio off. He was raging, Sir, it really annoyed him."

The judge interjected and spoke directly to Philip Pollard with a glum expression. "Was it Steve Wright?" he asked.

Pollard nodded.

"Hmmm." Said the judge. "Carry on."

The prosecutor was having a bad time and it was obvious to everybody in the court-room. His hands were shaking as he leafed through the paperwork on his lectern. The only sound in the court was the rustling of his case notes. The jury could almost hear the sigh of relief as he found the page that he'd been searching for.

"When you were interviewed by police officers on the day that you arrived at your mother's address in Aberdeen, you made a comment to the detectives. Do you recall telling them that 'Mr Pollard took you away so that he could teach you a lesson?"

"Yes Sir."

Suddenly, the prosecutor began to grow in confidence and his voice lifted several octaves. "Now bearing in mind that yourself and Mr Pollard had shared a very volatile, often difficult relationship within the school environment, did you not feel any sense of danger upon hearing such a vague comment?"

"No, Sir."

"You mean to say that you didn't wonder what Mr Pollard had meant, when he said that he wanted to 'teach you a lesson?"

"Yes Sir, I did."

"Ah, so you did wonder what he meant by that?"

"Yes. So, I asked him."

There was another uncomfortable moment in the court as several people stifled laughs, disguising their unfortunate, involuntary sounds with coughs and exaggerated throat clearing.

"And what was his response?"

"He said that he would show me what it was when we got to Scotland."

"And you were happy with such an ambiguous explanation?"

"What's does ambiguous mean?"

"It means, as I suspect you are already aware, that his answer was rather unclear and confusing."

"Oh right, well no, I just thought he'd tell me when he was ready, like he said."

"And did you ever find out what this so-called lesson

was?"

"Yes Sir."

"You did? Excellent! And would you care to share the same lesson with the rest of us?"

"Well, I will do. But I must warn you Sir, it was pretty boring to be honest." Darren smiled widely at the jury and a wave of laughter travelled through the court. Darren had skilful comic-timing and it was this, more than the actual things that he said which caught the audience off-guard. The judge looked at the jury with a stern expression of dissatisfaction.

"Well, to explain that, it would be easier to tell you about the last night in the motorhome. It was the Thursday night. Mr Pollard allowed me to cook the tea that night and after we'd eaten, he did the washing up. Then, he sat me down and explained the plan for the following day. He said he needed to leave the place where we were camped really early so he could get the motor-home back on time."

"Carry on," said the prosecutor, desperate to pounce on a detail that he could pick at.

"He told me how to get from the place where we were, to my mum's. He gave me some cash and said I could keep the mobile phone I'd been using all week, on the condition that I had to text him the moment I arrived outside mum's house."

"And where exactly were you at this point in time?"

"I'm not sure Sir, but he dropped me off the next morning at a bus stop and told me to catch a bus to Inverness, then catch a train from there to Aberdeen. He wrote it all down for me, the times and that. He said I had to keep my hood up and do a Scottish accent when I was getting on the bus."

"And was your Scottish accent convincing?"

"Aye, it wis, Sir, it wis."

"How long were you on the bus for?"

"I don't know, an hour, maybe two."

"And then when you arrived at Inverness railway station, you went in and you bought a ticket for Aberdeen?"

"Yes, well, I used the machine. And then I just waited on the platform for the train."

"Yes. And you arrived in Aberdeen in the afternoon.

How did you get to your mother's address from there?"

"I walked it Sir, because I had about two hours to spare, so I just took a stroll around town first, and then headed over to my mum's."

"Well that sounds like quite an adventure. But getting back to this lesson that Mr Pollard wanted to teach you. You said that he gave it to you the night prior?"

"Yes Sir. He started asking me loads of questions, he had them all written down on a piece of paper. It was all to do with the stuff we'd been doing all week. So, one of the questions would be about how to cook spaghetti Bolognese, which he'd taught me. Then he asked me why the Pennines are called that..."

"The Pennines, as in the vast range of hills and mountains which separate the north-west with Yorkshire?"

"Yes Sir. They go further than that though. They start just north of Birmingham and go all the way up into Scotland." Darren looked pleased to have out-smarted the posh legal bloke.

"Thank you. And would you like to share with us the answer to that question, of how the Pennines got their name? I'm sure we're all desperate to know?"

"Yes, well Penn is the old-fashioned name for a hill, it's what they were called in Anglo Saxon times. And there's nine of them."

This remark received a gentle laugh from the jury and even the prosecutor seemed quite endeared by the explanation, his wide smile displaying a warmth, for the first time, towards Darren Jenkins.

"And may I ask how you knew the answers to these questions that Philip Pollard was putting to you?"

"Yes, well we had a deal. He said that I could pick the places we went, but I had to tell him interesting things about the places, or I wouldn't get any tea. He gave me a phone to use and he said that I had to plan the route we were taking, and each day we had to visit an interesting place and I had to tell him all about it."

"And what other things did you discover on this trip?"

"Loads Sir. Like Scarborough, where we went on the

first day, there's a hotel there that was built especially for a visit from Queen Victoria. It's called The Grand and its shaped in a V for Victoria. It was built on a design to do with the calendar. It's got 365 bedrooms, one for each of the days in a year. It's got 52 chimneys, one for each week, there are 12 floors, one for each month, and it also has four towers, one for each season. It was the biggest hotel in Europe when it was built in 1867."

"Wow, well, I must say that was impressive." The prosecutor looked quite astounded by Darren's knowledge of the famous building on the Yorkshire coast. "And so, as you travelled around, Mr Pollard asked you to come up with facts about the places that you were travelling to. And then he did a test, is that right?"

"Yes Sir. And I got twenty-four out of twenty-five questions right." Darren looked quite chuffed with himself.

"And was this the lesson that he said he was going to teach you?"

"No Sir. There was more to it than that. I also had to learn the names of twenty famous people who were expelled from school."

The jury looked quite perplexed by this bizarre turn.

"And did you find twenty?"

"Yes Sir. There's a lot more actually, but I learnt them off by heart."

"And would you like to tell us a few of these names?"

"Yes Sir. I can tell you all of them. But I need a pen, so I can keep count."

The prosecutor took a pen from the desk behind him and found a piece of scrap paper. He walked across to the witness stand and handed them to Darren.

"Okay. And will we have heard of these people?"

"I think so Sir. You've heard of Albert Einstein?"

"Of course!"

"So, that's one, then there's Stephen Spielberg, Sir Richard Branson, Adele, Amy Winehouse, Guy Ritchie, Stephen Fry, Frank Skinner, Kevin Bridges, Lily Allen, Liz Hurley, that's eleven so far. Charlie Sheen. Marlon Brando, Russell Brand, Jon Bon Jovi, Eric Clapton, Johnny Rotten, Jackie Collins, Lewis

Hamilton and Keanu Reeves."

Darren looked pleased with his rendition.

"Well, I'm sure the jury will agree with me that is quite a list. There are a number of names there that I am profoundly shocked and surprised to hear."

"Yes Sir. I was surprised myself."

"And what was Mr Pollard trying to achieve, do you think, in making you do this research?"

"Well he made me do a few. He said I had to do one of famous people who have done well but don't have any qualifications."

"And was that list as shocking as the list of people who had been expelled?"

"Yes Sir. Some people you wouldn't expect. Like Sir Alan Sugar, Prince Harry, Jon Snow, Deborah Meaden, Simon Cowell, Jeremy Clarkson, Sir Phillip Green, Sir Richard Branson."

"Well, this is really fascinating, Darren."

"He was just trying to make me realise that school wasn't everything. I think he felt responsible for me getting expelled."

"And did these exercises make you feel a little better about that fact?"

"Yes Sir. He also said that the reason that I was always getting into trouble was because I probably had ADHD. I started arguing with him, you know, nobody wants to have that, and have to go to a special school, or take loads of drugs that make you docile."

"Was this a serious argument?"

"No Sir, Mr Pollard just told me to come up with a list of people who have got ADHD and I'd see that its not that bad. So I did."

"And was he right?"

"Sir, something you have to know about Mr Pollard is that he is always right."

This comment received a huge smile from the accused.

"He always says 'next time I'm wrong will be the first time."

"Okay, thank you Darren, I think we get the picture. Tell

us all about the ADHD list you came up with."

"Yes Sir. Some of the famous people who have ADHD are Michael Phelps, Will Smith, Jamie Oliver, Jim Carey, Stevie Wonder. There's loads of them, Sir."

"Go on," said the prosecutor, with an encouraging smile.

"I could be here all day..." said Darren, receiving a warm laugh from the jury. "No really, there's a lot. It's easier to break it down into professions. So, like from painters, it's basically the most famous ones. Leonardo Da Vinci, Picasso, Van Gogh."

It was clear from the faces of the jury and the people who filled the public gallery, that these comments from Darren Jenkins were surprising, to say the least.

"In music, there's John Lennon, Robbie Williams, Justin Timberlake, I've said Stevie Wonder, Cher, Ozzy Osbourne. In politics, there was Abraham Lincoln, John F Kennedy, Winston Churchill."

"This is a genuinely fascinating topic Darren, but I'm conscious of time. I feel we must move on..."

"Yes Sir. But the main thing that I learnt about ADHD was that the people who have it are the best hunters."

"The best hunters?"

"Yes, you see, human evolution is all thanks to people with ADHD. We're all here today, in this court, thanks to people who had ADHD two million years ago. It's always been around you see, it's just a thing, like shyness or being good at dancing. The earliest humans relied on the ones with ADHD to travel further hunting, climb higher up mountains, stay up later guarding the camp and the herd, fighting off other tribes and stuff. The ones with ADHD are automatically ready for risk taking, so they used to be put in charge of the hunting and gathering, building the rafts or the rope bridges that got them from one side of the valley to another."

"That's extremely interesting, but how can we possibly know this?"

"It's common sense, Sir. But there was a big study a few years ago into a nomadic tribe in Kenya. It discovered that the strongest and healthiest members of the tribe showed signs of

ADHD. They were just better than the rest at doing natural stuff, like climbing, hunting, swimming, fighting and stuff like that. It's the risk-takers that get things done. The professor who did the study says it is proof that people with ADHD shouldn't be locked up in schools because it's unnatural and that it's not the right environment for them, they need to be outside doing proper stuff, looking for new things and experiences. The study showed that the tribes-people with ADHD were always on the go but the ones who didn't have ADHD were better settlers. Then they tried teaching the tribes-people in a classroom and the ones who were the best at all the stuff they needed to be good at, they couldn't deal with the lessons, and learnt nothing. But the settlers were excellent students. You should read up about it, its proper interesting Sir. It explains why kids with ADHD are always struggling to stay still and keep quiet, but if you give them a bit of freedom and let them build something, or make something, or create something, they'll be no trouble because the part of the brain that's working faster than everybody else's is busy doing the task. The point is, ADHD people can't just sit in a class and learn, just like somebody who hasn't got ADHD can't paint a picture like Vincent Van Gogh, or create a song like Stevie Wonder, or win a war like Winston Churchill, Sir."

Everybody in the court-room seemed engrossed in Darren's information.

"In school, we're treated as though we're freaks and told that there's something wrong with us. But it's a load of rubbish. It's like saying there's something wrong with the fast runners, or the kids who find algebra easy. But because they don't cause a nuisance with their fast running and algebra, nobody says anything. It's all wrong, Sir."

"And I'm guessing that this was the lesson that Mr Pollard wanted to teach you?"

"No, Sir. I think Mr Pollard would be the best person to ask about that."

The prosecutor turned and faced the accused. Mr Pollard stared back from the dock.

"Mr Pollard?"

"Well, it's quite simple really. In the letter that Darren

wrote me, the one that I refused to read, and which set off this chain of events, he said that he couldn't do school anymore because he couldn't learn. He said he was thick and that it was a waste of time. But I think we have all seen today that this simply isn't true. In fact, nothing could be further from the truth! However, it was us, the teachers, the school system that had drummed that opinion into him, sending him out of class, treating him as a moron and constantly reinforcing the view that he is bad and that he is doomed to fail. Well, that's not entirely fair. Our teaching model is still based on the Victorian model of preparing children for the army, for taking orders and treating them all the same. Sit down, shut up and learn this. But that simplistic approach doesn't accommodate kids like Darren. Every single class has a kid like Darren, we established that already, you all remembered the Darren Jenkins in your own class. There are 25 thousand schools in this country, so we're talking about tens of thousands of kids in our schools today, right now, being tormented by teachers, parents, school-mates, simply for being themselves. I wanted to show Darren that it is the system that is wrong and that people like him can, and do, go on to achieve amazing things in life. But most importantly, I felt that I had a duty to demonstrate that Darren could learn, arguably better than most kids. But just in a different way."

Darren Jenkins was smiling at his teacher as he held his hand up, as though he was still in class. Mr Pollard nodded at him.

"He also told me that today's human beings are capable of putting satellites into space which beam TV channels down to earth and can build cars that don't need a driver and can swap a bad heart for a good heart inside a human body. But human beings haven't yet sussed out how to keep kids like me quiet in a classroom without expelling us or filling us with drugs. But he also said that if anybody can come up with a positive way of dealing with kids who aren't wired up for sitting still and writing down words from a book, it will probably be somebody who has got ADHD. Somebody like Albert Einstein, a man who had ADHD, failed his exams, got expelled from several schools and went on to give the world the Theory of Relativity."

There was a moment of silence as the jury members considered the information that Darren had provided, coupled with the words of Philip Pollard, who had explained that Darren hadn't believed that he was capable of learning.

The prosecutor was looking at his case notes and it was becoming quite obvious that he was stumped. Everything that he had built his prosecution case around had been explained and the information that had been presented to the court was credible. The major problem with this case was that Darren Jenkins had always maintained that Philip Pollard was not responsible for any offence. These statements had been made again, in the court, in great detail.

The prosecutor closed his file and walked across to the judge.

"Your honour, based on the information that we have heard here today, I wish to inform you that I am giving notice under section 23A of the Prosecution of Offences Act 1985 that the proceedings are to be discontinued."

The Judge nodded sombrely, he did not look remotely surprised by the decision. He looked at the accused, then at the witness, and finally across at the Jury. "Case dismissed," he said. "Court rise."

Chapter Forty

"Some breaking news that is reaching us here at Sky News centre, and in the past few moments, the court case against the school teacher Philip Pollard has just been dismissed. Our crime reporter Carole Lindsay is outside Preston Crown Court, Carole, this is a shocking turn-up?"

"Yes, well, maybe to the viewers at home, but it hasn't really come as a huge shock to those of us who were in court. The trial, which was scheduled to last two weeks has collapsed after just one day, as the prosecution service realised that there was no evidence of any crimes committed."

"This is a real surprise Carole. To remind our viewers, Philip Pollard was standing trial accused of abduction and child-grooming after taking his pupil, Darren Jenkins away in a motor-home for a week in May. There was lots of evidence that Philip Pollard did take the boy, so why has the case been dismissed?"

"Well, the boy in question has maintained throughout the investigation that no sexual contact, nor talk of sex was ever a part of the story, so the charge of sexual grooming was always going to be a difficult crime to prove. However, the charge of abduction did look much stronger because there was, as you say, plenty of evidence that Philip Pollard did indeed take the boy away in the motor-home without parental consent. However, it has been revealed today in court that Darren had effectively run away from home and he explained to the court that the reason Mr Pollard was with him that week was to look after him."

"If that's the case, that no crime has been committed, then why has Mr Pollard been on remand in prison for six months? Surely these matters should have been dealt with prior to any charges being brought against him?"

"Yes, well in normal circumstances, the Crown Prosecution Service would have made a decision as to whether the case against Mr Pollard was strong enough for a realistic chance of prosecution. However, as Mr Pollard gave police officers no information in any of his police interviews, choosing to provide 'no comment' answers to the investigating officers, the CPS went into this trial with none of the information which has come to light today. And, I'm... yes, I'm just hearing that Philip Pollard is about to come out of the court..." Carole Lindsay turned around and looked back at the huge glass doors at the entrance to Preston Crown Court.

There was a moment of confusion for Sky News' viewers, as they realised that this breaking news story was catching everybody by surprise, not least the broadcasters. After several awkward seconds of silence and camera focusing, Philip Pollard walked out of the building, alone, and into a rapturous round-of-applause from the crowd of people who had come up from Stalybridge to witness the trial for themselves. He waved, and smiled at them all, as one young lady ran towards him and gave him a hug and a kiss on the cheek.

He looked emotional and extremely drained as he approached the press, who were hastily creating a scrum before him.

"Hello!" he said, and smiled for the TV cameras. "Today, as you will be aware, the case against me has been dropped. I'd like to say that I have been extremely well treated by the police officers and by the prison service staff whilst I have waited for this trial."

People were streaming out of the court building behind him and a crowd began gathering around the back of Mr Pollard as he continued talking to the cameras, photographers and reporters.

"I'd just like to make a few points about my time in prison. Firstly, I know that it has probably been hard for my family and friends, hearing the press talking about me the way they have. But, I just want to say that I am glad that they did. The idea of a sexual motivation for my actions was a very plausible theory to explain what I did and I applaud those reporters who didn't shy away from making those assumptions public. If people with such influence had been fearless in speaking their minds so publicly during Cyril Smith's time as an MP, or when Jimmy Savile was abusing young people, or during the Rochdale and Rotherham grooming scandals, then a lot of innocent young people would have been saved from the horrors that they were left to endure. So, I applaud the press for being fearless in that regard, however inaccurate and baseless those theories turned out to be."

The crowd behind Mr Pollard began applauding and shouting encouraging remarks over his shoulder. The mood was jovial and victorious amongst many of them, former pupils and colleagues, who'd come up here to Preston, desperate to be proved right about their belief in Mr Pollard's innocence and his principles.

"When I came into teaching thirty-six years ago, I wanted to make a difference to the lives of the kids that I was going to teach. I have always wanted to make a difference and I think that in a small way today, I might have finally done that. If any teachers watching this news programme start to think a little differently, a little more positively about challenging students, then I think my six months in prison will have been a small sacrifice."

Once again, the crowd were cheering and applauding the former-teacher, lots of them were patting him on his back and shoulders.

"Schools, teachers, the whole education establishment is built around the foundations of right and wrong. What the teacher says is right, what the school says is right, and pupils are instructed very early on that nothing the school does is ever wrong. But that's not always true, as we all know. Gary Lineker, one of Britain's best loved football players of all time was told by his school master that 'he must devote less of his time to sport if he wants to be a success.' And that he 'can't make a living in football.' David Bowie was told by his tutor that 'he needs to learn that music will not make him a liveable wage.' John Lennon's school report stated that he was 'on the road to failure. He is hopeless.' These school reports were spectacularly wrong, as we all know. And the way that we educate some of our pupils is wrong, too. I'm so glad that I have had this opportunity to help one of my students, rather than turn a blind-eye to his problems. It is turning a blind-eye and excluding these kids, giving up on them and setting them up to fail which is encouraging the suicides, the homelessness and the addictions of so many thousands of people whose only crime was to be themselves inside an institution that hasn't worked out a way to include them, yet. Let's all try and remember that every class, in every year, in every school, has at least one kid who just isn't capable of learning in the same way as the others, just like one of the kids is better at singing, and one is better at drawing, and one is better at latin. Let's try and work out a better way of accepting that fact, and finding a positive solution, rather than tormenting them, and then throwing them on the scrap heap at fifteen years old. Thank you."

There was a round of deafening applause and cheers of jubilation all around as the crowd went crazy, several were chanting "for he's a jolly good fellow" jumping up and down behind Mr Pollard. One of the faces in the crowd suddenly stepped forward and took Phil Pollard's hand. It was Sandra Pollard.

He quickly pulled his hand away.

Chapter Forty-One

Miller was sat in his office, buried deep beneath a pile of files which he had ignored for far too long. He had been working on them all day, but the pile just didn't seem to be shrinking.

He looked pissed off when he heard a knock at his door, but nobody could see the expression, it was well hidden by the tower of paperwork.

"Hi Sir," said Rudovsky.

"Hi Jo," said Miller without looking up. He seemed in a mood.

"What's up with you?" she asked, picking up on the bad vibes.

"Aw, nowt. Sorry Jo. I just don't seem to be getting anywhere with this lot. It's doing my head in, I've been at it for five hours and the pile looks bigger now than it did when I started."

"Do I look like I work for The Samaritans?"

"Ha ha, sorry. What's up?" Miller smiled at Rudovsky, it wasn't her fault that he'd allowed this paper-work to build up so spectacularly.

"Just wondered what you're doing on Wednesday?"

"You know what I'm doing Jo... I'm in court."

"No, you're not!"

"Yes, I am. It's Philip Pollard's trial this week, possibly into next..."

"Think again. It's just collapsed. Prosecutor has just discontinued."

"Shut up!" Miller looked genuinely surprised by this unexpected, but good news.

"No, you shut up."

"Bloody hell! That's a turn-up!"

"I know, and it gets you out of court on Wednesday, so you can stop being a grumpy bum."

"What happened?"

"Well, not sure exactly, just got a news alert on my phone. But its looking as though Pollard has just done this to bring attention to kids being excluded or something. It was a stunt by all accounts."

"What... so that's why he no commented us! He told me and Keith it would all make sense when it came to court."

"Stick it on Sky News, come on."

"Aw Jo, I can't. Honestly mate, I need to get this sorted..."

"Come on Sir, don't be a drip."

"No, seriously, I'm in the zone here. I'll watch it when I get home, they'll have a better report then anyway, it's all a load of shit when it's breaking news."

"Fair enough. Well, anyway, I thought I should let you know..."

"Yes, I appreciate it. Oh, Jo, that reminds me, there's a parcel at reception for you. Forgot to tell you earlier."

Rudovsky looked surprised. Miller continued to look at the file he was reading.

"Have you ordered summat?"

"No."

"Oh, well, anyway, I passed the message on. See you later."

"Sir."

Rudovsky left Miller to his paperwork, surprised that he didn't seem too interested in the Pollard case collapsing at Preston Crown Court. She decided to head off down to reception and pick this parcel up.

"Hiya Judy, Miller said there's a parcel for me?" said Rudovsky to the kind-faced receptionist.

"What's your name and rank?" asked Judy. Rudovsky looked confused.

"You what?" asked Rudovsky, wearing a look of bemused confusion.

"I need your name and rank. It's procedure."

"Oh my days! Honestly! Where will the anally retarded formality in this place end? My name is the same as it was this morning, when you said, 'good morning Jo.' And my rank is the same too."

"I'm sorry, but I can't give out any packages unless I

have your full name and rank."

Rudovsky looked as though she was starting to get annoyed by this nonsense, but thought better of starting a row.

She rolled her eyes dramatically as she said, "Name Jo Rudovsky, rank, Detective Constable, SCIU."

Judy looked down under her desk the internal post was kept, then glanced back up. "No, I'm sorry, there's nothing for you."

Rudovsky looked at Judy and smiled. "Is this a prank? Miller just told me that there's a parcel here for me."

"No. I'm sorry. There's nothing for a detective constable here. There *is* a package for a Detective Sergeant Jo Rudovsky..."

"Detective Sergeant..."

Judy handed the package across. Sure enough, it was addressed to DS Jo Rudovsky.

"Congratulations, Jo." Judy started laughing as Rudovsky stared back at her, her mouth was wide-open.

Suddenly, a round of applause broke out from the balcony upstairs, as Miller and the rest of the team applauded their new DS.

Rudovsky was shaking and tears were streaming down her face as she looked up at her colleagues above. They were laughing and pointing at her, singing "for she's a jolly good fellow."

Jo ripped open the package and saw her new ID badge and warrant card, with her new title. For the first time ever, Jo Rudovsky was completely lost for words.

Epilogue

Darren Jenkins and his mother Dawn have moved into a council house in Aberdeen, not far from her parent's home. She continues to work in the Co-op. Darren has started an apprenticeship in helicopter maintenance at Aberdeen Heliport, and is doing very well. His father, Michael, hasn't been in touch with him, or Dawn since the trial. He is still on a final warning at work and is still convinced that ADHD is a made-up excuse for bad parenting. Nobody has had the heart to point out that if this was true, it means that he is a bad parent. And that his parents were bad parents too.

No action was taken against Daniel or Jess Pollard following the collapse of the case. The brother and sister are back to sending the occasional text here and there.

Philip Pollard has left the teaching profession and now spends his time visiting schools and talking to the pupils who find themselves on the wrong side of the tracks. He has appeared on several TV and radio shows talking about his experiences, and trying to promote a greater understanding of the problems that disruptive kids face in a classroom environment. He has written a best-selling book on the subject, which is part biographical and part self-help, aimed at teachers and parents of disruptive kids. He is planning to write another one for the pupils affected by the issues that he has championed.

The government have held several high-profile meetings with Mr Pollard in an attempt to gain a greater understanding into the issues involved in educating children who don't have the same response to mainstream education as the majority. Mr Pollard, and the education minister are confident that a positive solution to this recurring problem is found, and that the 35 pupil exclusions per day in England can become a thing of the past.

Philip and Sandra have separated for good.

The End

I'd like to dedicate this book to my mum, Mary Anne, who through no fault of her own, spent a lot of time in Headmaster's offices throughout my school days.

I had quite a lot in common with Darren Jenkins when I was a youngster. As I've got older, I've come to realise how frustrating it is to have a child who would rather make fart-noises by cupping their hand in their arm-pit, than working hard on getting great exam results.

Sorry. I won't do it again. I love you xxx

ALSO BY THIS AUTHOR:

Miller 1: One Man Crusade
A gunman is killing paedophiles. One by one.

Miller 2: Neighbours From Hell
Moving house ends in murder.

Miller 3: Road To Nowhere
Where the hell is Sergeant Knight?

Miller 4: Gone Too Far
Britain's most provocative celebrity has disappeared.

Miller 5: The Final Cut
Tables are turning in the war against the poor.

The Clitheroe Prime Minister
What if an ordinary working man became PM?

77499025R00184

Made in the USA
San Bernardino, CA
24 May 2018